A Woman in Berlin

A WOMAN IN BERLIN

Eight Weeks in the Conquered City

A DIARY

BY ANONYMOUS

Translated by Philip Boehm

Metropolitan Books

Henry Holt and Company · New York

Metropolitan Books
Henry Holt and Company, LLC
Publishers since 1866
175 Fifth Avenue
New York, New York 10010

Originally published in Germany in 2003 under the title
Eine Frau in Berlin by Eichborn AG, Frankfurt am Main

ISBN-13: 978-0-7394-6600-1

Designed by Victoria Hartman

Printed in the United States of America

Contents

Foreword

It is perhaps no accident that an extraordinary work like *A Woman in Berlin* has had a history that is no less amazing: first published in 1953, the book disappeared from view, lingering in obscurity for decades before it slowly reemerged, was reissued, and then became an international phenomenon—a full half century after it was written. The events described are also extraordinary: the author, a woman living in Berlin, took meticulous note of everything that happened to her as well as her neighbors and friends from late April to mid-June 1945—a time when Germany was defeated, Hitler committed suicide, and Berlin was occupied by the Red Army. While we cannot know whether the author kept the diary with eventual publication in mind, it's clear that the "private scribblings" she jotted down in three notebooks (and on a few hastily added slips of paper) served primarily to help her maintain a remnant of sanity in a world of havoc and moral breakdown. The earliest entries were literally notes from the underground, recorded in a basement where the author sought shelter from air raids, artillery fire, looters—and ultimately rape by the victorious Russians. With nothing but a pencil stub, writing by candlelight since Berlin had no electricity, she recorded her observations, which were at first severely limited by her confinement in the basement and the dearth of information. In the absence of newspapers, radio, and telephones, rumor was the sole source of news about the outside world. As a semblance of normalcy returned to the city, though, the author expanded her view, and began reporting on the life of her building, then of her street, then on the forced labor she had to perform and her encounters in other neighborhoods. Beginning in July, when a more permanent order was restored, she was able to copy the contents of her three notebooks on a typewriter. In the process, words became sentences, allusions were clarified, loose sheets were incorporated where they belonged. The result was 121 pages of gray war-issue paper. These pages—authenticated along with the original notebooks by a foremost expert on twentieth-century diaries—stand as a shattering indictment and complete our record of the time.

The author chose to remain anonymous for reasons that any reader can understand, and I feel bound to respect her wish, responsible as I am for the reissue of her text. What may be said, however, is that the woman who wrote this book was not an amateur but an experienced journalist. In the diary she alludes to several trips abroad as a reporter and to visiting the Soviet Union, where she picked up a basic knowledge of Russian. We may surmise that she worked for various periodicals after Hitler came to power: up until 1943–44 a number of magazines managed to avoid involvement in the propaganda demanded by Joseph Goebbels.

It is likely that through her professional contacts the author met Kurt W. Marek, a journalist and critic who facilitated publication of the diary. An editor at one of the first newspapers to appear in the new German state, he went on to work for Rowohlt, a major Hamburg publishing house. It was to Marek that the author entrusted her manuscript, agreeing to change the names of people in the book and eliminate certain revealing details. In 1954 Marek placed this version of the book with a publisher in the United States, where he had settled. Thus *A Woman in Berlin* first appeared in English (in an earlier translation) and then in seven other languages.

It took five more years for the German original to find a publisher and even then the company, Helmut Kossodo, was not in Germany but in Switzerland. But German readers were obviously not ready to face some uncomfortable truths, and the book was met with either hostility or silence. One of the few critics who reviewed it complained about the author's "shameless immorality." German women were not supposed to talk about the reality of rape; and German men preferred not to be seen as impotent onlookers when the Russians claimed their spoils of war. (According to the best estimates, more than 100,000 women were raped after the conquest of Berlin.) The author's attitude was an aggravating factor: devoid of self-pity, with a clear-eyed view of her compatriots' behavior before and after the Nazi regime's collapse, her book flew in the face of the reigning postwar complacency and amnesia. No wonder the diary was quickly relegated to obscurity.

By the seventies, the political climate had become more receptive, and photocopies of the text, which had long been out of print, began to circulate in Berlin among the radical students of 1968 and the burgeoning women's movement. By 1985, when I started my own publishing venture, I thought it was time to reprint *A Woman in Berlin*, but the project turned out to be fraught with difficulty. The author could not be traced, the original publisher had disappeared, and it was not clear who held the copyright. Kurt Marek had died in 1971. On a hunch I contacted his widow, Hannelore, who knew the identity of the author. She also knew that the diarist did not wish to see her book reprinted while she was alive—an understandable reaction given the dismal way it was originally received.

In 2001, Ms. Marek told me that the author had died and her book could now reappear. By then, Germany and Europe had undergone fundamental changes and all manner of repressed memories were reemerging. It was thus now possible to publish the diary in its full, complete form for the first time and restore passages that had previously been excluded, either to avoid touching on delicate matters or to protect the privacy of people still alive. At the same time, discussion of once-taboo issues had become acceptable. Subjects like the widespread collaboration in France, the Netherlands, and elsewhere; anti-Semitism in Poland; the saturation bombing of civilian populations; ethnic cleansing in postwar Europe—which for many years had been dwarfed by the German act of genocide—were now legitimate areas of inquiry. These are, of course, complex and morally ambiguous topics, easily exploited by revisionists; nonetheless, they belong on the historical agenda and deserve levelheaded discussion. And it is in this context that *A Woman in Berlin* ought to be read.

It is hardly remarkable that one of the best personal records of the war in Germany is a diary kept by a woman. After all, it was the women who preserved an oasis of sanity in a world run amok. While the men were fighting a murderous war, the women proved to be true heroines of survival. To the extent that a German resistance existed, women provided the logistics. And when their husbands and lovers returned, paralyzed by defeat, it was women who cleared the rubble. Of course, this is not to say that women had no part in the Nazi universe. The author of this diary would be the last to claim such high moral ground. She is a relentless observer, unwilling to tolerate any sentimentality or hypocrisy. Though she was unaware at the time of the enormity of the Holocaust, she nonetheless saw that Germans had brought their suffering on themselves by what they had done to others. An exceptional figure, this woman of Berlin managed to keep her nerve as well as her dignity intact throughout her trials. More than that, she never abandoned her fundamental sense of decency, a trait too rarely found amid the ruins of her time.

Hans Magnus Enzensberger

Introduction

In the early hours of April 16, 1945, civilians in the eastern quarters of Berlin were awoken by a distant rolling thunder. The vibrations were so strong that telephones began to ring on their own and pictures fell from their hooks. Women emerged slowly from their apartments and exchanged meaningful looks with neighbors. They hardly needed to speak. The long-awaited Soviet offensive had at last begun sixty miles to their east.

One and a half million Red Army soldiers of Marshal Zhukov's First Belorussian Front were bursting out from the bridgeheads on the west bank of the river Oder. Facing them were the desperate scrapings of the embattled Third Reich, mainly boys from the Hitler Youth and old men from the Volkssturm, groups of cadets from Luftwaffe military schools, and a smattering of veterans and SS. They had little ammunition, hardly any shells for their artillery, and insufficient fuel for their few remaining armored vehicles. Yet Goebbels, the Reich commissar for the defense of Berlin as well as minister of propaganda, had declared that the line of the Oder was a wall on which the "Asiatic hordes" would smash themselves. Surrender was out of the question. Himmler had just issued orders that any German male found in a house displaying a white flag be shot. The propaganda ministry organized graffiti squads, dressed as ordinary Germans, to paint slogans such as "We will never surrender!" and "Protect our women and children from the Red beasts!"

The argument for continuing the fight was largely based on Goebbels's own horror propaganda of enemy atrocities, which for once turned out to be no exaggeration. In the autumn of 1944, Soviet troops had made their first foray into East Prussia, laying waste to the village of Nemmersdorf before being repulsed by a German counterattack. Goebbels had rushed camera teams forward to film the corpses of women and girls who had been raped and murdered by drunken Red Army soldiers. The images on the Nazi newsreels had been so appalling that many women presumed they were part of a gross exaggeration by the "Promi," the propaganda ministry. But then in late January and early February, after the main Soviet assault on East Prussia and Silesia, refugees passing through Berlin recounted stories of rape, looting, and murder on a terrifying scale. Yet many Berlin women, while convinced that such things had indeed occurred in the countryside and isolated communities, refused to believe that mass rape was possible in the public view of a capital city. Others, increasingly nervous, began rapidly to instruct young daughters in the facts of life just in case the worst did happen.

Berlin at the time contained just over two million civilians, of whom the large majority were women and children. It was typical of the crazed irresponsibility of the Nazi regime at this time that Hitler rejected any idea of evacuating them while there was still opportunity. He openly disbelieved the military commander of Berlin who told him that there were 120,000 babies and infants left in the city and no provisions for a supply of milk. Consciously or unconsciously, Hitler appears to have imitated Stalin's refusal to allow the evacuation of civilians from Stalingrad in order to force his troops to defend the city more bravely.

THIS DIARY, WRITTEN by a thirty-four-year-old journalist begins on Friday, April 20, four days after the opening ground bombardment. It was Hitler's birthday. Nazi flags were raised over ruined edifices in the center of the city, where U.S. Air Force Flying Fortresses by day and RAF Lancasters by night had destroyed 90 percent of the buildings. Signs erected in Hitler's honor proclaimed: "The Fighting City of Berlin Greets the Führer." Even Hitler's military staff had no idea how close the front was. Soviet tanks had smashed their way through the German defenses and were starting to encircle the city. The first shells from long-range artillery would land in the northern suburbs that evening.

The diary continues for just over two months, until June 22, a period that covers the bombardment, the brief street fighting in most districts, Hitler's suicide on April 30, the surrender of the last pockets of resistance on May 2, and then the occupation of the city by the Russian conquerors.

First published anonymously in 1954 in an incomplete English translation in the United States and then in 1959 in German, the diary was highly controversial in Germany, where some accused it of "besmirching the honor of German women." Almost fifty years later, the complete book was reissued, again anonymously, but a few months after its publication Jens Bisky, a German journalist and critic, claimed to have discovered the identity of the anonymous diarist and revealed her name. A vehement controversy over exposing the author's identity raged in various German papers, throughout which Hannelore Marek, the executor of the estate, refused to confirm Bisky's claim. It is perhaps inevitable that in the absence of an author, some have raised doubts over the authenticity of the work, but experts on personal documents from the period have confirmed that the diary's transcript is original and completely genuine.

Such questions are to be expected, however, particularly after the scandal over the fake Hitler diaries, and after the great bestseller of the 1950s *Last Letters from Stalingrad* was found to be fictitious more than forty years following its initial appearance. On reading *A Woman in Berlin* for the first time in 1999, I instinctively compared my reactions to those I'd had to the Stalingrad letters, which had quite quickly made me uneasy. They were simply too good to be true. One, for example, milked the reader's emotions with a letter about a German concert pianist in Stalingrad whose fingers had been broken. As soon as I was able to read genuine last letters from Stalingrad kept in the German and Russian archives, I was certain that the published collection was false. Yet any such suspicions I might have had about *A Woman in Berlin* were soon discarded. The truth lay in the mass of closely observed detail. The anonymous diarist possessed an eye so consistent and authentic that even the most imaginative forger would never have been able to reproduce her vision of events. Just as importantly, other written and oral accounts that I had accumulated during my own research into the events in Berlin attest to the truth of the world she describes.

IF THE AUTHOR'S name is not known for certain, her character comes through clearly in her writing. In contrast to the totally closed mind of Nazi *Gleichschaltung*, she was liberal and receptive. She disliked the xenophobia of the regime as much as its military machismo. In her twenties, she had traveled around Europe and had even visited the Soviet Union, where she acquired some Russian. This was to prove vital once the Red Army arrived. Everyone in her apartment building turned to her, to save them from the depredations of usually drunken soldiers. Thus, she herself was placed on the front line. Again and again, the author shows bravery and resilience, her account revealing the close relationship between an inquiring mind and intellectual honesty. It is this quality that makes the diary so impressive and so important.

The only physical description of herself the diarist offers is of "a pale-faced blonde always dressed in the same winter coat," yet she is meticulous in recording her feelings out of an almost forensic curiosity. Her reason for writing all this is quite simple: "It does me good, takes my mind off things." She also thinks of showing her account to her erstwhile fiancé, Gerd, "if he comes back." Modest as her aspirations are, the author is nonetheless a brilliant observer, as much of the large historic events as of the daily life she shares with her fellow apartment dwellers. She vividly evokes the civilians trapped in Berlin and deprived of meaningful news. They know only that information from the western front, where the Americans have just reached the Elbe, is by then irrelevant. "Our fate is rolling in from the east," she writes. "It will transform the entire climate, like another Ice Age." She notes that horizons have narrowed: "My sole concern as I write these lines is my stomach. All thinking and feeling, all wishes and hopes begin with food." The lack of electricity and gas has reduced modern conveniences like lights and stores and hot water boilers to useless objects. "We're marching backwards in time," she writes, "cave dwellers."

Deference to the Nazi regime has collapsed along with an administration that can no longer protect its subjects. Ration cards may still be stamped, but only out of bureaucratic habit. Although a few diehards proclaim their confidence in Hitler, even they no longer speak of the Führer. They refer simply to "he" and "him." The propaganda ministry's promises of victory and a bright future fool nobody, yet many still suffer from that powerful human desire for hope in the face of all logic. The diarist is more realistic. She glimpses a few German soldiers: "That was the first time I saw real front-line men—dirty, gray-bearded, all of them old. The carts were pulled by Polish ponies, dark-coated in the rain. The only other freight they're hauling is hay. Doesn't look much like a Blitzkrieg anymore." Soon, everyone is looting stores and shops as the imminent Soviet onslaught and collapse of Nazi power leaves society disintegrating into communities formed and organized by building.

Beyond the breakdown of order, the biggest fear is what will happen when the Russians arrive. One "young man in gray trousers and horn-rimmed glasses" turns out on closer inspection to be a woman, attempting to save herself from the attention of Red Army soldiers. Other young women try to make themselves appear old and dirty in the vain hope of repelling lust. When somebody ventures that perhaps the Red Army soldiers are not so bad after all, a female refugee from East Prussia screams, "They'll find out all right." Everyone understands that the horrors she has witnessed and probably experienced were not just the ravings of the propaganda ministry.

Finally, on April 27, the Red Army reaches their street. "My stomach was fluttering," the diarist writes after seeing her first Russians through the window. "I felt the way I had as a schoolgirl before a math exam—anxious and uneasy, wishing that everything were already over." At first, things do not appear too bad. The soldiers in the street are playing with bicycles they have found, trying to learn to ride them. As almost all other eyewitness accounts confirm, the soldiers' first interest is in looting watches. Most have five or six strapped around each forearm. But once evening comes and they have drunk their ration of vodka, the "hunt" begins.

* * *

ONE OF THE MOST important aspects of this diary is its careful and honest reflection on rape in war. The whole subject of mass rape in war is hugely controversial. Some social historians argue that rape is a strategy of war and that the act itself is one of violence, not sex. Neither of these theories is supported by events in Germany in 1945. There have indeed been cases of rape being used as a terror tactic in war—the Spanish Civil War and Bosnia are two clear examples. But no document from the Soviet archives indicates anything of the sort in 1945. Stalin was merely amused by the idea of Red Army soldiers having "some fun" after a hard war.

Meanwhile, loyal Communists and commissars were taken aback and embarrassed by the mass rapes. One commissar wrote that the Soviet propaganda of hatred had clearly not worked as intended. It should have instilled in Soviet soldiers a sense of disgust at the idea of having sex with a German woman.

The argument that rape has more to do with violence than sex is a victim's definition of the crime, not a full explanation of male motive. Certainly, the rapes committed in 1945—against old women, young women, even barely pubescent girls—were acts of violence, an expression of revenge and hatred. But not all of the soldiers' anger came in response to atrocities committed by the Wehrmacht and the SS in the Soviet Union. Many soldiers had been so humiliated by their own officers and commissars during the four years of war that they felt driven to expiate their bitterness, and German women presented the easiest target. Polish women and female slave laborers in Germany also suffered.

More pertinent, Russian psychiatrists have written of the brutal "barracks eroticism" created by Stalinist sexual repression during the 1930s (which may also explain why Soviet soldiers seemed to need to get drunk before attacking their victims). Most important, by the time the Red Army reached Berlin, eyewitness accounts and reports show that revenge and indiscriminate violence were no longer the primary factors. Red Army soldiers selected their victims more carefully, shining torches in the faces of women in air-raid shelters and cellars to find the most attractive. A third stage then developed, which the diarist also describes, where German women developed informal agreements with a particular soldier or officer, who would protect them from other rapists and feed them in return for sexual compliance. A few of these relationships even developed into something deeper, much to the dismay of the Soviet authorities and the outrage of wives at home.

FOR OBVIOUS REASONS it has never been possible to calculate the exact number of rape victims in 1945. A general estimate given is two million German women; this figure excludes Polish women and even Soviet women and girls brought to Germany for slave labor by the Wehrmacht. But the figures for Berlin are probably the most reliable in all of Germany—between 95,000 and 130,000, according to the two leading hospitals. These can hardly be inflated figures if one takes into account that at least a dozen women and girls were raped in the single medium-sized apartment block where the author lived. Some pockets in the city escaped completely, but not many, considering that over a million troops either were billeted in the city or passed through it. Most of these men wanted what they saw as their fair share of loot in one form or another.

A number of victims, as the diary indicates, suffered grave psychological damage, but the author and the widow she comes to live with instinctively find the best means of self-preservation. "Slowly but surely we're starting to view all the raping with a sense of humor," she writes. "Gallows humor." The widow jokes to everyone they meet about the compliment she was paid by one rapist who declared that she was much better than any Ukrainian woman. The author's sense of humor is drier. She finally manages to wash her sheets. "They needed it," she notes, "after all those booted guests."

Rape in war is a "collective experience," she also observes, as opposed to in peacetime, when it is individual. "Each woman helps the other, by speaking about it, airing her woes." But, as she soon found out, the male half of the German population wanted the subject to be buried.

"These days I keep noticing how my feelings toward men— and the feelings of all the other women—are changing," she writes as Hitler's regime collapses. "We feel sorry for them; they seem so miserable and powerless. The weaker sex. Deep down we women are experiencing a kind of collective disappointment. That has transformed us. . . . Among the many defeats at the end of this war is the defeat of the male sex." Her optimism proved sadly premature. The late 1940s and the 1950s, after the men returned from prison camps, were a sexually repressive era in which husbands reasserted their authority. Women were forbidden to mention the subject of rape as if it somehow dishonored their men, who were supposed to have defended them. It remained taboo until the late 1980s, when a younger generation of women started to encourage their mothers and grandmothers to speak about their experiences.

A Woman in Berlin is a war diary unlike any other. This is a victim's eye view, a woman's perspective of a terrifying onslaught on a civilian population, yet her account is characterized by its courage, its stunning intellectual honesty, and its uncommon powers of observation and perception. It is one of the most important personal accounts ever written about the effects of war and defeat. It is also one of the most revealing pieces of social history imaginable.

Antony Beevor

Translator's Note

This translation, like every other, must reckon with certain challenges. Local terrain familiar to the author is foreign to us: streets and districts, outlying towns, and even the specific architecture of apartment buildings, which in Berlin are frequently built around a courtyard, with shops at street level, below the residences. In conveying this topography I have tried to make it as accessible as possible while preserving a sense of place. Most names of places and streets have been kept in German (Müncheberg, Berliner Strasse), although a few (Landwehr Canal instead of Landwehrkanal) have been anglicized for clarity. The district *Rathaus* is identified once as a town hall and remains "Rathaus." Most military terms have been rendered with the U.S. equivalent ("first lieutenant"), although some Nazi-era formations have been kept in German (*Schutzpolizei, Volkssturm*). *Schnaps* is a generic word of certain distilled spirits and has been variously translated as "liquor," "brandy," or "vodka," depending on the context. Russian words have been transliterated, with any necessary translations provided in the text.

—*P. B.*

A Woman in Berlin

*This chronicle was begun on the day
when Berlin first saw the face of war.*

Friday, April 20, 1945, 4:00 P.M.

It's true: the war is rolling toward Berlin. What was yesterday a distant rumble has now become a constant roar. We breathe the din; our ears are deafened to all but the heaviest guns. We've long given up trying to figure out where they are positioned. We are ringed in by barrels, and the circle is growing smaller by the hour.

Now and then whole hours pass in eerie silence. Then all of a sudden you remember that it's spring. Clouds of lilac perfume drift over from untended gardens and waft through the charred ruins of apartment houses. Outside the cinema, the acacia stump is foaming over with green. The gardeners must have snatched a few minutes between sirens to dig at their allotment plots, because there's freshly turned earth around the garden sheds up and down Berlinerstrasse. Only the birds seem suspicious of this particular April: there's not a single sparrow nesting in the gutters of our roof.

A little before three o'clock the newspaper wagon drove up to the kiosk. Two dozen people were already waiting for the delivery-man, who immediately vanished in a flurry of hands and coins.

Gerda, the concierge's daughter, managed to grab a few "evening editions" and let me have one. It's not a real paper anymore, just a kind of news sheet printed on two sides and damp on both. The first thing I read as I went on my way was the Wehrmacht report. New place-names: Müncheberg, Seelow, Buchholz—they sound awfully close, like from somewhere in the Brandenburg Mark. I barely glanced at the news from the western front. What does it matter to us now? Our fate is rolling in from the east and it will transform the entire climate, like another Ice Age. People ask why, tormenting themselves with pointless questions. But I just want to focus on today, the task at hand.

Little groups milling around the kiosk, people with pasty faces, murmuring.

"Impossible, who would have thought it would come to this?"

"There's not one of us here didn't have at least a shred of hope."

"Nothing the likes of us can do about it."

The talk turns to western Germany: "They've got it good. For them it's over and done with." No one uses the word *Russians* anymore. It refuses to pass our lips.

Back in the attic apartment. I can't really call it a home; I no longer have a home. Not that the furnished room I was bombed out of was really mine either. All the same, I'd filled it with six years of my life. With my books and pictures and the hundreds of things you accumulate along the way. My starfish from that last peacetime summer on Norderney. The kilim Gerd brought me from Persia. My dented alarm clock. Photos, old letters, my zither, coins from twelve different countries, a piece of knitting that I'd started. All the souvenirs, the old skins and shells—the residue and warm debris of lived-in years.

Now that it's gone and all I have is a small suitcase with a handful of clothes, I feel naked, weightless. Since I own nothing, I can lay claim to everything—this unfamiliar apartment, for instance. Well, it's not entirely unfamiliar. The owner is a former colleague, and I was a frequent guest before he was called up. In keeping with the times, we used to barter with each other: his canned meat from Denmark for my French cognac, my French soap for the stockings he had from Prague. After I was bombed out I managed to get hold of him to tell him the news, and he said I could move in here. Last I heard he was in Vienna with a Wehrmacht censorship unit. Where he still is now . . . ? Not that attic apartments are much in demand these days. What's more, the roof leaks as many of the tiles have been shattered or blown away.

I keep wandering around these three rooms, but I can't find any peace. I have systematically searched every single cupboard and drawer for anything usable, in other words, something to eat, drink, or burn. Unfortunately, there isn't much. Frau Weiers, who used to clean the place, must have beaten me to it. These days everything is up for grabs. People no longer feel so closely tied to things; they no longer distinguish clearly between their own property and that of others.

I found a letter wedged inside a drawer, addressed to the real tenant. I felt ashamed for reading it, but I read it all the same. A passionate love letter, which I flushed down the toilet. (Most of the time we still have water.) Heart, hurt, love, desire—how foreign, how distant those words sound now. Evidently a sophisticated, discriminating love life requires three square meals a day. My sole concern as I write these lines is my stomach. All thinking and feeling, all wishes and hopes begin with food.

Two hours later. The gas is running on a tiny, dying flicker. The potatoes have been cooking for hours. The most miserable potatoes in the country, good only for distilling into liquor, they turn to mush and taste like cardboard. I swallowed one half-raw. I've been stuffing myself since early this morning. Went to Bolle's to use up the pale-blue milk coupons Gerd sent me for Christmas. Not a moment too soon—I got the last drops. The saleswoman had to tilt the can; she said there'd be no more milk coming into Berlin. That means children are going to die.

I drank a little of the milk right there on the street. Then, back at home, I wolfed down some porridge and chased it with a crust of bread. In theory I've eaten better than I have in ages. In practice, the hunger is gnawing away at me like a savage beast. Eating just made me hungrier than ever. I'm sure there's some scientific explanation. Something about food stimulating the digestive juices and making them crave more. No sooner do they get going than the limited supply is already digested and they start to rumble.

Rummaging through the few books owned by the tenant of this apartment (where I also found the blank notebook I'm using to write this), I turned up a novel. The setting is English aristocratic, with sentences like: "She cast a fleeting glance at her untouched meal, then rose and left the table." Ten lines later I found myself magnetically drawn back to that sentence. I must have read it a dozen times before I caught myself scratching my nails across the print, as if the untouched meal—which had just been described in detail—were really there and I could physically scrape it out of the book. A sure sign of insanity. Onset of mild delusions brought on by lack of food. I'm sorry I don't have Hamsun's *Hunger* to bone up on the subject. Of course I couldn't read it even if I hadn't been bombed out, since somebody snatched my copy right out of my shopping bag over two years ago in the U-Bahn. It had a raffia cover; evidently the pickpocket mistook it for a ration card holder. Poor man! He must have been a very disappointed thief! I'm sure Hamsun would enjoy hearing that story.

Morning gossip at the baker's: "When they get here they'll go through the apartments and take whatever they can find to eat. . . . Don't expect them to give us a thing. . . . They've worked it all out;

the Germans are going to have to starve for two months. . . . People in Silesia are already running around the woods digging up roots. . . . Children are dying. . . . Old people are eating grass like animals."

So much for the vox populi—no one knows anything for sure. There's no *Völkischer Beobachter* on the stairs anymore. No Frau Weiers coming up to read me the headlines about rape over breakfast. "Old Woman of Seventy Defiled. Nun Violated Twenty-Four Times." (I wonder who was counting.) That's exactly what they sound like, too, those headlines. Are they supposed to spur the men of Berlin to protect and defend us women? Ridiculous. Their only effect is to send thousands more helpless women and children running out of town, jamming the roads heading west, where they're likely to starve or die under fire from enemy planes. Whenever she read the paper Frau Weiers's eyes would get big and glaze over. Something in her actually enjoyed that brand of horror. Either that or her unconscious was just happy it hadn't happened to her. Because she *is* afraid; I know for a fact she wanted to get away. I haven't seen her since the day before yesterday.

Our radio's been dead for four days. Once again we see what a dubious blessing technology really is. Machines with no intrinsic value, worthless if you can't plug them in somewhere. Bread, however, is absolute. Coal is absolute. And gold is gold whether you're in Rome, Peru, or Breslau. But radios, gas stoves, central heating, hot plates, all these gifts of the modern age—they're nothing but dead weight if the power goes out. At the moment we're marching backwards in time. Cave dwellers.

Friday, probably around 7:00 P.M. Went for one last quick ride on the streetcar headed for the Rathaus. The air is full of rolling and rumbling, the constant thunder of heavy guns. The woman tram conductor sounded pathetic shouting over the din. I studied the other passengers. You could read in their faces what they weren't saying out loud. We've turned into a nation of mutes. People don't talk to one another except when they're safe in their basements. When's the next time I'll ride a streetcar? Will I ever? They've been pestering us with these Class I and Class II tickets for the past several weeks, and now the news sheet says that as of tomorrow only people with the red Class III tickets will be allowed to use public transportation. That's about one in four hundred—in other words, no one, which means that's it.

A cold evening, dry faucets. My potatoes are still simmering on the tiny gas flame. I poked around and managed to fill some shopping bags with split peas, pearl barley, flour, and ersatz coffee, then stashed the bags in a box. More luggage to drag down to the basement. After I'd tied it all up I realized I'd forgotten the salt. The body can't do without salt, at least not for long. And we'll probably be holed up down there for a while.

Friday, 11:00 P.M., by the light of an oil lamp in the basement, my notebook on my knees. Around 10:00 P.M. there was a series of three or four bombs. The air-raid siren started screaming. Apparently it has to be worked manually now. No light. Running downstairs in the dark, the way we've been doing ever since Tuesday. We slip and stumble. Somewhere a small hand-operated dynamo is whirring away; it casts giant shadows on the wall of the stairwell. Wind is blowing through the broken panes, rattling the blackout blinds. No one pulls them down anymore—what's the point?

Shuffling feet. Suitcases banging into things. Lutz Lehmann screaming, "Mutti!" To get to the basement shelter we have to cross the street to the side entrance, climb down some stairs, then go along a corridor and across a square courtyard with stars overhead and aircraft buzzing like hornets. Then down some more stairs, through more doors and corridors. Finally we're in our shelter, behind an iron door that weighs a hundred pounds, with rubber seals around the edges and two levers to lock it shut. The official term is air-raid shelter. We call it cave, underworld, catacomb of fear, mass grave.

The ceiling is supported by a forest of rough timbers. You can smell the resin despite the closeness of the air. Every evening old Herr Schmidt—Schmidt the curtain man—launches into a structural analysis to demonstrate that the forest will hold up even if the building overhead collapses—assuming that it collapses at a certain angle and distributes its weight in a certain way. The landlord, who should know about that kind of thing, isn't around to tell us. He took off to Bad Ems and is now an American.

In any case, the people here are convinced that their cave is one of the safest. There's nothing more alien than an unknown shelter. I've been coming here for nearly three months and still feel like a stranger. Every place has its own set of quirks and regulations. In my old basement they were obsessed with having water on hand in case of fire. Wherever you turned you bumped into pots and pails and buckets and barrels full of murky fluid. And still the building burned like a torch. You might as well have spit on the fire for all that water would have done.

Frau Weiers told me that in her shelter it's the lungs. At the first sound of a bomb they all bend forward and take very shallow breaths, their hands pressed against their bodies. Someone told them this would help prevent blast lungs. Here in this basement they're all fixated on the walls. They sit with their backs against the outside wall—except in front of the ventilation flap. At the first explosion they move on to the next obsession: cloths—everyone has a cloth handy to wrap around their mouths and noses and then tie behind their heads. I haven't seen that in any other basement. I don't know how the cloths are supposed to help. Still, if it makes people feel better!

Apart from these ticks it's the usual cave dwellers on the usual chairs, which range from kitchen stools to brocade armchairs. We're mostly upper- and lower-middle class, with a sprinkling of workers. I look around and take stock:

First is the baker's wife, two plump red cheeks swaddled in a lambskin collar. Then the pharmacist's widow, who finished a training course in first aid and who sometimes lays out cards on two chairs pushed together and reads them for the other women. Frau Lehmann, whose husband is missing in the East and who is now a pillow for the sleeping infant on her arm and four-year-old Lutz asleep on her lap, his shoelaces dangling. The young man in gray trousers and horn-rimmed glasses who on closer inspection turns out to be a young woman. Three elderly sisters, all dress-makers, huddled together like a big black pudding. The refugee girl from Königsberg in East Prussia, wearing the few old rags she's managed to piece together. Then there's Schmidt, who was bombed out and reassigned here, Schmidt the curtain wholesaler without curtains, always chatting away despite his years. The bookselling husband and wife who spent several years in Paris and often speak French to each other in low voices . . .

I've just been listening to a woman of forty who was bombed out of her home in Adlershof and moved in here with her mother. Apparently a high-explosive bomb buried itself in her neighbor's garden and completely demolished her own house, which she had bought with her savings. The pig she'd been fattening up was flung all the way into the rafters. "It wasn't fit to eat after that." The married couple next door to her also met their maker. People retrieved what parts of them they could from the rubble of the building and the mess in the garden. The funeral was very nice. An all-male choir from the Tailors' Guild sang at the graveside. But everything ended in confusion when the sirens cut in right during the "Rock of Ages" and the grave diggers had to practi-cally throw the coffin in the ground. You could hear the contents bumping about inside. And now for the punch line, the narrator chuckling in advance, although so far her story hasn't been all that funny: "And imagine, three days later their daughter is going through the garden looking for anything of use, and right behind the rain barrel she stumbles on one of her papa's arms."

A few people give a brief laugh, but most don't. I wonder: did they bury the arm as well?

Continuing with my inventory: Across from me is an elderly gentleman, a businessman, wrapped in blankets and sweating feverishly. Next to him is his wife, who speaks with a sharp Hamburg *s*, and their eighteen-year-old daughter, whom they call Stinchen, with the same *s*. Then comes the blonde who was recently reassigned here and whom no one knows, holding hands with her lodger, whom no one knows either. The scrawny retired postmaster and his wife, who is forever lugging around an artificial leg made of nickel, leather, and wood—a partial Pietà since its owner, their one-legged son, is (or was, nobody knows for sure) in a military hospital in Breslau. The hunchbacked doctor of chemistry from the soft drink company, slumped over in his armchair like a gnome. Then the concierge's family: a mother, two daughters, and a fatherless grandson. Erna and Henni from the bakery, who are staying with their employer because it was impossible for them to make their way home. Antoine the Belgian with his curly black hair, who puts on a big show of being a baker's apprentice and has something going with Henni. The landlord's housekeeper, who got left behind and who in open defiance of all airraid regulations is carrying an aging fox terrier. And then there's me, a pale-faced blonde always dressed in the same winter coat—which she managed to save just by chance—who was employed in a publishing house until it shut down last week and sent its employees on leave "until further notice."

One or two other people, colorless, unremarkable. A community of discards, unwanted at the front, rejected by the Volkssturm, the civil defense. A few of our group are missing: the baker, who's gone out to his garden plot to bury his silver (he's the only one in the building with a red Class III ticket), and Fräulein Behn, a brash spinster who works in the post office, who just raced off to get today's news sheet during a lull in the bombing. Another woman left for Potsdam to bury seven of her family who died in the heavy bombardment there. The engineer from the fourth floor is also absent, along with his wife and son. Last week he boarded a barge that was to take him and his household goods along the Mittelland Canal to Braunschweig, where his armaments factory has been moved. The entire workforce is heading for the center of the country. It must be dangerously overpopulated—unless the Yanks have already arrived. We no longer know a thing.

Midnight. No power. An oil lamp is smoking away on the beam above me. A sudden spike in the constant drone outside sets off our mania, and we all wrap our cloths around our mouths and noses. A ghostly Turkish harem, a gallery of half-veiled death masks. Only our eyes are alive.

Saturday, April 21, 1945, 2:00 A.M.

Bombs that made the walls shake. My fingers are still trembling as I hold my pen. I'm covered in sweat as if from heavy labor. Before my building was hit I used to go down to the shelter and eat thick slices of bread with butter. But since the night I helped dig out people who'd been buried in the rubble, I've been preoccupied, forced to cope with my fear of death. The symptoms are always the same. First the sweat beads up around my hairline, then I feel something boring into my spine, my throat gets scratchy, my mouth goes dry, my heart starts to skip. I've fixed my eyes on the chair leg opposite and am memorizing every turned bulge and curve. It would be nice to be able to pray. The brain clings to set phrases, fragments of sentences: "Pass lightly through this world, for it is nothing . . . and each one falls as God desires. . . . *Noli timere.*" And so on, until this wave of bombers passes.

As if on command, everyone starts chattering feverishly, laughing, joking, shouting over one another. Fräulein Behn steps up with the news sheet and reads Goebbels's speech in honor of the Führer's birthday (the date had slipped most of our minds). She reads with a new intonation, a mocking, sarcastic voice we haven't heard down here before: "Golden fields of grain . . . a people at peace." "How about that," say the people from Berlin. Or: "That would be nice!" High-blown phrases that now fall on deaf ears.

Three in the morning. The basement is snoozing away. Several all clears sound, immediately followed by new alarms. No bombs, though. I'm writing. It does me good, takes my mind off things. And Gerd needs to read this if he comes back—if he's still—no, cross that out, musn't jinx things.

The girl who looks like a young man just snuck up and asked what I'm writing. "Nothing special. Just some private scribbling. Gives me something to do."

After the earlier wave of bombs, "Siegismund" turned up, an elderly gentleman from the neighborhood. His nickname comes from *Sieg,* victory: he keeps talking about the victory at hand, the certain victory, *Sieg* this and *Sieg* that, which is presumably why he was kicked out of his own basement. Siegismund genuinely believes that salvation is at hand and that "that man" (as we now call A. H.) knows exactly what he's doing. Whenever he talks the people sitting nearby exchange silent, meaningful glances. No one challenges Siegismund. Who wants to argue with a madman? Besides, madmen can be dangerous. The only person who agrees with him is the concierge's wife, and she is fervent in her support, pronouncing through her fanglike teeth that you can count on "that man" as if he were God himself.

Nine in the morning, up in the attic apartment. (I can only guess at these times; as long as there's no clock in sight my life is timeless.) Gray morning, pouring rain. I'm writing at the windowsill, using it as a stand-up desk. The all-clear sounded shortly after three. I came upstairs, took off my shoes, slipped out of my dress, and collapsed onto my bed, which is always turned back and ready. Five hours of deep sleep. The gas is out.

Just counted my cash, 452 marks. No idea what I'll do with all that money—the only things left to buy cost no more than a few pfennigs. I also have about a thousand in the bank, again because there's nothing to buy. (When I opened that account, in the first year of the war, I was still thinking of saving for peacetime, maybe even taking a trip around the world. That was a long, long time ago.) Recently people have been running to the bank—assuming they can find one that's still open—to withdraw their money. What for? If we go down, the mark goes with us. After all, money, at least paper money, is only a fiction and won't have any value if the central bank collapses. Indifferent, I run my thumb over the wad of bills, which probably won't be worth anything except as souvenirs, snapshots of a bygone era. I assume the victors will bring their own currency and let us have some. Or else they'll print some kind of military scrip—unless they decide not to give us even that, and force us to work for just a helping of soup.

Noontime. Endless rain. Walked to Parkstrasse and got some more paper money to add to my wad of souvenirs. The head clerk paid me last month's salary and made my "vacation" official. The whole publishing house has dissolved into thin air. The employment office has also breathed its last; no one is looking for help anymore. So for the moment we're all our own bosses.

Bureaucracy strikes me as a fair-weather friend: the whole civil service shuts down at the first sign of shrapnel. (By the way, it's very peaceful just now. Alarmingly peaceful.) We're no longer being governed. And still, everywhere you look, in every basement, some kind of order always emerges. When my house was hit I saw how even people who'd been injured or traumatized or buried in the rubble walked away in an orderly manner. The forces of order prevail in this basement as well, a spirit that regulates, organizes, commands. It has to be in our nature. People must have functioned that way as far back as the Stone Age. Herd instinct, a mechanism for preservation of the species. With animals they say it's always the males, the lead bull, the lead stallion. But in our basement lead mares would be closer to the truth. Fräulein Behn is a lead mare, so is the woman from Hamburg, who keeps very calm. I'm not one, and I wasn't in my old basement either. Besides, back there we had a lead bull bellowing around, dominating the field, a retired major who brooked no rivals. I always hated having to huddle together down there, always tried to find a corner of my own to sleep in. But when the herd leader calls I follow willingly.

On the way home I walked alongside the tram. I couldn't get on, since I don't have a Class III ticket. And it was nearly empty, too; I counted eight passengers in the car. Meanwhile hundreds of people were trudging right next to it in the pouring rain, even though the tram could easily have picked them up—it has to run anyway. But no—see above under: Order. It's rooted deep inside us; we do as we are told.

I bought some rolls at the bakery. The shelves still appear to be stocked, you don't see any panic-buying. After that I went to the ration card office. Today they were stamping potato coupons 75 to 77 for people with my last initial. The line went surprisingly quickly, although there were only two women on duty with rubber stamps instead of the usual group. They didn't even look at the coupons, just stamped them automatically, like machines. Why all this stamping? No one knows, but we all go there, assuming that there's some sense in it. The last group—X to Z—is to report April 28th, according to the posted schedule.

Carts covered with sopping wet canvas were trundling through the rain into the city. Under the tarps are soldiers. That was the first time I'd seen the real men from the front line—dirty, gray-bearded, all of them old. The carts were pulled by Polish ponies, dark-coated in the rain. The only other freight they're hauling is hay. Doesn't look much like a motorized Blitzkrieg anymore.

On the way home I went behind the black ruins where Professor K. used to live, and broke into his abandoned garden, where I picked several crocuses and tore off a few lilac branches. Took some to Frau Golz, who used to live in my old apartment building. We sat across from each other at her copper table and talked. Or rather, we shouted above the gunfire that had just resumed. Frau Golz, her voice breaking: "What flowers, what lovely flowers." The tears were running down her face. I felt terrible as well. Beauty hurts now. We're so full of death.

This morning I wondered how many dead people I've seen in my life. The first was Herr Schermann. I was five at the time, he was seventy, silver-white hair on white silk, candles at his head, raised casket, the whole scene full of meaning. So death, then, was something solemn and beautiful. At least until 1928, when Hilde and Käte P. showed me their brother Hans, who'd died the day before. He lay on the sofa like a bundle of rags, a blue scarf tied high around his chin, his knees bent—a piece of dirt, a nothing. Later came my own dead relatives, blue fingernails among the flowers and rosaries. Then the man in Paris who'd been run over and was lying in a pool of blood. And the frozen man on the Moskva River.

Dead people, yes, but I've never seen anyone actually die. I expect that won't be long in coming. Not that I think it could happen to me. I've had so many narrow escapes; I feel I lead a charmed life. Which is probably the way most people feel. How else could they be in such high spirits, surrounded by so much death? What's clear is that every threat to your life boosts your vitality. My own flame is stronger; I'm burning more fiercely than before the air raids. Each new day of life is a day of triumph. You've survived once again. You're defiant. On the one hand you stand taller, but at the same time your feet are planted more firmly on the ground. When the first bombs started to hit I remembered a verse from Horace, which I penciled on the wall of my room:

> *Si fractus illabatur orbis*
> *Impavidum ferient ruinae.*
>
> *[Should Nature's pillar'd frame give way,*
> *that wreck would strike one fearless head.]*

Back then you could still write to people abroad. I quoted those lines in a letter to my friends the D.s in Stockholm, flexing my muscles—in part to make myself feel strong—by telling them how intense it was to live here, amid all the danger. I felt a kind of forbearance writing that, as if I were an adult initiated into the deep secrets of life, speaking to innocent children in need of protection.

I was upstairs in bed, dozing away as the wind blew through the shattered panes. I had a brick at my feet that had taken hours to warm over a tiny gas flame. Around 8:00 P.M. Frau Lehmann knocked on the door. "Come on down, the alarms are out, no sirens anymore. Everybody else is already in the basement."

A breakneck rush down the stairs. I was scared to death when my heel caught on the edge of a step; I barely managed to grab hold of the railing in time. My knees went weak, but I went on, heart pounding, slowly groping my way through the pitch-dark passage. Finally I found the lever to the basement door.

Our cave looked different. Everybody was bedded down. There were pillows everywhere, quilts, deck chairs. I just managed to squeeze my way to my usual spot. The radio's dead: no signal, not even from the airport. The kerosene lantern is flickering dimly. A cluster of bombs, then things go quiet. Siegismund shows up, still waving his flag, claiming that the tide's about to turn—even as Curtainman Schmidt is muttering something about Russians in Bernau and Zossen. We stay put, the hours crawl by, we listen to the artillery thudding away, sometimes far off, sometimes quite close. The pharmacist's widow turns to me. "You better not go back to that fifth-floor apartment of yours," she warns. She offers to let me spend the night in her apartment on the second floor. We clamber up the back stairs, formerly designated "for servants and deliveries"—a narrow spiral staircase. The glass shards crunch underfoot, wind whistles through the open windows. She shows me to a small room next to the kitchen; a couch by the door welcomes me and grants me two hours of sleep under an unfamiliar-smelling woolen blanket. Until sometime around midnight, when bombs start hitting nearby and we take refuge back in the basement. Long, miserable hours in the middle of the night. Right now I'm too tired to go on writing, down here.

Next morning, a little before 10:00 A.M., upstairs in the attic apartment. We stuck it out in the basement until about 4:00 A.M. Then I climbed up here, warmed some turnip soup on what gas there was, peeled a couple of potatoes, boiled my last egg—it was practically liquid when I ate it—and dabbed on the last drops of cologne. It's strange to be doing all these things for the last time, at least for the foreseeable future, until further notice, for what's sure to be a long time. Where am I supposed to come up with another egg? Or more perfume? I treat myself to these pleasures deliberately, consciously, reverently. After that I crawled into bed with all my clothes on, slept in fits and starts, uneasy dreams. Now I have to run, do shopping.

Back in the attic, 2:00 P.M. Torrents of rain outside. No more newspapers. Even so, people pushed to line up right on time at the distribution center; apparently some leaflet or extra edition had run an announcement. News is now spread by word of mouth, and every new item gets quickly passed around.

They're handing out what are officially called advance rations—meat, sausage, processed foods, sugar, canned goods, and ersatz coffee. I took my place in line and waited in the rain for two hours before finally getting 250 grams of coarse-ground grain, 250 grams of oatmeal, 2 pounds of sugar, 100 grams of ersatz coffee, and a can of kohlrabi. There still isn't any meat or sausage or real coffee. A crowd is milling about the corner butcher's, an endless line on both sides, people standing four abreast in the pouring rain. What a mess! My line was abuzz with rumors: we've just surrendered Köpenick, they've taken Wünsdorf, the Russians are already at the Teltow Canal. The women seem to have reached an unspoken agreement—all of a sudden no one is bringing up "that subject."

Talking in the line, I find myself coming down a level both in the way I speak and in what I say, immersing myself in the general emotion—though this always leaves me feeling a little slimy and disgusting. And yet I don't want to fence myself off, I want to give myself over to this communal sense of humanity; I want to be part of it, to experience it. There's a split between my aloofness, the desire to keep my private life to myself, and the urge to be like everyone else, to belong to the nation, to abide and suffer history together.

What else can I do? I have to sit it out and wait. Our days are accented with flak and artillery fire. Now and then I wish it were all over. These are strange times—history experienced firsthand, the stuff of tales yet untold and songs unsung. But seen up close, history is much more troublesome, nothing but burdens and fears.

Tomorrow I'll go look for nettles and get some coal. Small as it is, our new stock of provisions will keep us from starving. I fret over it the way rich people worry about their money. The food could be bombed or stolen, eaten by mice or looted by the enemy. Finally I have everything crammed into one more box for the basement. I can still carry all my earthly possessions up and down the stairs with hardly any effort.

Late evening, twilight. I paid Frau Golz another visit. Her husband was there, too, sitting in his coat and scarf, since the room was cold and gusty. They were both quiet, depressed. They don't understand the world anymore. We hardly spoke. Outside the building we could hear a constant, tinny rattle, punctuated by the drumlike flak. As if someone were beating a gigantic carpet that hung all the way down from the sky.

The courtyards echo the sound of the gunfire. For the first time I understand the phrase *thunder of cannon*, which until now has always sounded like a hollow cliché, such as *courage of a lion* or *manly chest*. But thunder is an apt description.

Showers and storms outside. I stood in the doorway and watched some soldiers pass by our building, listlessly dragging their feet. Some were limping. Mute, each man to himself, they trudged along, out of step, toward the city. Stubbly chins and sunken cheeks, their backs weighed down with gear.

"What's going on?" I shout. "Where are you headed?"

At first no one answers. Then someone mutters something I can't make out. Then someone else mumbles something, but the words are clear enough: "Führer, command! And we will follow, even unto death."

They all seem so miserable, so little like men anymore. The only thing they inspire is pity, no hope or expectation. They already look defeated, captured. They stare past us blindly, impassively, as we stand on the curb. They're obviously not too concerned about us, us *Volk* or civilians or Berliners or whatever we are. Now we're nothing but a burden. And I don't sense they're the least ashamed of how bedraggled they look, how ragged. They're too tired to care, too apathetic. They're all fought out. I can't bear watching them anymore.

The walls are marked with chalk, by now smeared and running, evidently directing the soldiers to specific assembly points. Two cardboard placards are tacked onto the maple tree across the street, announcements, neatly penned by hand in blue and red letters, with the names *Hitler* and *Goebbels* on them. One warns against surrender and threatens hanging and shooting. The other, addressed "To the People of Berlin," warns against seditious foreigners and calls on all men to fight. Nobody pays any attention. The handwriting looks pathetic and inconsequential, like something whispered.

Yes, we've been spoiled by technology. We can't accept doing without loudspeakers or rotary presses. Handwritten placards and whispered proclamations just don't carry the same weight. Technology has devalued the impact of our own speech and writing. In the old days one man's call to arms was enough to set off an uprising—a few hand-printed leaflets, ninety-five theses nailed to a church door in Wittenberg. But today we need more, we need bigger and better, wider repercussions, mass-produced by machines and multiplied exponentially. A woman reading the placards summed it up nicely: "Well, just look what those two have come to."

In the basement, 10:00 P.M. After my evening soup I allowed myself a little rest in the bed upstairs before trotting back down. The full assembly had already gathered. There was less shelling today and there has been no air raid yet, though this is the time they usually come. Nervous merriment. All sorts of stories making the rounds. Frau W. pipes up, "Better a Russki on top than a Yank overhead." The joke seems not very appropriate to her mourning crape. Next comes Fräulein Behn: "Let's be honest for once. None of us is still a virgin, right?" No one says anything; I wonder who among us might be. Probably the concierge's younger daughter—she's only sixteen and ever since her older sister went astray they keep her under close guard. If I'm any judge of young girls' faces, then eighteen-year-old Stinchen with the Hamburg *s* slumbering away over there is another. As for the girl who looks like a young man, I have my doubts. But she could be a special case.

We have a new woman in the basement: up to now she's been going to the public bunker six blocks away, which is supposed to be secure. She lives by herself in her apartment, but I don't know yet whether she's abandoned, widowed, or divorced. She has a patch of weeping eczema over her left cheek. She tells us, at first in a whisper but then out loud, that she's secured her wedding ring to her panties. "If they get that far then the ring won't matter much anyway." General laughter. Still, her weeping eczema might prove just the thing that saves her. Which is worth something these days.

Monday, April 23, 1945, 9:00 A.M.

The night was amazingly quiet, with hardly any flak. We have a new resident, the husband of the woman who was bombed out of her home in Adlershof and who moved in here with her mother. He showed up very quietly, still in uniform; an hour later he was wearing civilian clothes. How could he get away with it? No one even noticed, or else they don't care. Anyway, no one's saying anything. A hard-boiled soldier from the front, he still looks pretty strong. We're happy to have him.

Deserting suddenly seems like a perfectly understandable thing to do—a good idea, in fact. I can't help thinking of Leonidas and his three hundred Spartans standing their ground at Thermopylae and falling in battle as their law demanded. We learned about them in school; we were taught to admire their heroism. And I'm sure that if you looked hard enough you could find three hundred German soldiers willing to do the same. But not three million. The larger the force and the more random its composition, the less chance of its members opting for textbook heroism. We women find it senseless to begin with; that's just the way we are— reasonable, practical, opportunistic. We prefer our men alive.

Toward midnight I was so tired I almost fell off my chair (where am I supposed to come up with a bed?), so I staggered up the glass-strewn stairs and made my way to the second floor and the widow's couch, where I slept until nearly 6:00 A.M. Afterward I was surprised to learn there'd been a series of bombs. I slept right through it.

There were rolls at the baker's, the last ones. My last ration cards for bread, too. No new cards in sight. No decrees and no news, either. Nothing. Not a soul cares about us anymore. We're suddenly mere individuals, no longer members of the tribe, the German Nation. Old ties are broken; friendships don't extend farther than three buildings away. There's only the group of us, huddled in the cave, a clan, just like in prehistoric times. The horizon has shrunk to three hundred paces.

At the baker's I heard the Russians were in Weissensee and Rangsdorf. How many times have I gone swimming in the lake at Rangsdorf? "The Russians in Rangsdorf": I say it out loud, just to try it out, but it doesn't sound right. Today the eastern sky was burning red with the constant fires.

Back from getting coal, 1:00 P.M. Heading south I could feel I was literally marching toward the front. They've already closed off the S-Bahn tunnel. The people standing outside said a soldier had been hanged at the other end, in his underwear, a sign with the word *traitor* around his neck. His body was dangling so close to the ground you could spin him around by the legs. The person who said this had seen it himself; he'd chased off the street kids who'd been amusing themselves that way.

Berliner Strasse looked desolate, half torn up and barricaded off. Lines in front of the stores. Blank faces amid the flak. Trucks were rolling into town. Filthy figures in shabby bandages trudged alongside, their bodies sprayed with dirt, their faces empty. A baggage train of hay carts, gray-haired men on the boxes. Volkssturm units are posted at the barricade, in motley uniforms hastily pieced together. You see very young boys, baby faces peeping out beneath oversized steel helmets; it's frightening to hear their high-pitched voices. They're fifteen years old at the most, standing there looking so skinny and small in their billowing uniform tunics.

Why are we so appalled at the thought of children being murdered? In three or four years the same children strike us as perfectly fit for shooting and maiming. Where do you draw the line? When their voices break? Because that's what really gets me the most, thinking about these little boys: their voices, so high, so bright. Up to now being a soldier meant being a man. And being a man means being able to father a child. Wasting these boys before they reach maturity obviously runs against some fundamental law of nature, against our instinct, against every drive to preserve the species. Like certain fish or insects that eat their own offspring. People aren't supposed to do that. The fact that this is exactly what we are doing is a sure sign of madness.

No one was at the publishing house; the building was completely abandoned, the basement full of coal. The woman relocated in our building had a problem and plied me with questions about what to do. Her oldest daughter is the mother of an eight-week-old infant; it seems that yesterday she stopped giving milk, so that all of a sudden she can no longer nurse her baby, and the little one has been bawling. Everyone's worried how the mother will pull the child through, now that there's no more cow's milk. I suggested to the young mother that eating some wild vegetables might help bring on her milk. Together we bent over the grass in the garden, which was soaked through with rain, and pulled up the young nettle shoots along the wall, using handkerchiefs to protect our hands. Then dandelions, the few we could find. Smells of plants and soil, primrose stars, red hawthorn, spring. But the flak keeps yapping away.

I filled a pack with hard coal and probably carried off fifty pounds. Yet even with the load I managed to overtake another troop of soldiers on my way back. I saw my first weapons in several days: two bazookas, one submachine gun, ammunition boxes. Young guys wearing their cartridge belts like some barbarian adornment.

A little before noon there was a burial on our street, or so I was told; the pharmacist's widow had been there. A seventeen-year-old girl: grenade, shrapnel, leg amputated, bled to death. Her parents buried her in their garden in back of some currant bushes. They used their old broom closet as a coffin.

So now we're free to bury our dead wherever we wish, just as in ancient times. It makes me think of the time a huge Great Dane died in my old apartment building and wound up being buried in the garden. But what a scene beforehand—the landlord, the concierge, the other tenants, everybody fought against it. And now they bury a human being and nobody gives it a second thought; in fact, I think the parents find comfort in their daughter's being so close. And I catch myself assigning graves in our own little bit of garden.

4:00 P.M. in the attic. I just had an amazing experience. I was visiting Frau Golz and started playing with the telephone, just for fun. To my amazement I could hear something despite the fact the line has been dead for days. I dialed Gisela's number and managed to get through even though she lives an hour away in Berlin W. We were so eager to hear what the other had to say we couldn't stop talking. It turns out her company has just collapsed. Her boss gave a rousing speech and then fled to the west, leaving the little people to fend for themselves. We're completely forgotten. We strain our ears to the void. We are all alone.

Gisela told me she's exactly as old as her father was when he fell at Verdun in the First World War almost to the day. She never saw her father. Now she says that she can't stop thinking about him; she talks with him in spirit, as if her time were coming, as if she was going to meet him soon. We never spoke about such things before; we would have been embarrassed to bare our hearts like that. Now the deepest layers are pushing to the surface. Farewell, Gisela. We've each lived our thirty years or so. Maybe we'll see each other again someday, safe and sound.

Back in the cave, Monday, 8:00 P.M. Today the first artillery hit our corner. Whizzing, hissing, howling: *uuueee*. Flames flashing up. Terrified shouts in the courtyard. Stumbling downstairs, I could hear the shells landing right outside the cinema. The enemy is shooting at us. Incidentally, people say the Russians are sticking to the smaller guns. And we're beginning to feel a little less terrified about the American carpet bombing, since at least here in Berlin they'd wind up hitting Russians as well.

A new rumor floats around the basement, which the wife of the liquor distiller heard from a reliable, very secret source and announces with a heaving bosom: the Yanks and Tommies have quarreled with Ivan and are thinking of joining with us to chase Ivan out of the country. Scornful laughter and heated discussion. The woman is offended and gets so angry she slips into her native Saxon dialect. She just returned yesterday to her apartment—and our basement—from their (somewhat small) distillery behind Moritzplatz, where she and her husband had been spending the nights, so she could hold the fort at home. Her husband stayed with the bottles and vats—and a redhead named Elvira, as everyone in the basement knows.

People are still taking care of business. Just before the stores closed I managed to get another 150 grams of coarse grain. Suddenly I heard excited screams around the corner and the sound of running feet: a wagon was being unloaded near Bolle's; barrels of butter—all rancid—were being carried into the building for distribution. One pound per person and—here's what's frightening—for free! All you have to do is get your card stamped. Is this the first sign of panic or is it the voice of reason speaking from beyond the bureaucratic files? Right away people started crowding outside the shop door, pounding one another with umbrellas and fists. I joined in the pushing, too, for a few minutes, and in the process overheard talk of reserves, reinforcements, and German tanks from somewhere—one woman claimed to have picked up something like that last night over the radio detector. Then I decided to let butter be butter—I don't want to get into a fistfight over it, at least not today. But maybe I'll have to learn how soon.

Silent night. Distant pounding. Not a peep from the cave dwellers, not a word—they're too exhausted. Only snoring and the short, shallow breaths of the children.

Tuesday, April 24, 1945, around noon

No news. We're completely cut off. Some gas but no water. Looking out the window I see throngs of people outside the stores. They're still fighting over the rancid butter—which is still being given away, but now it's down to a quarter pound per ration card. The Schutzpolizei is just now getting things under control—I see four of them. And on top of that it's raining.

At the moment I'm sitting on the window seat in the widow's apartment. She just stormed in, all keyed up. A shell hit outside Hefter's meat market, right in the middle of the line. Three dead and ten wounded, but they're already lining up again. The widow demonstrated how people were using their sleeves to wipe the blood off their meat coupons. "Anyway, only three people died," she said. "What's that compared with an air raid?" No question about it: we're spoiled, all right.

Even so, I'm astounded at how the sight of a few beef quarters and hog jowls is enough to get the frailest grandmother to hold her ground. The same people who used to run for shelter if three fighter planes were spotted somewhere over central Germany are now standing in the meat line as stolid as walls. At most they'll plop a bucket on their head or perhaps a helmet. Standing in line is a family business, with every member on shift for a couple hours before being relieved. But the line for meat is too long for me; I'm not yet ready to give it a go. Besides, meat has to be eaten right away; it won't keep for more than a meal. I think they're all dreaming of eating their fill one last time, a final meal before the execution.

2:00 P.M. Just caught a glimpse of the sun. Without giving it a second thought I strolled out to the balcony overlooking the court-yard and sat down in my wicker chair, basking in the sun—until a formation of bombers whizzed by overhead and one explosion merged into the next. I'd actually forgotten there was a war on. As it is, my head is oddly empty—just now I jerked up from my writing, something fell close by, and I heard the clink of shattering glass. Once again I'm having hunger pangs on a full stomach. I feel the need to gnaw on something. What's the baby who's still nursing supposed to live off now, the baby who can't get any milk? Yesterday the people in line were talking about children dying. One old lady suggested that a piece of bread chewed up and full of saliva might help the little ones when they can't get milk.

An infant in the city is a sorry thing indeed when its elaborately constructed supply of milk has been disrupted. Even if the mother manages to find something for herself and get halfway nourished, the source is bound to run dry soon enough, given what is approaching us so mercilessly. Fortunately the youngest child in our basement is already eighteen months old. Yesterday I saw someone slip the mother a couple of cookies for the baby—in what was likely the only recent act of giving. Mostly people squirrel away whatever they have and nobody thinks about sharing anything with anybody.

Back in the basement, 9:00 P.M. Toward evening a woman we didn't know showed up and asked the widow and me to go with her to help in the field hospital.

Smoke and red skies on the horizon. The east is all ablaze. They say the Russians have already reached Braunauer Strasse—ironic, considering that it was in Braunau that Adolf first saw the light of day. That reminds me of a quip I heard yesterday in the basement: "Just think how much better off we'd be if his old lady'd had a miscarriage."

When we reached the hospital, the whole place was filled with smoke. Men were running about wildly, screaming and hollering.

An ambulance driver: "Hey, we've got a shot lung with an impacted bullet!"

"Move, go away, didn't you hear? We don't have a single bed left."

The driver is fuming: "This is where they told me to go."

"Go away or else!" The sergeant threatens with his fists. The driver storms off, cursing.

Lightly wounded men go slinking through the corridor, one barefoot, his bleeding hand wrapped in his socks. Another, also barefoot, leaves bloody footprints as he walks; the soles of his feet squish as he lifts them off the ground. Waxy yellow faces peek out of head bandages with rapidly spreading stains of red. We look into two or three other rooms.

It's very stuffy, a smell of men, bivouacs, nervous apprehension. One man snarls at us: "What do you want?"

The woman who'd come to get us answers shyly that a man in a truck had driven by shouting that the field hospital needed women to help.

"That's nonsense. We don't have anything for you to do here. Go back home."

So they don't want female help, but what a peculiar tone, so dismissive, disdainful. As if we wanted to get our hands on the guns or play at being soldiers. Once again, I have to relearn everything I've been taught about women in war. Once our role was to play the ministering angel. Scraping up lint for bandages. A cool hand on a man's hot brow, at a healthy distance from the shooting. Now there's no difference between a regular hospital and a field hospital. The front is everywhere.

Admittedly this particular hospital is trying to remain a kind of island in the midst of the storm. The roof is painted with gigantic crosses and white sheets have been spread out in the form of a cross in the yard in front of the building. But aerial mines are impartial and the carpet of bombs is tightly woven, with no holes for compassion. Which they know in the field hospital—otherwise they wouldn't have crammed everyone down in the basement the way they have. Men's faces peer out of every barred window.

Back in the shelter, the cave dwellers are feverish with excitement, agitated, nervous. The woman from Hamburg tells me with her sharp *s*'s that they've managed to phone some friends on Müllerstrasse in north Berlin. "We're already Russian," her friend shouted into the telephone. "The tanks just rolled in down below. Masses of people are lining the streets, the Ivans are all laughing and waving and holding up babies." It could be true—that's an old Communist district known as Red Wedding. Her story immediately sets off a heated argument. Some people wonder whether our propaganda has simply made fools of us. So "they" aren't as bad as we thought, after all? But then the refugee from East Prussia, who otherwise never says a word, starts yelling in her dialect. Broken sentences—she can't find the right words. She flails her arms and screams, "You'll find out all right," and then goes silent once again. As does the entire basement.

The distiller's wife is peddling yet another rumor: von Ribbentrop and von Papen have just flown to Washington to negotiate with the Americans in person. No one answers her.

The basement is full of gloom. The kerosene lantern is smoldering. The phosphor rings painted at eye height on the beams so no one bumps into them in the dark give off a greenish glow. Our clan has increased: the book dealers have brought their canary. The cage is hanging off a joist, covered with a towel. Shelling outside and silence within. All dozing or asleep.

Wednesday, April 25, 1945, afternoon

To recapitulate: around 1:00 A.M. I left the basement again to go up to the second floor and dump myself on the couch. All of a sudden there was a fierce air raid; the flak started raging. I simply lay there and waited, too sleepy to care. The windowpane is already broken, and the wind is blowing in, along with the stench of fires. I felt an idiotic sense of security under the bedcovers, as if the sheets and blankets were made of iron—though they say bedding is extremely dangerous. Dr. H. once told me how he'd had to treat a woman who'd been hit in bed; the bits of feather had lodged so deeply in her wounds he could barely remove them. But there comes a time when you're so mortally tired you stop being afraid. That's probably how soldiers sleep on the front, amid all the filth.

I got up at 7:00, and the day began with quaking walls. Now the fighting is moving in our direction. No more water, no gas. I waited for a minute that was halfway calm and raced up the four flights of stairs to my attic apartment. Like an animal backing into his lair I crept into one room at a time, always on the lookout, ready to beat a hasty retreat. I grabbed some bedclothes and toiletries and fled back downstairs to the second floor, to the widow. We get along well. These days you come to know people quickly.

Buckets in hand, I made my way to the pump through the garden plots, which were in full bloom. The sun was beating down, very warm. A long line at the pump, everyone pulling for himself—the lever was squeaky and difficult to move. Then the fifteen-minutes walk back with splashing buckets. "We are all of us fine sumpter asses and she-asses" (Nietzsche, I think). Outside Bolle's they're still shoving one another on account of the free butter. And in front of Meyer's there's an endless dark line, all men; they're selling liquor there, half a liter per ID card, anything they have.

Right away I turned around and made a second trip for more water. A sudden air raid on my way home, a column of smoke and dust rising over the patch of grass outside the cinema. Two men threw themselves flat on the ground, right in the gutter. Some women bolted for the nearest entranceway and ran down any stairs they could find, with me at their heels, into a completely unfamiliar basement that didn't have a trace of light. And all the time I couldn't let go of those buckets, otherwise they'd be stolen. A crowd inside the pitch-dark room, startled, very eerie. I heard a woman's voice moaning: "My God, my God . . ." And then things went quiet again.

Was she praying? I remember an event from about two years ago, see myself back in that hole, the most pitiful basement imaginable, under a one-story cottage. A village of 3,000, a place of no significance, but conveniently located on the way to the Ruhr Valley. A candle was burning in the dark, and the women (there were hardly any men) were reciting the rosary, the sorrowful mysteries. I can still hear their droning: "and for us was cruelly scourged . . ." And then more: the Lord's Prayer, the Ave Maria, monotonous, muted, soothing, freeing, just like I imagine the "Om mani padme hum" of the Tibetan prayer wheels. Only broken by the occasional hum of motors and once by a series of bombs that set the candle flame shivering. And then they went on: "and for us carried his heavy cross." Back then I could literally feel the prayer spreading its coat of oil over the troubled faces, helping, making things better. Since that time I haven't been inside another shelter where people prayed. Here in Berlin, in this motley mix of five-story tenements, you'd be hard pressed to find a group of people willing to come together and say the Lord's Prayer. Of course, people whisper prayers even here, perhaps more than it seems. And people do moan "My God, my God . . ." But the woman moaning probably doesn't understand what she's really saying; she's only grasping at empty phrases, repeating the words by rote, without meaning.

I never liked the proverb "Need teaches prayer"—it sounds so haughty, like "Need teaches begging." Prayers extorted by fear and need from the lips of people who never prayed when times were good are nothing more than pitiful begging.

There is no proverb that says "Happiness teaches prayer," but a genuine prayer of thanks ought to rise as high and as freely as fragrant incense. But this is all speculation. The fact that our German word for praying—*beten*—is so close to our word for begging—

betteln—obviously means something. After all, there was a time when beggars were as much a fixture at the church door as the handle, as legitimate as the king himself and every bit as graced by God, so that the king would have his exact opposite here on earth and so that whoever prayed to God in supplication would have someone to whom he in turn could extend divinely sanctioned charity. But I never will find out whether the moaning in the dark basement really was a prayer. One thing is certain: it's a blessing to be able to pray easily and unabashedly amid the oppression and torture, in all our despair and fear. People who can do it are lucky. I can't, not yet. I'm still resisting.

After I came back from getting water, the widow sent me to the meat line to find out what's going on. People were cursing; evidently they keep postponing the deliveries of meat and sausage, which maddens these women more than the entire war. That's our strength—we women always focus on the task at hand. We're happy whenever we can flee into the present to escape worrying about the future. And for these women the task at hand is sausage, and the thought of sausage alters their perspective on things that may be much more important but are nevertheless much further away.

Back in the cellar, around 6:00 P.M. I couldn't lie down upstairs any longer—there were some hits close by and I got scared when thick pieces of plaster started falling on my blanket. I dozed down here until Henni came from the baker's and reported that a bomb had landed right on the drugstore next to the cinema. The owner was killed on the spot, though it was impossible to say whether by shrapnel, the blast, or a heart attack. According to Henni, he didn't bleed. One of the three elderly pudding sisters got up and asked, with elegantly pursed lips, "If you don't mind—how did he get finished off?" That's the way we talk these days, that's how far we've fallen. The word *shit* rolls easily off the tongue. It's even spoken with satisfaction, as if by saying it we could expel our inner refuse. We are debasing our language in expectation of the impending humiliation.

Thursday, April 26, 1945, 11:00 A.M.

My fingers are shaking as I write this. Thirty minutes ago we took a direct hit on the fifth floor. We're still breathing the dust from the plaster. I'm out of breath, having just raced down from my apartment in the attic. The place looks like a dump, full of shattered plaster and splinters and broken glass. Farewell, my fleeting bit of home; I hardly had a chance to know you. For the moment you've been rendered uninhabitable.

I grabbed what I could: a pot, some towels, some gauze for bandages—things we need. My throat is parched, still burning from the dust. I don't have anything to drink down here. And countless gallons of water have just drained out of the radiators upstairs. We spent—

Wait, first I want to recount everything that's happened— there's been so much, and it's so long since I last wrote. It all started yesterday around 7:00 P.M., when someone came to our basement and announced that they were selling pudding powder at the corner store. I went along with everyone else and stood in line. Then out of the blue, Russian bombs. At first the line merely regrouped in the ruins of the building next door, as if the broken walls would protect us from the bombs. Smoke and flames were coming from Berliner Strasse. Another series of bombs exploded closer by. I gave up on the pudding powder and hurried across the street and back to the basement. A man called out to me, "Stick to the wall!" Rattling gunfire, flying debris. Back in the shelter at last, pudding or no pudding. The wife of the concierge started wailing that her daughter was still at the corner store; she probably hadn't felt it was safe to cross the street under fire.

She showed up half an hour later, also without any pudding powder. She was pretty darn lucky, as she put it, having just managed to squeeze into the shop's basement when a bomb fell right outside. A teenage boy who hadn't made it inside caught a fragment in his skull. She had to step over his body on her way out. She pointed to her temple and showed us how the wound was gushing white and red. Tomorrow they're supposed to resume selling the pudding. Evidently the store has plenty left.

The cave dwellers went to sleep around 9:00 P.M. The widow has made a sort of bed for me as well, in the front area of the basement, since there isn't any space left close to the support timbers, but it's soft and warm. I slept until the bombs woke me up. My hand was dangling over my bed and I felt something licking it—Foxel, our absent landlord's terrier. There, Foxel, good dog, don't be afraid. We're alone here in this front room. There's no support structure, but the air is cleaner and nobody bothers us with snores and groans.

Up early in the morning to fetch water at the pump. I read my first printed text in days, hot off the press, too. A newspaper called *The Armored Bear*. Someone pasted one next to the baker's display window. It had Tuesday's official Wehrmacht report, which meant it was two days old. According to the report: a) the enemy was pushing ahead and b) German reinforcements were on the way. The *Bear* also said that Adolf and Goebbels were still in Berlin and would stay here. One very smug piece told of a soldier named Höhne who had deserted and was now dangling from a rope at the Schöneberg station for all to see.

Breakfast in the basement. Everyone is trying as best they can to re-create some semblance of family life. A cozy morning meal served on trunks, crates, and chairs, with paper napkins and little tablecloths. Pots of hot drinks cooked over wood fires or spirit stoves are lifted out of their cloth warmers. You see butter dishes, sugar bowls, jam servers, silver spoons, everything. The widow conjured up some real coffee and cooked it on a fire made of broken champagne crates—that did us good. But people are fidgety, cranky, getting on one another's nerves.

A little before 10:00 A.M. a trunk-sized bomb landed on the roof of our building. A terrible jolt, screams. The concierge's wife staggered in, pale as a sheet, bracing herself against one of the support beams. Then came eighteen-year-old Stinchen with the Hamburg *s*, leaning on her mother. Her hair was gray with plaster dust, completely tangled and covering her young face, which was streaked with trickles of blood—she'd been hit while crossing the courtyard. Even the canary in its cage felt the general agitation, zigzagging back and forth as it cheeped away.

It wasn't until fifteen minutes later that someone noticed that the radiators were losing water. We ran upstairs. Well, not all of us. The postmaster's wife, for example, brandished a medical certificate and shouted that her husband had a heart condition and couldn't come along. And Curtainman Schmidt lost no time pressing his old spotted paw against his heart. Others hesitated as well, until Fräulein Behn bellowed like a lead mare, "You dopes are sitting here babbling while your homes are about to float away," and charged ahead without turning around to see who followed. I joined some fifteen others in going after her.

Up on the fourth floor a whole ocean of water was rushing out, without stopping. We waded up to our ankles, wrung out the rugs, slaved away as it continued to pour from upstairs. We used dustpans to scoop it up and then we dumped it out the window just like that into the street, so brightly lit by the sun and so utterly deserted. Shells kept exploding the whole time, many of them quite close. Once a flurry of shattered glass and bits of plaster splashed into the water, but no one was hurt.

After that we headed back to the basement, damp but quite excited. I hunkered down, squatting on wet socks—my feet still inside them, of course—and wondered whether the whole effort had been a smart thing to do. I'm not sure. In any case, it was very soldierly. Lieutenant Behn had charged ahead, an assault troop of volunteers followed, and everyone risked their lives to secure the endangered position—all under enemy fire. (It clearly wasn't just about possessions, either, about people rescuing their carpets, since practically none of the ones who went had any more to do with those apartments than I did.) We followed orders blindly, without looking to save our skins. Except that there will be no books or songs to celebrate this deed, and no one will receive the Iron Cross. Still, I now know one thing: in the heat of battle, in the thick of the action, you don't think—you don't even feel afraid because you're so distracted and absorbed.

Were we brave? Most people would probably say we were. Was our lead mare, Fräulein Behn, a hero? If she really were a lieutenant she would have definitely been given the Iron Cross. In any case I have to rethink my ideas about heroism and courage under fire. It's only half as bad as I thought. Once you've taken the first step, you just keep charging ahead.

It's also typical that while I was slogging through all that water I didn't give my own apartment a second thought—not until some others mentioned the possibility that it might have been hit. So I flew upstairs and found the dump described above. That means that from here on out I'll have to stay with the widow. It's perfectly fine with her; she's afraid of being alone in her apartment. In March they came and took her tenant to serve in the Volkssturm.

Who knows whether he's still alive or not. But that's just a thought, not something you say out loud.

Four hours later, 3:00 P.M., back in the basement. Once again I'm out of breath, once again my fingers are shaking, and with good reason.

Around noon things calmed down a little outside, so I went to the entryway to warm my damp back in the sunlight. The baker was next to me. A man came running past. He was coming from the former police barracks, most recently used by the Luftwaffe, and was carrying a loin of beef, dripping fresh. "Better be quick, they're giving it all away."

We looked at each other and took off just as we were, without a rucksack, without anything. Henni, from the bakery, who always has her nose to the wind, came running behind us. The sun was burning, and the shooting started up again, very faintly. We ducked, hurrying along close to the buildings. Some gray-haired soldiers, probably Volkssturm, were crouching on the curb by the corner. They were resting their heads on their knees, and never even glanced at us. A crowd outside the barracks, with baskets, sacks, bags. I run inside the first hall I come to. It's dark and cool and completely empty, evidently the wrong one.

I dash back, hear people ahead of me groping and gasping, then someone shouting, "Here! Over here!" I grab a crate that's lying around and drag it behind me.

Feeling my way, I bump into some people and get kicked in the shin. All of a sudden I'm in a basement that's completely pitch-black, full of people panting, shrieking in pain. A boxing match in the dark. This isn't distribution—it's sheer plunder.

Someone switches on a flashlight. I can see shelves with cans and bottles, but only down below; the upper shelves have already been cleaned out. I bend over, drop to the ground, rummage in the lowest compartment, pull out five, six bottles, and stuff them in my crate. In the dark I get hold of a can, but someone steps on my fingers and a man's voice shouts, "Those are mine!"

I leave with my things, head for the door, go into the next room. There's a faint shimmer of light coming through a crack in the wall. I can make out loaves of bread, rows and rows, once again only on the lowest levels. I grab a few, kneel back on the ground, and grope and dig for more. I'm kneeling in a pool of wine—you can smell it. Shattered glass is everywhere. I cram all the bread I can inside my box. Since I can't lift it anymore I have to drag it out through the door, into the corridor, and toward the exit, which beckons at the other end of the dark tunnel like a brightly lit stage.

Outside I run into the baker. He has also managed to get some bread and packs it into my box. Then he hurries back for more. I stay right by my crate and wait. He comes back with canned food, porcelain plates, coarse towels, and a ball of bright blue knitting wool, very frizzy and felted.

All at once Antoine the Belgian is there, the little baker's apprentice, with a leg of beef, and then Henni with Chartreuse in thick-bellied bottles. She's angry: "They have everything inside, everything. Coffee, chocolate, brandy. They were living it up, all right, that little band of brothers!" And she disappears back inside. I guard my crate. A man comes up; he's made his jacket into a sack to carry several bottles of alcohol. He looks longingly at the bread in my box. "Can I have one of those?"

"Sure," I say, "for some brandy."

We trade one loaf of whole-grain bread for a bottle of Steinhäger, both very pleased with the exchange.

Wild scenes are taking place all around in the dazzling sunlight. Now and then a few shells hit, two of them close. Men smash bottles against the walls, drinking in greedy gulps. Antoine and I each grab a side of my crate and head back.

It's full and heavy and hard to carry, so we frequently have to set it down. I'm very thirsty and do just like the others: I take a bottle of red wine and smash the neck against the gutter (the ones I got were all Burgundy, all French labels). The jagged edge cuts my lower lip; I didn't even notice until Antoine pointed it out and wiped off the blood with his handkerchief, all the while standing watchfully astride our box. The blood had already dribbled down below my neckline.

The baker comes puffing up behind us, carrying the bluish leg of beef, smeared with horse manure, pressing it against him like a baby. The sun is scorching, I'm dripping with sweat. A few close hits. Then, farther off, the *tacktacktack* of strafing and the *bangbangbang* of the light antiaircraft guns.

Outside our house we divvy up the loot. The idiotic blue wool managed to get into everything. My share consists of five bottles of Burgundy, three jars of preserved vegetables, one bottle of Steinhäger, four loaves of whole-grain bread, six packs of pea flour, which the baker generously gave me from his own stores, and one unlabeled can of I-don't-know-what. Now I've lugged everything upstairs to the widow's.

Hot and sweaty, I recount my adventures to about a dozen people as I stand next to the stove, plate in my left hand, and wolf down a few spoonfuls of the mashed potatoes that the widow fixed. A number of families have chipped in for fuel. More bombs hit outside. The others are eyeing my loot but don't dare go to the barracks, which have undoubtedly been emptied of their plunder by now.

Several hours later, around 6:00 P.M., back in the basement. I was able to get a little sleep, the widow and I having finished the open bottle of Burgundy. When I woke up I felt giddy, with a bitter taste in my mouth, and it took a while to connect to the kerosene flicker of the underworld. Not until I saw people run-

ning out and heard them calling for sacks: "Come on, they're taking potatoes out of the barracks!"

I rush over with the widow. The enemy is taking a break, and
things are fairly quiet, which explains the sudden mass of people
milling about streets normally deserted in the middle of the day.
Two women pass by pulling a child's toy wagon with a whole barrel on top that smells of sauerkraut. Young and very old alike run
like mad in the direction of the barracks. The widow and I have
grabbed all the buckets we could find, two for each of us. The way
is strewn with trampled potatoes and rotting carrots—you just
have to follow them and you can't go wrong. But right by the stone
steps is a patch of blood. I shrink back . . . but the widow just
laughs. "That's marmalade!" And that's exactly what it is, too;
people are rolling it out by the barrel.

We push through the crowd in the corridor, stumble down the
slippery steps, land in a stinky pile of rotting potatoes. By the light
of the narrow skylights we dig around in the mush with our hands
and shoes, picking out whatever we can use. We leave the carrots
and muddy rutabagas and fill our buckets with potatoes. We find a
half-filled sack, and without asking whose it is we grab it and carry
it up the stairs, down the street, into our building, and up to the
second floor.

More rattling and booming. Nobody cares—they're all
gripped by plunder fever. We turn around and run right back, this
time returning with buckets full of briquettes. Mobs of people
everywhere, running and snatching.

Now they've begun to loot the abandoned shops as well. A
white-haired man—"gentleman" would be a better description—
is hauling a drawer full of boxes of soap powder. The drawer is la-
beled "Rice."

Up to the second floor. We sit around on the living room
couch. Our arms are stiff, our legs shaky. What windowpanes are

still left are quivering slightly. A gentle warmth is wafting through the broken windows—that and the smell of fire. Now and then we hear a *voo-oommm!* Then a prolonged echo, from the heavy antiair-craft guns. After that comes a *pinng!*—a short blow right to the eardrum—heavy artillery. And then, far away, an occasional *knackvoom-knackvoom,* very fast, accompanied by howling and bark-ing. I have no idea what it is. The widow claims they're katyusha rockets, the so-called Stalin Organs. Incidentally, up to now the Russians have been using individual bombs rather than a carpet.

In the end the two of us go off to see whether there's any pud-ding powder left at the corner store that was hit yesterday. It turns out there are still a few customers, and yes, they're still selling. There's a price printed on the powder—thirty-eight pfennigs, I think. The person selling, who also owns the store and lives right there, insisted on giving every customer exact change, so he kept running up and down the line asking who had small coins and could help him. And that while under fire! Only here. We'll be counting our change right into the grave.

Just for fun we peeked around the corner to see what was up at the butcher's, since I still hadn't used up my ration. There, too, they were selling, with more supply than demand—at most a dozen people were in the store. So we were able to get some good pieces, boneless pork, fairly weighed.

As we walked out of the store a truck drove by with German troops, red tabs, meaning antiaircraft. They were headed away from us, toward the center of town. They sat there mute, staring off into the distance. A woman called out to them, "Are you leaving?" No one answered her. We looked at each other and shrugged our shoulders. The woman said, "They're just poor souls themselves."

These days I keep noticing how my feelings toward men—and the feelings of all the other women—are changing. We feel sorry for them; they seem so miserable and powerless. The weaker sex.

Deep down we women are experiencing a kind of collective dis-appointment. The Nazi world—ruled by men, glorifying the strong man—is beginning to crumble, and with it the myth of "Man." In earlier wars men could claim that the privilege of killing and being killed for the fatherland was theirs and theirs alone. Today we women, too, have a share. That has transformed us, emboldened us. Among the many defeats at the end of this war is the defeat of the male sex.

Later in the basement, intelligent conversations over supper. Cozy still lifes—in one square yard per household. Here tea with bread and butter, there mashed potatoes. Stinchen with the Ham-burg *s* wields her knife and fork flawlessly as she pokes at her pickle. Her wounded head has been neatly bandaged. The book-selling wife asks, "May I serve you some?"

"Yes, please, if you'd be so kind," answers Curtainman Schmidt, softly.

A towel is spread over the canary's cage. The deserter comes and announces that the Russians are scouting out the cinema. Our corner is currently under fire from small guns. The ex-soldier tells us we can't have anyone wearing a uniform in the basement; otherwise under martial law we'll all be subject to execution.

Palaver about the notices in the *Armored Bear*. Two armies really do seem to be heading to relieve Berlin, Schörner from the south and some other one from the north. Teuenbrietzen, Oranienburg, and Bernau are said to have been liberated.

And us? Very mixed feelings, and a sense of fright. "So now they'll be back and forth and we're caught right in the middle. Are we supposed to stay here for months? We're lost one way or the other. If things don't work out for Ivan, then the Americans will come from the air. And God have mercy if they start in with car-pet bombs. We'll be buried alive in this basement."

A new announcement from the street: the Volkssturm has

retreated, Ivan is pushing right toward us. German artillery has pulled up on our corner; the explosions are booming through the basement. Meanwhile six women are sitting around a little table; the widow is reading the distiller's wife's cards. She's very good at it, too: "In the short run you will experience a disappointment in connection with your husband." (He's still holding his post in the distillery—together with the redheaded Elvira.)

I want to go to sleep right away. I'm looking forward to it. The day's been packed to the brim. The net result: I'm healthy, bold, and bright; for the moment my fear is mostly gone. My brain is full of vivid images of greed and rage. Stiff back, tired feet, broken thumbnail, a cut lip that's still smarting. So the saying's true after all: "What doesn't kill you makes you stronger."

One more thing. An image from the street: a man pushing a wheelbarrow with a dead woman on top, stiff as a board. Loose gray strands of hair fluttering, a blue kitchen apron. Her withered legs in gray stockings sticking out the end of the wheelbarrow. Hardly anyone gave her a second glance. Just like when they used to ignore the garbage being hauled away.

Friday, April 27, 1945,
Day of catastrophe, wild turmoil—
recorded on Saturday morning

It began with silence. The night was far too quiet. Around twelve o'clock Fräulein Behn reported that the enemy had reached the gardens and that the German line of defense was right outside our door.

It took a long time for me to fall asleep; I was going over Russian phrases in my head, practicing the ones I thought I'd soon have a chance to use. Today I briefly mentioned to the other cave dwellers that I speak a little Russian, a fact I'd been keeping to myself. I explained that I'd been to European Russia when I was younger, one of the dozen or so countries I visited in my travels.

My Russian is very basic, very utilitarian, picked up along the way. Still, I know how to count, and to say what day it is, and I can read the Cyrillic alphabet. I'm sure it will come back quickly now that practice is near at hand. I've always had a knack for languages. Finally, counting away in Russian, I fell asleep.

I slept until about 5:00 A.M., when I heard someone wandering around the front of the basement—it was the bookselling wife, who had come in from the outside. She took my hand and whispered, "They're here."

"Who? The Russians?" I could barely open my eyes.

"Yes. They just climbed through the window at Meyer's"— meaning the liquor store.

I finished dressing and combed my hair while she delivered her news to the others. Within minutes the whole basement was on its feet.

Taking the back stairs, I felt my way up to the second floor in order to hide our meager provisions, at least whatever wasn't already squirreled away. Before going inside I put my ear to the back door, which was in splinters and could no longer be locked. All quiet, the kitchen empty. Keeping close to the floor I crept over to the window. It was a bright morning outside, our street was under fire; you could hear the whistle and patter of the bullets.

A Russian antiaircraft battery was turning the corner, four barrels, four iron giraffes with menacing necks tall as towers. Two men were stomping up the street: broad backs, leather jackets, high leather boots. Jeeps pulling up to the curb. Fieldpieces rattling ahead in the early light. The pavement alive with the din. The smell of gasoline drifted into the kitchen through the broken windowpanes.

I went back to the basement. We ate our breakfast as if in a nightmare, although I did manage to consume several slices of bread, much to the amazement of the widow. Even so, my stomach was fluttering. I felt the way I had as a schoolgirl before a math exam—anxious and uneasy, wishing that everything were already over.

After that the widow and I climbed upstairs. We dusted her apartment, wiped down the counters, and swept and scrubbed with our next-to-last bucket of water. The devil knows why we slaved away like that. Probably just to exercise our limbs a little, or maybe we were simply fleeing again into a palpable present to escape an uncertain future.

As we worked we kept creeping up to the window and peeking out at the street, where an endless supply train was passing by. Stout mares with foals running between their legs. A cow drearily mooing to be milked. Before we knew it they had set up a field kitchen in the garage across the street. And for the first time we could make out faces, features, individuals—sturdy, broad foreheads, close-cropped hair, well fed, carefree. Not a civilian in sight. The Russians have the streets entirely to themselves. But under every building people are whispering, quaking. Who could ever imagine such a whole other world hidden here, so frightened, right in the middle of the big city? Life sequestered underground and split into tiny cells so that no one knows what anyone else is doing.

Outside, a bright blue, cloudless sky.

Sometime around noon—the woman from Hamburg and I were just getting the second pot of barley soup, cooked at the baker's for the entire clan—the first enemy found his way into our basement. A ruddy-cheeked farmer, he blinked as he sized us up by the light of the kerosene lantern. He hesitated, then took a step, two steps toward us.

Hearts pounding. Scared, people offered him their bowls of soup. He shook his head and smiled, still silent.

That's when I uttered my first Russian words, or rather rasped them, since I suddenly went hoarse: *"Shto vy zhelaete?"* What do you want?

The man spins around, stares at me in amazement. I sense I've taken him aback. He doesn't understand. Evidently he's never heard one of us "mutes" address him in his own language. Because the Russian word for Germans, *nemtsy*, means "mutes." Presumably it dates from the Hanseatic League, over five hundred years ago, when German merchants used sign language to trade textiles and lace for beeswax and furs in Novgorod and elsewhere.

Anyway, this Russian doesn't say a thing, answers my question with a mere shake of his head. I ask whether he wants something to eat. With a little smile he says, in accented German, *"Schnaps"*—brandy.

The cave dwellers shake their heads: regrettably they have no brandy or alcohol of any kind. Whoever has any left keeps it well hidden. So Ivan wanders back off, trying to find his way through the labyrinth of passageways and courtyards.

Cheerful bustle of soldiers on our street. Along with two or three other women I venture out to watch. A young man is polishing a motorcycle in our entranceway, a German Zündapp, nearly new. He holds out the cloth, gestures at me to go on buffing. I tell him in Russian that I don't want to, even manage a laugh; he looks at me in surprise and then laughs back.

Some Russians are wheeling freshly stolen bicycles up and down the driveway. They're teaching one another to ride, sitting on their seats as stiffly as Susi the bicycle-riding chimpanzee in the zoo. They crash into the trees and laugh with pleasure.

I feel some of my fear beginning to dissipate. It turns out that Russian men, too, are "only men"—i.e., presumably they're as susceptible as other men to feminine wiles, so it's possible to keep them in check, to distract them, to shake them off.

The sidewalks are full of horses that leave their droppings and spray their pee. A strong scent of stalls. Two soldiers ask me to show them to the nearest pump—the horses are thirsty. So we traipse through the gardens for fifteen minutes. Friendly voices, good-natured faces. And questions that will keep coming back, heard now for the first time: "Do you have a husband?" If you say yes, they ask where he is. And if you say no, they ask if you wouldn't want to "marry" a Russian. Followed by crude flirting.

These two first address me using the familiar *du*, but I dismiss the impropriety by sticking with the formal form. We walked down the deserted green path as artillery shells arc across the sky. The German line is ten minutes away. No more German planes, though, and hardly any German flak. No more water in the taps, no electricity, no gas. Only Russians.

Back with the buckets, now full of water. The horses drink as the two men look on contentedly. I stroll around, talking to this Russian and that. It's past noon, the sun so hot it feels like summer. There's something strange in the air, though, something I can't put my finger on, something evil, menacing. A few men look past me shyly, exchanging glances. One young man, small and sallow and reeking of alcohol, gets me involved in a conversation. He wants to coax me off into the courtyard, shows me two watches on his hairy arm, he'll give one to me if I . . .

I draw back to the passage that leads to our basement, then sneak out to the inner courtyard, but just when I think I've shaken him he's standing next to me and slips into the basement along with me. Staggering from one support beam to the next, he shines his flashlight on the faces, some forty people all together, pausing each time he comes to a woman, letting the pool of light flicker for several seconds on her face.

The basement freezes. Everyone seems petrified. No one moves, no one says a word. You can hear the forced breathing. The spotlight stops on eighteen-year-old Stinchen resting in a reclining chair, her head in a dazzlingly white bandage. "How many year?" Ivan asks, in German, his voice full of threat.

No one answers. The girl lies there as if made of stone. The Russian repeats his question, now roaring with rage, "How many year?"

I quickly answer, in Russian: "She's a student, eighteen." I want to add that she's been wounded in the head, but I can't find the right words so I resort to the international word *kaput*. "Head *kaput*, from bomb."

Next comes a conversation between the Russian and myself, a rapid back and forth of questions and answers that would be senseless to record, for the simple reason that it was senseless. All about love: true love, passionate love, he loves me, do I love him, whether we want to make love. "Maybe," I say, and start heading toward the door. He falls for it. The people all around are still paralyzed with fear, don't have the faintest idea what's going on.

I flirt with fluttering hands, hardly able to speak because my heart is pounding so. I look the man in his black eyes, amazed at his yellow, jaundiced eyeballs. We're outside in the hall, it's nearly dark, I prance backwards ahead of him, he doesn't know his way in this labyrinth, he follows. I whisper: "Over there. Very beautiful there. No people." Three more paces, then two stairs . . . and we're back out on the street, in the bright afternoon sun.

Right away I run to my two horse handlers, who are now combing and currying their steeds. I point at my pursuer: "He's a bad egg, that one, ha-ha!" The man looks daggers at me and takes off. The horse grooms laugh. I talk with them a while and catch my breath. Little by little my hands calm down.

As I was chatting away, a number of heroes visited our basement, but they were more interested in watches than in women. Later I would see many an Ivan with whole collections on both arms—five or six pieces, which they would constantly compare, winding and resetting, with childlike, thieflike joy.

Our street corner has become an army camp. The supply train is billeted in the shops and garages. The horses munch their oats and hay; it's comic to watch them stick their heads out the broken display windows. There's a hint of relief in the air—oh well, there go the watches. "*Voyna kaput*," as the Russians say. The war is kaput. And for us it *is* kaput, finished, all over. The storm has rushed past and now we're safely in its wake.

Or so we thought.

Things started happening around 6:00 P.M. A man built like a bull came into the basement, dead drunk, waving his pistol around and making for the distiller's wife. No one else would do. He chased her with his pistol up and down the basement, shoved her ahead of him, toward the door. She fought back, hitting him, howling, when all of a sudden the revolver went off. The bullet went right through the supports and hit the wall; no one was hurt. The basement broke into a panic, everyone jumped up and started screaming. The hero seemed to have frightened himself and slipped off into the corridors.

Around 7:00 P.M. I was sitting upstairs with the widow, peacefully eating our evening porridge, when the concierge's youngest daughter burst in yelling, "Come quick, you have to talk to them in Russian. There's more of them after Frau B." The distiller's wife again. She's by far the plumpest woman in our group, very buxom. People say they like that. Fat means beautiful; the more woman there is, the more her body differs from that of a man. Primitive people are said to have had particular respect for women who are fat, as symbols of abundance and fertility. Well, these days they'd have a hard time finding such symbols here. The older women in particular who had once been quite plump have shrunken terribly, at least for the most part. Of course, the distiller's wife is an exception. Since the war began she hasn't lacked for things to trade. And now she's paying for her unmerited fat.

When I came down she was standing in the doorway whimpering and shaking. She had managed to run out and escape. But she didn't dare go back to the basement, nor did she dare go up the four flights of stairs to her apartment, since the German artillery was still firing occasional shells. She was also afraid the Russians might follow her upstairs. Digging into my arm so firmly that her nails left marks, she begged me to go with her to the "commandant" to request an escort, some kind of protection. I couldn't imagine what she was thinking of.

A man came by with stars on his epaulettes and I tried to explain to him how afraid the woman was but couldn't think of the word for "afraid." He just shrugged us off impatiently. "Don't worry, nobody's going to do anything to you, go on home." Finally the distiller's wife staggered upstairs, sobbing. I haven't seen her since; she must have snuck off somewhere. And a good thing, too—she was too compelling a decoy.

No sooner was I back upstairs than the concierge's girl— evidently the designated messenger—came running in for the second time. More men in the basement. Now they're after the baker's wife, who's also managed to keep a bit of flesh on during the years of war.

The baker comes stumbling toward me down the hall, white as his flour, holding out his hands. "They have my wife . . ." His voice breaks. For a second I feel I'm acting in a play. A middle-class baker can't possibly move like that, can't speak with such emotion, put so much feeling into his voice, bare his soul that way, his heart so torn. I've never seen anyone but great actors do that.

In the basement. The lantern is no longer burning; it's probably out of kerosene. By the flickering light of a so-called Hindenburg lamp—a wick in tallow encased in cardboard—I see the baker's wife in a recliner, her ashen face, her twitching mouth. Three Russians are standing next to her. One is jerking her up by the arm, but when she tries to get up, another shoves her back in the chair as if she were a puppet, a thing.

All three are talking to one another very quickly, evidently arguing. I can't understand much; they're speaking in slang. What to do? "Commissar," the baker stammers. Meaning, find someone who has some authority. I go out on the street, now peaceful, calmed down for the evening. The shooting and burning are far away. As luck would have it, I run into the same officer who had been so dismissive with the distiller's wife. I speak to him in my most polite Russian, ask him for help. He understands what I'm saying and makes a sour face. Finally he follows me, reluctant and unwilling.

The people in the basement are still scared stiff and silent as if they all, men, women, and children, had turned to stone. It turns out that one of the three Russians has backed off. The other two are still standing next to the baker's wife, arguing.

The officer joins the conversation, not with a tone of command but as among equals. Several times I hear the expression "*ukaz Stalina.*" Stalin's decree. Apparently Stalin has declared that "this kind of thing" is not to happen. But it happens anyway, the officer gives me to understand, shrugging his shoulders. One of the two men being reprimanded voices his objection, his face twisted in anger: "What do you mean? What did the Germans do to our women?" He is screaming. "They took my sister and . . ." and so on. I can't understand all the words, only the sense.

Once again the officer speaks, calming the man down, slowly moving toward the door, and finally managing to get both men outside. The baker's wife asks, hoarsely, "Are they gone?"

I nod, but just to make sure I step out into the dark corridor. Then they have me. Both men were lying in wait.

I scream and scream . . . I hear the basement door shutting with a dull thud behind me.

One of them grabs my wrists and jerks me along the corridor. Then the other is pulling as well, his hand on my throat, so I can no longer scream. I no longer want to scream, for fear of being strangled. They're both tearing away at me; instantly I'm on the floor. Something comes clinking out of my jacket pocket, must be my key ring, with the key to the building. I end up with my head on the bottom step of the basement stairs. I can feel the damp coolness of the floor tiles. The door above is ajar and lets in a little light. One man stands there keeping watch, while the other tears my underclothes, forcing his way—

I grope around the floor with my left hand until I find my key ring. I hold it tight. I use my right hand to defend myself. It's no use. He's simply torn off my garter, ripping it in two. When I struggle to come up, the second one throws himself on me as well, forcing me back on the ground with his fists and knees. Now the other keeps lookout, whispering, "Hurry up, hurry."

I hear loud Russian voices. Some light. The door opens. Two, three Russians come in, the last a woman in uniform. And they laugh. The second man jumps up, having been disrupted in the act. They both go out with the other three, leaving me lying there.

I pull myself up on the steps, gather my things, drag myself along the wall toward the basement door. They've locked it from the inside. "Open up," I say. "I'm all alone, there's no one else."

Finally the two iron levers open. Everyone stares at me. Only then do I realize how I look. My stockings are down to my shoes, my hair is disheveled, I'm still holding on to what's left of my garter.

I start yelling. "You pigs! Here they rape me twice in a row and you shut the door and leave me lying like a piece of dirt!" And I turn to leave. At first they're quiet, then all hell breaks loose behind me, everyone talking at once, screaming, fighting, flailing about. At last a decision: "We'll all go together to the commandant and ask for protection for the night."

And so finally a small platoon of women, along with a few men, heads out into the evening twilight, into the mild air smelling of fire, over to where the commandant is said to be staying.

Outside it's quiet. The guns are silent. A few men are sprawled in the entranceway—Russians. One of them gets up as we approach. Another mumbles, "They're just Germans," and turns back over. Inside the courtyard I ask to speak to the commandant. A figure breaks away from the group of men standing in the door that leads to the rear wing of the building. "Yes, what do you want?" He's tall, with white teeth and the features of someone from the Caucasus.

He looks at the pitiful group of people come to complain and laughs, laughs at my stammering. "Come on, I'm sure they didn't really hurt you. Our men are all healthy." He strolls back to the other officers. We hear them chuckling quietly. I turn to our gray assembly. "There's no point."

We leave and return to our basement. I don't want to go back, don't want to look at their faces anymore. I climb upstairs, together with the widow, who's hovering over me as if I were sick, speaking in hushed tones, stroking me, watching my every move to the point where it's annoying. I just want to forget.

I undress in the bathroom—for the first time in days—and wash up as well as I can with the little water I have, and brush my teeth in front of the mirror. Suddenly a Russian appears in the door frame, as still as a ghost, pale and tender. "Where, please, the door?" he asks in a quiet voice—in German, too. He's evidently strayed into the apartment. Frozen in shock, wearing nothing but my nightgown, I point the way to the front door, which leads to the stairwell, without saying a word. "Thank you," he says politely.

I hurry into the kitchen. Yes, he broke in through the back door, which the widow had blocked off with a broom closet—he simply pushed it aside. The widow is just coming up the back stairs from the basement. Together we barricade the door again, this time more thoroughly, piling chairs in front and shoving in the heavy kitchen buffet for good measure. That should do it, says the widow. As always she bolts the front door and turns the lock twice. We feel a little secure.

A tiny flame is flickering on the Hindenburg lamp, casting our overlarge shadows on the ceiling. The widow has set up a place for me in her living room, on the sofa bed. For the first time in ages we don't let down the blackout blinds. What for? There won't be any more air raids this Friday night, not for us—we're already Russian. The widow perches on the edge of my bed and is just taking off her shoes when all at once we hear a clatter and din.

Poor back door, pitifully erected bulwark. It's already crashing down, the chairs rumbling against the floor tiles. Scraping of feet and shoving and several rough voices. We stare at each other. Light flickers through a crack in the wall between the kitchen and the living room. Now the steps are in the hall. Someone pushes in the door to our room.

One, two, three, four men. All heavily armed, with machine guns on their hips. They look at the two of us briefly, without saying a word. One of them walks straight to the chest, rips open the two drawers, rummages around, slams them back, says something dismissive, and stomps out. We hear him going through the next room, where the widow's tenant used to live, before he was drafted into the Volkssturm. The three others stand around murmuring among themselves, sizing me up with stolen glances. The widow slips back into her shoes, whispering to me that she's going to run upstairs for help from the other apartments. Then she's gone; none of the men stop her.

What am I to do? Suddenly I feel insanely comical, standing there in front of three strange men in nothing but my candy-pink nightgown with its ribbons and bows. I can't stand it any longer, I have to say something, do something. Once again I ask in Russian, "*Shto vy zhelaete?*"

They spin around. Three bewildered faces, the men lose no time in asking, "Where did you learn Russian?"

I give them my speech, explain how I traveled across Russia, drawing and photographing, at such and such a time. The three warriors plop down in the armchairs, set aside their guns, and stretch their legs. As we chat I keep my ear cocked for any noise in the hallway, waiting for the widow to return with the neighbors and the promised help. But I hear nothing.

Meanwhile the fourth soldier comes back and leads number three into the kitchen. I hear them busy with the dishes. The other two speak quietly to each other; evidently I'm not supposed to understand. The mood is strangely restrained. Something is in the air, a spark, but where will it land?

The widow doesn't come back. I again try to draw the two men into conversation, as I get under my quilt, but nothing comes of it. They look at me askance and shift around. That's a sign things are about to happen—I read about it in the papers, when there still were some—ten or twenty times, what do I know? I feel feverish. My face is burning.

Now the other two men call them from the kitchen and they get up clumsily and stroll over there. I crawl out of bed very quietly, put my ear to the kitchen door, and listen a moment. They're obviously drinking. Then I slink down the pitch-dark corridor, silently, on bare feet, grab my coat off the hook, and pull it on over my nightgown.

I cautiously open the front door, which the widow has left unbolted. I listen at the stairwell, silent and black. Nothing. Not a sound, not a shimmer of light. Where could she have gone? I'm just about to go up the stairs when one of the men grabs me from behind. He's snuck up without a sound.

Huge paws. I can smell the brandy. My heart is hopping like crazy. I whisper, I beg: "Only one, please, please, only one. You, as far as I'm concerned. But kick the others out."

He promises in a low voice and carries me in both arms like a bundle through the hall. I have no idea which of the four he is, what he looks like. In the dark front room with hardly any windows he unloads me on the former tenant's bare bedstead. Then he shouts a few short phrases to the others, shuts the door, and lies down beside me in the dark. I'm miserably cold, I beg and plead for him to let me back into the made-up bed in the next room. He refuses, seemingly afraid the widow might come back. Not until half an hour later, when things are quiet, can I get him to move there.

His automatic clanks against the bedpost; he's hung his cap on the bedpost knob. The tallow light has gone on burning quietly, for itself. Petka—that's his name—has a pointy head, a widow's peak of bristly blond hair; it feels like the nap on a sofa. A gigantic man, broad as a bear, with the arms of a lumberjack and white teeth. I'm so tired, exhausted, I barely know where I am. Petka fumbles around, tells me he's from Siberia—well, well. Now he's even taken off his boots. I feel dizzy, I'm only half present, and that half is no longer resisting. It falls against the hard body smelling of curd soap. Peace at last, darkness, sleep.

At four o'clock I hear the crowing of a rooster, part of the supply train. Right away I'm wide awake, pull my arm out from under Petka. He smiles, showing his white teeth. He gets up quickly, explaining that he has guard duty but he'll definitely be back at seven, absolutely! In parting he practically crushes my fingers.

I crawl back under the blanket and sleep fitfully, in fifteen-minute intervals. Once I think I hear the word "Help!" and jump up, but it's only the rooster. Now the cow is mooing as well. I unwrap our alarm clock (it's really the widow's, but I now consider myself part of the household)—just to be safe we keep it wrapped in a terry cloth towel, far back in the chest. We never look at it unless we're completely alone and safe. We don't want to lose it to some Ivan.

It's five o'clock. I can't sleep any more. I get up and smooth out the bed, shove the crates and chairs back against the rear door with its broken lock, clear the empty bottles the men have left behind, and check to see whether we still have our Burgundy in the kitchen cupboard, hidden in the old bucket. Thank God they didn't find that.

A reddish gray light shining through the window means the war is still on outside. A distant rumble and hum. The front is now rolling into the center of town. I get dressed, wash myself as best I can, and listen carefully to the morning quiet of the stairwell. Nothing but silence and emptiness. If only I knew where the widow snuck off to! I don't dare knock on any doors, don't want to frighten anyone.

The next time I stick my ear out, I hear voices. I run up, they're already coming my way, a whole group of women, with the widow in the lead, sobbing lamentably, "Don't be angry with me!" (As of yesterday we've been calling each other with the familiar *du*.) A number of women around her are sobbing as well. I just laugh in the face of all the lamentation. "What's the matter, I'm alive, aren't I? Life goes on!"

As we head up to the next floor, to the booksellers', the widow whispers in my ear about how she knocked on several doors and asked people to take us in and give us shelter for the night. In vain. No one opened. At the postmaster's they hissed through the chained door, "The girl? That would be asking for trouble. No, we don't want to be luring them this way!" After that it was pitch-dark when some Russian came up and grabbed her, threw her on the floorboards . . . A mere child, she whispers, no beard at all, smooth-skinned and inexperienced—a smile breaks on her face, so swollen with sobbing. I don't know her age exactly. I'm not even sure she would tell me. Probably between forty and fifty; she dyes her hair. But for them any woman will do, when they're grabbing in the dark.

Some fifteen people have holed up at the booksellers', bringing their bedclothes and spreading out on the sofas, the floor, wherever there's room. The doors of the apartment have patent deadbolts and extra reinforcements anchored in the floor. On top of that, the front door has a metal backing on the inside.

We sit around the unfamiliar kitchen table, all of us hollow-eyed, greenish pale, worn out for lack of sleep. We speak in whispers, our breathing is forced, we gulp down the hot malt coffee (which the bookseller cooked on the stove over a fire of Nazi literature, as he tells us).

We keep staring at the back door, locked and barricaded, hoping it will hold. Hungry, I stuff myself with someone else's bread. We hear steps coming up the back stairs, then those unfamiliar sounds, to our ears so coarse and animal-like. The table freezes, falls silent. We stop chewing, hold our breath. Hands clenched over hearts. Eyes flickering wildly. Then silence once again as the steps fade away. Someone whispers, "If things go on like this . . ."

No one answers. The refugee girl from Königsberg throws herself across the table: "I can't take any more! I'm going to end it all!" She'd been through it several times in the night, up under the roof, where she had fled an entire troop of pursuers. Her hair in tangles, covering her face, she refuses to eat or drink.

We sit, wait, listen, as the missiles pipe away overhead like an organ. Shots whip through our street. It's seven o'clock by the time I creep down to our apartment, together with the widow, carefully checking to see the stair landings are secure. We stop to listen outside our door, which I left ajar—when suddenly it opens from inside.

A uniform. Shock. The widow clutches my arm. Then a sigh of relief—it's only Petka.

The widow listens to our conversation without saying a word. A minute later I, too, am standing there speechless. Petka is beaming at me, his small blue eyes glittering. He shakes my hands, assuring me that he missed me while he was away, that he hurried over as fast as he could after guard duty, that he searched the entire apartment for me, that he's happy, so happy to see me again. And he presses and squeezes my fingers with his lumberjack paws, so hard I have to pull them away. I stand there like an idiot, in the face of these unambiguous symptoms, listen to this Petka-Romeo babble on, until he finally, finally disappears—promising he'll be back soon, very soon, just as soon as he can.

I'm rooted in place, open-mouthed. The widow didn't understood a word Petka was saying, but she read his face perfectly, she knew what was up. She shakes her head. "Well . . ." Both of us are completely stunned.

And now I'm sitting here at our kitchen table. I've just refilled my pen, and am writing, writing, writing all this confusion out of my head and heart. Where will this end? What will become of us? I feel so slimy, I don't want to touch anything, least of all my own skin. What I'd give for a bath or at least some decent soap and plenty of water. That's it—enough of these fantasies.

I remember the strange vision I had this morning, something like a daydream, while I was trying in vain to fall asleep after Petka left. It was as if I were flat on my bed and seeing myself lying there when a luminous white being rose from my body, a kind of angel, but without wings, that floated high into the air. Even now as I'm writing this I can still feel that sense of rising up and floating. Of course, it's just a fantasy, a pipe dream, a means of escape—my true self simply leaving my body behind, my poor, besmirched, abused body. Breaking away and floating off, unblemished, into a white beyond. It can't be me that this is happening to, so I'm expelling it all from me. Could I be raving? But my head feels cool at the moment, my hands heavy and calm.

Tuesday, May 1, 1945, 3:00 P.M.
Looking back on Saturday, Sunday, Monday

I haven't written since Saturday morning, April 28—three days ago, three days crammed with so many frenzied images, fears, and feelings that I don't know where to begin, what to say. We're deep in the muck now, very deep. Every minute of life comes at a high price. The storm is passing overhead, and we are leaves quaking in the whirlwind, with no idea where we're being blown.

An eternity has passed since then. Today is May Day, and the war is still on. I'm sitting in the armchair in the front room. The widow's tenant is here, too, lying in bed—Herr Pauli, now discharged from the Volkssturm. He showed up on Saturday, without warning, carrying a sixteen-pound lump of butter wrapped in a towel. At the moment he's sick with neuralgia.

The wind is whistling through the windows, tugging and rattling the scraps of cardboard tacked on so pitifully; the daylight comes flickering inside, making the room now bright, now dark. But it's always bitter cold. I've wrapped myself in a wool blanket and am writing with numb fingers while Herr Pauli sleeps and the widow wanders through the building looking for candles.

Russian sounds come bouncing in from outside. Some Ivan is talking to his horses, which they treat far better than they do us; when they talk to the animals their voices sound warm, even human. Now and then the horses' scent comes wafting in as well, and you can hear a chain clinking. Somewhere someone is playing an accordion.

I peer through the flapping cardboard. The army is camped outside; horses on the sidewalks, wagons, drinking pails, boxes of oats and hay, trampled horse droppings, cow paddies. A small fire stoked with broken chairs is burning in the entranceway across the street. The Russians crouch around it in quilted jackets.

My hands are shaking, my feet are ice. Yesterday a German grenade broke the last panes we had. Now the apartment is completely defenseless against the east wind. Good thing it's not January.

Our walls are riddled with holes. Inside we scurry back and forth, listening anxiously to the clamor outside, gritting our teeth at every new noise. The splintered back door is open; we gave up barricading it long ago. Men are forever traipsing down the hall, through the kitchen, in and out of our two rooms. Half an hour ago a complete stranger showed up, a stubborn dog, who wanted me but was chased away. As he left he threatened, "I'll be back."

What does it mean—rape? When I said the word for the first time aloud, Friday evening in the basement, it sent shivers down my spine. Now I can think it and write it with an untrembling hand, say it out loud to get used to hearing it said. It sounds like the absolute worst, the end of everything—but it's not.

Saturday afternoon around 3:00 two men banged on the front door with their fists and weapons, shouting in raw voices, kicking the wood. The widow opened the door. She's always worried about her lock. Two gray-haired soldiers come careening in, drunk. They thrust their automatics through one of the hall windows, shattering the last remaining pane and sending the shards clattering into the courtyard. Then they tear the blackout shades to shreds, kick the old grandfather clock.

One of them grabs hold of me and shoves me into the front room, pushing the widow out of the way. Without a word, the other plants himself by the front door and points his rifle at the widow, keeping her in check. He doesn't touch her.

The one shoving me is an older man with gray stubble, reeking of brandy and horses. He carefully closes the door behind him and, not finding any key, slides the wing chair against the door. He seems not even to see his prey, so that when he strikes she is all the more startled, as he knocks her onto the bedstead. Eyes closed, teeth clenched.

No sound. Only an involuntary grinding of teeth when my underclothes are ripped apart. The last untorn ones I had.

Suddenly his finger is on my mouth, stinking of horse and tobacco. I open my eyes. A stranger's hands expertly pulling apart my jaws. Eye to eye. Then with great deliberation he drops a gob of gathered spit into my mouth.

I'm numb. Not with disgust, only cold. My spine is frozen: icy, dizzy shivers around the back of my head. I feel myself gliding and falling, down, down, through the pillows and the floorboards. So that's what it means to sink into the ground.

Once more eye to eye. The stranger's lips open, yellow teeth, one in front half broken off. The corners of the mouth lift, tiny wrinkles radiate from the corners of his eyes. The man is smiling.

Before leaving he fishes something out of his pants pocket, thumps it down on the nightstand without a word, pulls the chair aside, and slams the door shut behind him. A crumpled pack of Russian cigarettes, only a few left. My pay.

I stand up—dizzy, nauseated. My ragged clothes tumble to my feet. I stagger through the hall, past the sobbing widow, into the bathroom. I throw up. My face green in the mirror, my vomit in the basin. I sit on the edge of the bathtub, without daring to flush, since I'm still gagging and there's so little water left in the bucket.

Damn this to hell! I say it out loud. Then I make up my mind.

No question about it: I have to find a single wolf to keep away the pack. An officer, as high-ranking as possible, a commandant, a general, whatever I can manage. After all, what are my brains for, my little knowledge of the enemy's language?

As soon as I am able to move again, I grab a bucket and drag myself down the stairs and out into the street. I wander up and down, peering into the courtyards, keeping my eyes open, then go back into our stairwell, very cautiously. I practice the sentences I will use to address an officer, wondering if I don't look too green and miserable to be attractive. Physically I feel a little better, though, now that I am doing something, planning something, determined to be more than mere mute booty, a spoil of war.

For half an hour there's nothing—no epaulettes with stars. I don't know their rankings and insignia, only that the officers wear stars on their caps and generally have overcoats. But all I see is a shabby mass of uniform green. I'm just about to give up for the day, am already knocking at our door, when I see a man with stars coming out of an apartment across the street (the former tenant having managed to escape just in time). Tall, dark hair, well fed. He sees me with the bucket, then laughs and says in broken German, "Du, Frau." I laugh back and shower him with my best Russian. He's delighted to hear his own language. We chatter away, silly, just fooling around, and I learn that he's a first lieutenant. Finally we arrange to meet that night at 7:00 P.M. at the widow's. He's busy until then. His name is Anatol So-and-so—a Ukrainian.

"Will you definitely come?"

"Of course," he says, reproachfully. "As fast as I can."

But as it happened, another man showed up first, around 5:00 P.M., someone I'd almost forgotten, Petka from the previous night, with the blond bristle and the Romeo babble. He's brought two buddies, too, whom he introduces as Grisha and Yasha. Soon all three are sitting at our round table, like a bunch of farm boys invited into a house well above their class. Only Petka acts as if he's at home, showing me off to the others with clear pride of possession. The three men stretch out on the armchairs; they feel good. Yasha pulls out a bottle of vodka, and Grisha produces some herrings and bread wrapped in a greasy page of *Pravda* (the front page—unfortunately it's old). Petka calls for glasses as if he were master of the house. He pours the vodka, then slams his fist on the table and commands, "*Vypit' nado!*" You have to drink up!

The widow and I, and even Herr Pauli, who showed up out of the blue half an hour earlier, have no choice but to sit and drink with the boys. Petka sets a slice of dark, moist bread on the table in front of each of us, then divides the herrings, right there on the polished mahogany, using his thumb to press it onto the bread, all the while beaming at us as if this were a special favor and delicacy.

The widow, appalled, runs for some plates. Grisha is the silent type, with a permanent smirk; his voice has a deep rasp. He makes sure each person receives an equal portion of bread and herring. Yasha is short, with a crew cut; he smiles and nods all around. Both are from Kharkov. Little by little I start talking to them, acting as interpreter between them and Herr Pauli. We drink to one another's health. Petka from Siberia is loud and fully at ease.

I keep listening for the door and checking the dainty lady's wristwatch on Yasha's arm. Any minute I expect First Lieutenant Anatol to show up as arranged. I'm worried because I suspect there'll be a fight. Petka is strong as an ox, of course, and clean, but he's primitive, uncouth—no protection. A first lieutenant, on the other hand, ought to guarantee a kind of taboo, or so I imagine. My mind is firmly made up. I'll think of something when the time comes. I grin to myself in secret, feel as if I'm performing on the stage. I couldn't care less about the lot of them! I've never been so removed from myself, so alienated. All my feelings seem dead, except for the drive to live. They shall not destroy me.

Meanwhile Grisha has let it be known that he's an "accountant." Then Herr Pauli, who works as an industrial salesman, makes a similar declaration. Both men have drunk a good deal, and they fall into an embrace, shouting for joy, "Me accountant, you accountant, we accountants!" And the first kiss of German-Russian brotherhood smacks across Herr Pauli's cheek. Soon the widow's tenant is completely drunk. He calls out to us, elated, "These guys are great, these Russians, full of vim and vigor!"

Another round. Here's to international accountancy. Now even the widow is feeling merry, for the moment having forgotten about the herrings being sawed right on her polished table. (None of the boys bother with the plates.) I drink very measuredly, secretly switching glasses; I want to keep my wits about me for later. Still, the mirth at the table is tainted, especially for us two women—we want to forget what happened three hours before.

Outside, the sun is setting. Yasha and Petka sing a melancholy song, with Grisha chiming in. Herr Pauli is in a blessedly relaxed mood. It's a bit much for him; after all, only this morning he was courting death with the Volkssturm, until his troop had the sense to disband and, lacking both weapons and any orders to the contrary, dismissed themselves and went home. Suddenly he belches, falls forward, and throws up on the carpet. The widow and fellow accountant Grisha immediately spirit him into the bathroom. The others shake their heads, express their sympathy. Then Herr Pauli crumples into bed in his room next door, where he spends the rest of the day and, as it turns out, the foreseeable future. A lame duck—probably his subconscious wants him that way. Neuralgia of the soul. Even so, his simple male presence keeps things somewhat in check. The widow swears by him and his rare pronouncements about the world situation and massages his back.

Twilight, a distant howling along the front. The widow has managed to get hold of a candle; we light it and stick it onto a saucer. A meager pool of light on the table. Soldiers come and go—evening is when things get busy. People hammering on the front door, pushing through the back into the kitchen. But we are unafraid; nothing can happen to us as long as Petka, Grisha, and Yasha are sitting at our table.

Suddenly Anatol is standing in the room, filling the space with his masculine self. A regular soldier is trotting behind him carrying a canteen full of brandy and a round dark loaf of bread under his arm. The men are all at their best-fed, strong and strapping, their uniforms clean, practical, and rugged, their movements broad, very self-assured. They spit inside the room, toss their long cigarette filters on the floor, scrape the herringbones off the table onto the carpet, and plop down into the armchairs.

Anatol reports that the front has reached the Landwehr Canal, and I have to think of that dreary old tune "Es liegt eine Leiche im Landwehrkanal . . ." A body floats down the Landwehr Canal. Lots of bodies at the moment. Anatol claims that 130 German generals have surrendered in the past few days. He takes a cellophane bag, pulls out a map of Berlin, shows us the progress of the front. The map, printed in Russian, is very exact. It's a strange feeling when, complying with Anatol's request, I show him where our house is located.

So . . . Saturday, April 28, 1945 . . . the front at the Landwehr Canal. As I write this, it's Tuesday, May 1. The rockets are singing overhead, the oily drone of Russian airplanes. Long rows of Stalin Organs are stacked in the school across the street; the Russians call them by the tender name Katyusha—"little Kate"—and the title of a popular song among the soldiers. When they're fired they howl like wolves. They don't look like much—upright balusters, made of thin tubes. But they howl and shriek and wail so loud they nearly break our eardrums as we stand in line for water, not far away. And they spew bundles of fiery streaks.

They were howling overhead this morning when I stood in line for water. The sky was full of bloody clouds. Smoke and steam rising over the center of town. The lack of water brings us out of our holes. People come creeping from all sides, miserable, dirty civilians, women with gray faces, mostly old—the young ones are kept hidden. Men with stubbly beards and white armbands to show they've surrendered stand and watch the soldiers fill bucket after bucket for their horses. Naturally the military always has priority. Still, there's never any quarrel. Quite the contrary: one time the handle broke while a civilian was using it, and a Russian nailed it right back together.

They're camped out in the garden plots, under the flowering trees. Fieldpieces mounted in the flower beds. Russians sleeping outside the sheds. Others give water to their horses, which are stabled inside the sheds. We're amazed to see so many women soldiers, with field tunics, skirts, berets, and insignia. They're regular infantry, no doubt about it. Most are very young—small, tough, their hair combed back smooth. They wash their things in tubs. Shirts and blouses dance together on hastily strung clotheslines. And overhead the organs howl away, their wall of thick black smoke cutting off the sky.

This morning was like yesterday. On my way home I ran into Herr Golz, loyal Nazi to the end. Now he's adapted. He spotted a Russian with bright rows of decorations on his breast, all wrapped in cellophane, and asked, "Ribbons?" (It's the same word in Russian and German, as he informed me, not realizing how much Russian I understand.) He gave me a little notebook, a German-Russian dictionary for soldiers, assuring me he could get hold of some more. I've looked it over; it has a lot of very useful words like *bacon, flour, salt*. Some other important words are missing, however, like *fear* and *basement*. Also the word for *dead*, which I never used on my travels but which I find myself reaching for quite often in recent conversations. Instead I substitute the word *kaput*—which works well for a lot of other things, too. The dictionary also contains a number of expressions for which I have no use at all now, despite my best intentions, such as "Hands up!" and "Halt!" At most we might hear those words being used on us.

Getting back to Saturday evening, the twenty-eighth. Around 8:00 P.M. Petka and his entourage left—official business of some sort. Petka mumbled something about coming back soon, in a low voice, so the first lieutenant wouldn't hear. Then he crushed my fingers again and tried to look me in the eye.

Incidentally, the officer's stars seem to have strangely little effect on the enlisted men. I was disappointed. No one felt any need to restrain their happy mood because of Anatol's rank, and he himself simply sat alongside the others very peacefully and laughed and carried on with them, filling up their glasses and sharing his pot of liquor. I'm worried about my taboo. Apparently the strict Prussian order of ranks we're so used to doesn't apply here. The ones with stars don't come from any special class; they're by no means superior to the others in background or education. Nor do they have any special code of honor—especially when it comes to women. Western traditions of chivalry and gallantry never made it to Russia. As far as I know, they never had any jousting tournaments, no minnesingers or troubadours, no train-carrying pages. So why should they be expected to be chivalrous? They're all peasants, including Anatol. Of course, my Russian isn't good enough for me to tell from a given man's speech and vocabulary what his education or profession is. And I've scarcely been able to speak with any of them about literature and art. But I have the feeling that, deep inside, all these simple, undiscriminating men feel insecure in front of me, despite their blustering. They're children of the people.

Still, at least Anatol is a full two hundred pounds. So maybe his size will help even if his stars don't. In any case, I'm not changing my mind. He moves like a comet, with a tail of young people, boy-like soldiers, who in the meantime have found shelter in the apartment abandoned by the pudding sisters. One of Anatol's entourage really is just a child—Vanya, sixteen years old, with a stern face and intense black eyes. The widow takes me aside and whispers that he could have been the one, back then on the stairs; his face was small and smooth, his body slender. For his part, Vanya doesn't show any sign of recognition, although that's to be expected since he never even saw the woman he took in such a clumsy, juvenile fashion—he only felt her. Still, I have the sense he knows who she is. After all, he heard her voice; the widow told me how she sobbed and begged. In any event, Vanya follows her around like a puppy, carrying fresh glasses and washing out the dirty ones.

I drank a lot that evening. I wanted to drink a lot, wanted to get drunk, and I did. That's why I only remember bits and scratches: Anatol next to me again, his weapons and things scattered around the bed . . . All his buttons and all his bags and everything in them . . . Friendly, helpful, childlike . . . But born in May—a Taurus, a bull . . . I felt like I was a doll, no sensation, shaken, shoved around, made of wood . . . All of a sudden someone is standing in the dark room, shining a flashlight. And Anatol's yelling at him roughly, shakes his fists, and the man disappears. Or did I dream that?

Early in the morning I see Anatol standing by the window, looking outside. A reddish glow is flaming into the room, a yellow light tugs at the wallpaper. I hear the katyushas howling away, as Anatol stretches his arms and says, *"Petukh paiot."* The cock is singing. It's true—between shells you can actually hear a rooster crowing down below.

As soon as Anatol left I got up, washed myself in the bath with what water was left, scrubbed down the table, swept away the cigarette butts, herring tails, and horse droppings, rolled up the carpet, and stowed it in the chest. I looked in the next room, where the widow had set up camp under the protection of her tenant; both were snoring away. Ice-cold air was blowing through the cardboard on the windows. I felt rested and refreshed after five hours of deep sleep. A little hungover, but nothing more. I'd made it through another night.

I figured out that it was Sunday, April 29. But Sunday is a word for civilians, at the moment without meaning. There are no Sundays on the front.

The first part of the day was filled with the constant whiplike popping of rifle fire. Trucks rolling up down below, trucks driving away. Hoarse shouts, neighing, clinking of chains. The field kitchen sends its smoke right through our missing kitchen window, while our own oven, stoked with nothing but a few broken crates and pieces of lath, is smoking so much it makes us cry.

The widow asks me through the smoke, "Aren't you scared?"

"You mean of the Russians?"

"That, too. But it's really Anatol I'm thinking of. Such a great big bull of a man."

"I've got him eating out of my hand."

"While he gets you with child," the widow responds, poking at the fire.

Ah yes. She's right, that threat is looming over us all, though until now I haven't been very worried about it. Why not? I try to explain to the widow with a saying I once heard: "No grass grows on the well-trodden path."

The widow disagrees; she doesn't think that logic applies here. So I continue: "I don't know, I'm simply convinced it couldn't happen to me. As if I could lock myself up—physically shut myself off from something so unwanted."

The widow's still not satisfied. Her husband was a pharmacist; she knows what she's talking about. Her medicine chest is well stocked; unfortunately, she doesn't have anything that would help me protect myself, as she puts it.

"And you?" I ask back.

Next thing I know she's running to her purse, which is on the kitchen cabinet, fishing out her ID card, and showing it to me, pointing to her date of birth, as self-conscious as if she were undressing in front of me. Sure enough, she's turning fifty this year. I had pegged her as about six years younger.

"That's at least one worry I don't have," she says. "Anyway, we should start thinking about whom to go to in case it does happen." She assures me that she has connections, thanks to her late husband. "Let me handle it. I'll figure things out. You'll be able to get rid of it, no question." She nods as if that were that and, having finally brought the water to a boil, pours it over the ersatz coffee. And I stand there, my hands on my belly, feeling stupid. But I'm still convinced that my sheer aversion can prevent such a tragedy, that I can will my body shut.

It's strange how the men always start by asking, "Do you have a husband?" What's the best way to answer? If you say no they start making advances right away. If you say yes, thinking they'll leave you in peace, they just go on with their grilling: "Where is he? Did he stay in Stalingrad for good?" (Many of our troops fought at Stalingrad; they wear a special medal.) If you have a real live man around, one you can actually show them (as the widow does with Herr Pauli, even though he's her tenant and nothing more), they'll back off a bit—at first. But they don't really care; they take what they can get, married or not. However, they prefer to keep the husband out of the way for as long as needed, by sending him off somewhere or locking him up or doing something else. Not because they're afraid. They've already noticed that none of the husbands here are very likely to fly into a rage. But having one around makes them uncomfortable—unless they're completely plastered.

As it happens, I don't know how to answer that question even if

I wanted to be completely honest. Gerd and I would have married long ago if it hadn't been for the war. But once he was called up that was it, he didn't want to anymore. "Bring another war orphan into the world? Not a chance. I'm one myself, I know what it's like." And that's the way it's been up to now. Even so, we feel just as tied to each other as if we were married. Except I haven't heard from him for over nine weeks; his last letter was posted from the Siegfried Line. I hardly know what he looks like anymore. All my photos were bombed, except the one I had in my purse, and I tore that one up on account of the uniform. Even if he was just an NCO, I was afraid. The whole building got rid of anything that had to do with soldiers, anything that might upset the Russians. They all burned books, too, but at least when the books went up in smoke they provided some warmth, a little hot soup.

We'd barely managed to drink our ersatz coffee and eat a few buttered slices of the plundered bread when Anatol's men marched in. Our place has become a kind of restaurant for them, albeit one where the guests bring their own food. This time they brought a decent man along, the best I've met so far: Andrei, a sergeant, a schoolteacher by profession. Narrow forehead, icy blue eyes, quiet and intelligent. My first political conversation. That's not as difficult as it sounds, since all the words having to do with politics and the economy have Latin or Greek roots, so they sound similar in both languages. Andrei is an orthodox Marxist. He doesn't blame Hitler personally for the war; instead he faults capitalism, which spawns the Hitlers of the world and stockpiles war materiel. He thinks that Russia and Germany make a good economic match, that Germany can be a natural partner for Russia, once it has been built up along socialist lines. The conversation did me a lot of good, and not so much because of the subject, which I'm not as well versed in as Andrei, but simply because one of them treated me as an equal, without once touching me, not even with his eyes. He didn't see me as a mere piece of female flesh, like all the others up to now.

People were coming and going throughout the morning, while Andrei sat on the sofa writing his report. As long as he's there we feel secure. He brought a Russian army newspaper; I deciphered the familiar names of Berlin districts. There's not much left of our city that's still German.

Other than that we feel completely at the mercy of anyone and everyone. When we're alone we jump at every noise, every step. The widow and I huddle around Herr Pauli's bed, the way we are right now as I am writing this. We linger for hours in the dark, icy room. Ivan has driven us to the very depths—even literally, in some cases; there are still a few groups on our block that haven't been discovered, families who have been living in their basements since Friday, who only send people out early in the morning for water. I think our men must feel even dirtier than we do, sullied as we women are. In line at the pump one woman told me how her neighbor reacted when the Russians fell on her in her basement: he simply shouted, "Well, why don't you just go with them, you're putting all of us in danger!" A minor footnote to the Decline of the West.

I'm constantly repulsed by my own skin. I don't want to touch myself, can barely look at my body. I can't help but think about the little child I was, once upon a time, the little pink-and-white baby who made her parents so proud, as my mother told me over and over. And when my father had to become a soldier in 1916, when he said good-bye to my mother at the train station, he reminded her never to forget to put my lace bonnet on to protect me from the sun. So that I would have a lily-white neck and a lily-white face; that was the fashion of the times for girls from good homes. So much love, so much bother with sunbonnets, bath thermometers, and evening prayers—and all for the filth I am now.

Back to Sunday. It's difficult to recollect everything, my mind is such a jumble. By 10:00 A.M. all the usual guests were gathered: Andrei, Petka, Grisha, Yasha, and little Vanya as well, who once again washed our dishes in the kitchen. They ate, drank, and chatted away. At one point Vanya told me, his child's face turning very serious, "We humans are all bad. Me, too, I've done bad things."

Then Anatol shows up, lugging a record player—I have no idea from where—with two of his entourage carrying the records. And what do they keep playing over and over, at least a dozen times? After quickly sampling and rejecting records like *Lohengrin* and Beethoven's Ninth, Brahms, and Smetana? An advertising jingle! A record that the C&A Textile Company on the Spittel-markt used to give customers for buying a certain amount: "Stroll on down to C & A and see what's in our store today . . ." Followed by a list of their entire collection crooned to the rhythm of a fox-trot. But that's just what Ivan wants—they started warbling along, happy as larks.

Once again the brandy is going around the table. Anatol gets the familiar glint in his eye, and finally kicks everybody out under fairly obvious pretenses. This particular door doesn't even have a lock; he simply shoves the wing chair against it. Meanwhile I can't stop thinking about my conversation with the widow, this morning at the oven. I make myself stiff as stone, shut my eyes, concentrate on my body's veto, my inner No.

He moves the chair back away from the door to let the widow in with the soup tureen. She and I take our places at the table. Even Herr Pauli comes hobbling in from his room, perfectly shaved and manicured, in a silk robe, but Anatol stays sprawled across the bedstead, his legs dangling in their boots, his black hair tousled. He sleeps and sleeps, gently exhaling.

For three hours he sleeps, like a baby, all alone with us three enemies. But we feel safer even when he's sleeping; Anatol is our earthwork, our rampart. He saws away, his revolver stuck in his holster. And outside there's war, the crackle of gunfire, the center of town all in smoke.

The widow takes out a bottle of the Burgundy I looted from the police barracks and serves it to us in coffee cups—just in case of Russians. We talk very quietly, so as not to wake Anatol. It does us good to be together like this, polite and friendly; we enjoy an hour of calm, the chance to be nice to one another. Our souls recover somewhat.

Around 4:00 P.M. Anatol wakes up and rushes out, head over heels, to attend to some duty. A little later we hear loud banging on the front door. We tremble, my heart skips a beat. Thank God it's only Andrei, the schoolteacher with the icy blue eyes. We beam at him; the widow hugs him with relief. He smiles back.

We have a good conversation, this time about humanity, not politics. He lectures, about himself, about how he sees women as comrades and not mere female bodies, how he disapproves of "that kind of thing"—and here he looks past me, awkward and embarrassed. Andrei is a fanatic; his eyes are far away as he says this. He is convinced that his dogma is infallible.

There are times now when I have to wonder whether my knowing some Russian is a good thing or a bad thing. On the one hand, it gives me a degree of assurance the others don't have. What they consider animal grunting and screaming is for me a real human tongue—the richly nuanced, melodious language of Pushkin and Tolstoy. Of course I'm afraid, afraid, afraid (though a little bit less because of Anatol), but at least I speak with them as one person to another, at least I can tell who's truly evil from who is bearable, can picture them as separate human beings, distinguish them as individuals. For the first time I also have a sense of being a witness. There probably aren't many in this city who can talk to them, who've seen their birch trees and their villages and the peasants in their bast sandals and all the new, hastily constructed buildings they're so proud of—and that are now, like me, nothing more than filth beneath their boots. By the same token, it's also easier for those who don't understand a word of Russian. For them the Russians are more alien; they can talk themselves into the idea that these men aren't people but savages, mere animals. They can bury their feelings deeper. I can't do that. I know they're people, just like we are—less highly developed, perhaps, as it seems to me, and younger as a nation, but closer to their roots. This is probably how the Teutons acted when they sacked Rome, snatching the perfumed Roman ladies, with their pedicures and manicures and artificial curls. Being conquered means having salt rubbed in your wounds.

Around 6:00 P.M. there was a sudden shouting in the stairwell. A knock at the door, the prearranged dactyl. "They've looted the basement!" Andrei, who's sitting on our sofa, nods. He tells us that he's known about it for hours, advises us to go right away and see to our things.

Absolute chaos below: wooden partitions battered down, locks torn off, trunks slit open and trampled. We stumble over things that don't belong to us, tread on laundry that's still clean and crisply creased. We hold up a candle stump to light our corner, salvage this and that—a few towels, a side of bacon on the string. The widow complains that the big trunk with all her best clothes is missing. In the corridor she dumps out someone else's suitcase that's been slit open and starts filling it with the few things she has left, using her hands to shovel flour that's spilled on the floor, as if she's lost her mind. Left and right the neighbors rummage about by flickering candlelight. Shrill cries and wailing. Eiderdown whirls through the air, the place reeks of spilled wine and excrement.

We drag our things upstairs. Andrei is clearly embarrassed about the looting. He consoles us by saying that he's sure they were only looking for alcohol and that even though everything else has been turned upside down there shouldn't be anything missing. Then, half in Russian, half in German, Vanya the Child, who has shown up in the meantime as well, promises the widow with a serious expression in his black eyes that he'll go with us in the morning when it's daylight and stay by our side until we've found everything that belongs to us.

The widow cries, sobbing afresh each time she recalls a specific item from her trunk—her good suit, her knitted dress, her well-made shoes. I, too, am despondent. We have no rights; we're nothing but booty, dirt. We unload our rage on Adolf. Anxiously we ask where the front is, when there will be peace.

While we whisper among ourselves at Herr Pauli's bed, where he retreated once again after eating his midday meal, Andrei holds a war council with his comrades at the mahogany table. Suddenly all the window casements fly open, pieces of cardboard whiz through the room, an explosion throws me against the opposite wall. Something crunching, grinding, then a cloud of dust in the room . . . and a wall comes crashing down somewhere outside. As we learn from a neighbor half an hour later, a German mortar shell hit the house next door, wounding several Russians and killing a horse. We find the animal in the courtyard the next morning—the meat neatly removed and lying on a bloody sheet, the fatty entrails coiled on the wet red earth beside it.

Exactly how the evening passed escapes me at the moment. Presumably brandy, bread, herring, canned meet, coitus, Anatol. Now I have it: a whole tableful of Russians, known and unknown.

They keep pulling out their watches, comparing the time, the Moscow time they brought with them, which is an hour ahead of ours. One of the men has a thick old turnip of a watch, an East Prussian brand, with a shiny yellow, highly concave dial. Why are they so fixated on watches? It's not because of the monetary value; they don't ogle rings and earrings and bracelets the same way at all. They'll overlook them if they can lay their hands on another watch. It's probably because in their country watches aren't available for just anyone and haven't been for a long time. You have to really be somebody before you can get a wristwatch, that is, before the state allots you something so coveted. And now they're springing up like radishes ripe for the picking, in undreamt-of abundance. With every new watch, the owner feels an increase in power. With every watch he can present or give away back home, his status rises. That must be it. Because they can't distinguish a cheap watch from an expensive one. They prefer the ones with bells and whistles—stopwatches or a revolving face beneath a metal case. A gaudy picture on the dial also attracts them.

I look at the men's hands resting on our table, and feel a sudden twinge of disgust at their bald show of strength. What is clinging to those hands? I chase the feeling down with some brandy. They shout, "*Vypit' nado!*" whenever I put the glass to my lips, and celebrate each swallow as if it were a deed worthy of distinction. This time there's red wine in addition to the brandy, probably from the basement. A candle fixed to a saucer provides a flickering light, casting the Slavic profiles on the wall.

For the first time we have a real discussion, with at least three highly talented debaters: Andrei with the icy blue eyes, schoolteacher and chess player, composed and quiet as always. Then a man from the Caucasus, with a hook nose and a fiery gaze. ("I'm not Jewish, I'm from Georgia," was how he introduced himself to me.) He's amazingly well read, able to quote fluently both verse and prose, very eloquent, and as adroit as a fencing master. The third intellectual is also here for the first time—a lieutenant, extremely young, wounded this evening by some shrapnel. He has a makeshift bandage on his shin and limps around with a German hiking pole decorated with all sorts of badges from well-known destinations in the Harz Mountains. He is pale blond and has an ominous look and a nasty way of speaking. He starts to say, "As an intelligent person, I—" whereupon the Georgian interrupts him.

"There are other intelligent people here, too—the *nyemka*, for example" (meaning me).

We talk about how the war started; they see the root cause in Fascism, in a system driven toward conquest. Shaking their heads, they explain that there was absolutely no reason for Germany to go to war at all—such a wealthy country, so cultured, so well tended, even now, despite the destruction. For a while the discussion turns to the stunted form of early capitalism that was inherited by the October Revolution and to the later stage that is evident in Germany, where capitalist society is more advanced, in wealth as well as decadence. Suddenly cautious, they put forward tentative arguments for why their country is on the verge of a great development, and therefore should be considered, critiqued, and compared only from the perspective of the future.

One of the men points to the nineteenth-century-style furniture in the room as an example of a superior culture. Finally they come to the subject of "degeneration" and argue whether we Germans are degenerate or not. They enjoy the gamesmanship, the lively back and forth of the debate. Andrei guides the conversation with a gentle rein and a quiet voice.

Every now and then the wounded lieutenant directs a vicious outburst against me personally. Scorn and ridicule for Germany's plans of conquest, for its defeat. The others, displaying a sense of tact more becoming to a victor, refuse to follow suit, quickly changing the subject and telling him to watch his language.

Then in the middle of all this talk Anatol comes bursting in, yawning, exhausted from work. He sits down a while but soon gets bored. He can't keep up with the others. He's from the country-side, from the kolkhoz—he's told me that he was in charge of milk, a kind of dairy manager.

"How interesting," I said.

"It's all right, you know, but milk, all the time, nothing but milk . . ." And he sighed.

Half an hour later he goes, leaving the others to debate.

Herr Pauli is sleeping in the next room. Once again the widow has set up her improvised bed close to him. Otherwise the situation is clear: the apartment is open to a few friends of the house, if that's what they can be called, as well as to the men Anatol brings from his platoon, and no one else. But only their chief, only Ana-tol, has the right to spend the night. It seems that I really am taboo, at least for today. But who can say about tomorrow? Anatol comes back around midnight, whereupon the debaters disperse on their own. The last one out is the blond lieutenant, who limps away with his hiking pole, sizing me up with evil eyes.

Now there are holes in my memory. Once again I drank a great deal, can't recall the details. The next thing I remember is Monday morning, the gray light of dawn, a conversation with Anatol that led to a minor misunderstanding. I said to him, "You are a bear." (I know the word well—*medvede'*—which was also the name of a well-known Russian restaurant on Tauentzienstrasse.)

Anatol, however, thought I was getting my words mixed up, so he corrected me, very patiently, the way you'd speak to a child: "No, that's wrong. A *m'edv'ed* is an animal. A brown animal, in the forest. It's big and roars. I am a *chelovek*—a person."

Looking back on Monday, April 30, 1945

The day breaks gray and pink. The cold blows through the empty window sockets, filling our mouths with the taste of smoke. Once again the roosters. I have this early hour all to myself. I wipe everything down, sweep away cigarette butts, bread crumbs, fish bones, rub the brandy rings from the tabletop. Then a frugal wash in the tub, with two cups of water. This is my happiest time, between five and seven in the morning, while the widow and Herr Pauli are still asleep—if *happy* is the right word. It's a relative happiness. I do some mending and then soap up my extra shirt. We know from experience that no Russians come at this early hour.

But from 8:00 A.M. on, the back door is open to the usual traffic. Unknown men of all descriptions. Two or three burst in out of the blue, start pestering the widow and me, randy as goats, try to grab hold of us. But now it's the custom for one of our recent acquaintances to come and help us shake them off. I heard Grisha mentioning Anatol by name, affirming the taboo. And I'm very proud I actually managed to tame one of the wolves—most likely the strongest in the pack, too—to keep away the others.

Around 10:00 A.M. we climb up to the booksellers', where a dozen of the local tenants are still being sheltered, behind the excellent security locks. We give the special knock, the door opens, we join the other residents for the arranged meeting.

A jostle of men and women. It takes me a while to recognize individual cave dwellers; some of them look unbelievably different.

Overnight practically all the women have gray or gray-streaked hair—they can't get their usual hair dye. Their faces, too, look unfamiliar, older, distraught.

We draw around the table, hastily, for fear the Russians will discover our "assembly" and misinterpret it. Very quickly, as fast as I can speak, I report what news I've gleaned from the Russian papers and from the Russians themselves—mostly Andrei and Anatol: Berlin is completely encircled. All the outlying districts are occupied; the only places still resisting are Tiergarten and Moabit. Huge numbers of generals have been captured. They say that Hitler is dead but give no details, that Goebbels has committed suicide, that the Italians have shot Mussolini. The Russians have reached the Elbe, where they've met up and are fraternizing with the Americans.

Everyone listens eagerly; it's all news to them. I look around, ask the woman from Hamburg about her daughter, eighteen-year-old Stinchen with the bandaged head. She answers—with her sharp *s*—that the girl has moved into the crawl space above the false kitchen ceiling in their apartment and spends every night and most of the day up there under the real ceiling. The Russians don't know about crawl spaces and false ceilings—they don't have that kind of thing back home. In the old days people would store their trunks there; before that they were used as maids' quarters—or so they say. So now Stinchen is vegetating away in that cramped, stuffy space, equipped with bedclothes, a chamber pot, and some eau de cologne. Her mother says that at the first sign of footsteps or any other noise she quickly shuts the hatch. At least she's still a virgin.

We feel our way back downstairs. Our building has long since become a regular barracks. The stench of horses is everywhere, the whole place sprinkled with horse droppings tracked in by the soldiers. These victors also feel free to piss on any wall any time they choose. Puddles of urine in the stairwell, on the landings, in the entrance hall. Evidently they do the same in the abandoned apartments that they now have entirely to themselves.

Vanya the child is already waiting in our kitchen, erect as a sentry, his machine gun at the ready. With the look of a loyal dog he offers to escort us to the basement. So once again we go down into the dark. Several Russians are still sprawled out in the back hallway, slumbering into the day, on proper bedding, too, which they've managed to get hold of somewhere. One of them is lying right under the spiral staircase, blocking our way, in his own little puddle still trickling from his body. Vanya kicks him and he moves aside, muttering under his breath. Even though he's just sixteen, Vanya is a sergeant and demands that his rank is respected. Andrei has told me that Vanya was sent to labor on an estate in East Prussia but joined the advancing Russian army, and quickly climbed the ranks thanks to various heroic deeds.

We grope around the basement, looking for the widow's things. Things that I wouldn't recognize and that the widow doesn't want to identify too carefully, as she is simply grabbing whatever she feels might come in useful. By the faint glow from the upper windows, amplified by Vanya's flashlight, we gather potatoes and onions and even find a number of jars of preserves, still intact, which we take down off one of the shelves.

A man comes up, eyes like slits, makes some lewd comments mixed with German words. Whereupon Vanya says, as if to no one in particular, "All right, that's enough." And the slit-eyed man moves on.

The midday meal. We still have more than enough to eat. Compared to my meager meals alone in the attic, I'm living high on the hog. No more nettles; now there's meat, bacon, butter, peas, onions, canned vegetables. Even on his bed of pain, Herr Pauli manages to eat like a horse—until he starts cursing when he bites into a stewed pear and pulls a long, sharp splinter of glass out of his mouth. I find myself chewing on something jagged as well—evidently one of the jars we brought from the basement was chipped.

Outside the war is still on. And we have a new morning and evening prayer: "For all of this we thank the Führer." A line we know from the years before the war, when it was printed in praise and thanksgiving on thousands of posters, proclaimed in speeches. Today the exact same words have precisely the opposite meaning, full of scorn and derision. I believe that's what's called a dialectic conversion.

A quiet afternoon. Anatol is out with his men. Evidently they're preparing a May Day celebration. That makes us anxious; supposedly all Russians are to get an extra ration of liquor.

No Anatol. But around 9:00 P.M. someone else shows up instead, a small man, on the older side, pockmarked and with scarred cheeks. My heart pounds. What a terrible-looking face!

But it turns out he has good manners, uses highly refined language, and is very solicitous. He's also the first soldier to address me as "grazhdanka"—meaning "citizen"—which the Russians use for foreign women whom they can't refer to as "comrade." He introduces himself as Anatol's new orderly, charged with informing us that his superior will be joining us for supper and with procuring the necessary provisions. He tells me all of this from outside the door, which I haven't unchained.

I let him in, offer him a seat. Clearly he was hoping to get into a conversation with me. He's bound to realize that his face isn't one to inspire confidence, so he's twice as eager to please in some other way. He mentions that he's from the Caucasus, from an area that Pushkin visited and where he found much inspiration. I can't understand everything, since the man is using very sophisticated expressions and constructing long, elaborate sentences. Still, I take my cue from "Pushkin" and manage to name a few titles—*Boris Godunov* and *The Postmaster*. I tell him that they made a film of *The Postmaster* in Germany a few years back; the orderly is clearly pleased to hear it. In short, a genuine parlor conversation, very unusual. I don't know how to read these men and am always taken aback at how they surprise us.

A sudden noise, men's voices in the kitchen. Anatol? The little orderly doesn't think so. We both rush to the kitchen, run into the widow, who is fleeing in visible terror:

"Watch out, it's Petka!"

Petka? My God, so he's still around. Petka with the blond bristles and the lumberjack paws that shook so much when he launched into his Romeo babble.

The three of us advance into the room. A small Hindenburg lamp on the pantry is giving its last light. Apart from that there's a flickering gleam from a dying flashlight, swung by a Russian I've never seen before. The other man is Petka, no doubt about it; I can tell from his voice. Since the day before yesterday (hard to believe, but it really was just two days ago), his love for me has turned to hate. As soon as he catches sight of me, the spurned Siberian comes lunging my way. His bristles are standing on end (who knows where his cap is). His small eyes are glistening. He's dead drunk.

There's a sewing machine in the corner, next to the window. Petka picks the whole thing up by its locked cover and hurls it across the kitchen at me. The heavy piece goes crashing onto the tiles. I duck and call out to the orderly, "Go get Anatol!" Then I dash behind the other soldier, the one I don't know who came in with Petka, beg him to help me ward off the drunken man. Petka starts swinging at me with his fists but keeps missing because he's so drunk. Then without warning he blows out the Hindenburg lamp. The flashlight battery dies as well; we're completely in the dark. I hear Petka panting, smell the alcohol on his breath. I'm not frightened, not at all—I'm too busy trying to dodge him, trying to trip him, and I sense that I have allies near at hand. Finally we manage to maneuver him to the back door. The flashlight gives one or two final flashes. We shove Petka down the spiral staircase, hear him falling down several steps. As he stumbles he calls out to me how bad I am, nothing but filth, tells me to take my mother and . . .

It's 1:00 A.M., so it's already Tuesday—May Day. Exhausted, I plop down in the wing chair. The small orderly goes back out, this time to get Anatol for sure. I keep my ears perked, doze a bit . . . The widow and Herr Pauli are bound to have gone to sleep a long time ago. But I don't dare to, so I wait.

At last there's a knock at the front door. It's the orderly again, now loaded with bacon, bread, herring, a canteen full of vodka. Teetering with fatigue, I search the kitchen for some plates and glasses, then set the table with his help. The herring fillets are fully boned and daintily curled. I yawn. The orderly consoles me: "Anatol will be right over."

And he really does show up ten minutes later, along with the pale blond lieutenant, still limping on his German hiking pole. Anatol pulls me on his knee and yawns: "Ahhh, to sleep . . ."

No sooner have the four of us sat down to eat and drink than there's another knock at the door. One of Anatol's men, sent to bring Anatol and his orderly to their commander. Something seems to be going on, or maybe it has to do with the May Day celebration. Anatol sighs, gets up, goes out. The little orderly takes a hefty bite of bacon sandwich and follows his superior, still chewing.

They're gone, leaving me alone with the blond lieutenant. Restless, he hobbles around the room leaning on his stick, sits back down, fixes me with his eyes. The candle is flickering. I'm so tired I nearly fall off my chair. I can't think of a single word in Russian.

He gapes in front of him, announces that he wants to stay here. I start to show him to the back room. No, he wants to stay in this room. I put a blanket on the sofa. No, he wants the bed. He whines, on one note, stubborn, like an overly tired child. Fine, let him go ahead. I lie down on the sofa just as I am, fully dressed. No, I should go to bed with him. But I don't want to. He starts to pester me on the sofa. I threaten with Anatol. He laughs crudely. "He won't be coming back tonight."

I get up to move to the front room, or in with the widow, some-where. He gives in, says he's content to take the sofa, wraps him-self in the blanket. So I lie down on the bed and take off my shoes.

A little later I jump up, startled, hearing his pole tapping in the darkness, nearer and nearer. He's back, wants to get in bed with me. I'm drunk with fatigue. I resist, babble something, that I don't want to. With a dull, dogged, cheerless insistence, he refuses to give up, peevishly repeating, "But I'm young." He can't be more than twenty.

Once, as I'm resisting, I manage to hit his wounded leg. He groans, curses me, takes a swing at me with his fist. Then he bends over the edge of the bed, feeling for something on the floor. A mo-ment later I realize that he's looking for his hiking pole, which he left next to the bed. A knobby wooden stick. One blow on the head with that and I'm done for. I try to grasp his hands, pull him away from the edge of the bed. He starts trying to nuzzle me again. I say, keeping my voice low, "That's just like a dog."

That turns out to please him immensely. He repeats my words, sullenly, tenaciously: "Yes—that's good—just like dogs—very good—the way dogs love—just like dogs love." Meanwhile both of us are so exhausted we fall asleep for a few minutes, then he starts rooting around and pushing again . . . I'm so sore, so wrecked; I go on resisting, stupefied, half asleep. His lips are very cold.

Around 5:00 A.M., at the first cockcrow, he gets up, with difficulty, rolls up his pant leg, and pulls the grubby bandage off his jagged wound. I shrink back involuntarily, then ask, "Can I help?" He shakes his head, stares at me a while—then spits right in front of my bed, spits contempt. He leaves. One nightmare fades away. I sleep like a log for three hours more.

Tuesday, May 1, 1945, afternoon

We started off anxious and apprehensive, sitting in the kitchen from 8:00 A.M., already worn out, waiting for whatever new evil the day might bring. But it began the same as always. Suddenly the kitchen was full of men—some familiar, some we'd never seen. One dressed in a white smock introduced himself as a baker and quietly promised flour and bread, much flour and much bread, if I would . . . (most of them say "love" or even "marry" or sometimes simply "sleep with," but all this man did was look off to the side).

Some shouting came up from the street, and they all rushed out of the kitchen. A little later they were lined up in two rows right in full view under the maple tree. Anatol was pacing in front of them, every inch the first lieutenant but clearly in high spirits: he was giving a speech, his hands stuck in the pockets of his leather jacket. I could make out a few bits and pieces: "The first of May . . . victory at hand . . . enjoy yourselves but remember what Comrade Stalin has decreed," etc. Then he gave his men a roguish wink, and the men grinned back. Andrei stepped up, asked a question, and got an answer. Two or three others raised their hands as well, just like in school, then they started asking questions, and speaking without restraint. I saw no signs of military discipline—no tight ranks or smart saluting. Comrade First Lieutenant was acting very comradely indeed. Throughout the ceremony the katyushas by the school kept howling away, leaving trails of fire across the sulfur-yellow sky.

I was miserable, sore, barely dragging myself around. The widow got her medicine chest out from the crawl space where she'd hidden it and gave me a tin with some remnants of Vaseline.

I couldn't help thinking about how good I'd had it, until now—the fact that love had always been a pleasure and never a pain. I had never been forced, nor had I ever had to force myself. Everything had been good the way it was. But what's making me so miserable right now is not so much the excess itself, extreme though it is; it's the fact that my body has been mistreated, taken against its will. And pain is how it responds to the abuse.

I'm reminded of a girlfriend from school, now married, who confessed to me at the beginning of the war that in a certain way she felt physically better without her husband, who had been drafted, than she had earlier in the marriage. Consummation of the marriage had always been painful and joyless, though she did the best she could to keep this from her husband. That's probably what they mean by frigid. Her body wasn't ready. And frigid is what I've been during these encounters. It can't be otherwise, nor should it be; as long as I'm nothing more than a spoil of war I intend to stay dead and numb, without feeling.

Around noon I was able to save two lives, just by chance. It started when a German, an older man I didn't know, knocked on our front door and called out for "the lady who knows Russian," meaning me.

I have to admit I was reluctant to go with him, since he was mumbling something about revolvers and shooting, but in the end I followed him downstairs. To my relief I saw that the Russians were Anatol's men, mostly NCOs. (Thanks to Anatol's basic instruction I'm now pretty good at distinguishing the ranks.) The elderly postmaster was there as well, in his slippers, completely silent, his face to the wall, his shoulders slumped, his head sunk. His wife, beside him, had turned around and kept yammering the same words over and over, very fast.

What was going on? Apparently the refugee girl who had been staying at the postmaster's, who just this past Saturday morning had been moaning to us about not being able to go on anymore and ending it all—apparently she'd been caught in the stairwell with a revolver in her coat pocket. She probably brought it all the way from Königsberg, no one really knows for sure. Anyhow, she broke away from her pursuers, raced up the stairs, and somehow vanished in the maze of attic rooms. No one's seen her since. So they ransacked the postmaster's whole apartment and found— God forbid!—a photo of her . . . next to a soldier from the SS. The Russians have the picture right there; they show it to me. I have to verify that it is indeed the girl from Königsberg. The SS man could be her fiancé or most likely her brother, since he has the same large head.

So the Russians have detained the elderly couple as hostages and now they've threatened to shoot them if they don't produce the girl, if they don't say where she is hiding.

I can start by clearing up a misconception. The Russians think the postmaster and his wife are the girl's parents—evidently these men are still used to proper families, they don't realize how jumbled and scattered our homes have become, aren't familiar with our patchwork households. As soon as they learn that the girl was only lodging there, that she was a complete stranger, they change their tone. And right away the old woman, who's been watching us closely, her frightened eyes going back and forth between the Russians and me—right away she takes advantage of a lull in the conversation and starts cursing and vilifying the girl from Königsberg, hoping to curry favor with the Russians: they'd been forced to take the girl in, they're fed up with her, she's nothing but trouble, they aren't surprised at anything. And if the woman knew where the girl was hiding she'd say. After all, she has no reason to keep it a secret. And so on.

She really would give the girl away, if she could—no doubt about it. She keeps repeating the same nonsense, her voice shaking with fear, while her husband keeps standing there with his face to the wall, impassive and inert.

Meanwhile I talk and talk, explaining to the Russians that the girl couldn't possibly have intended to kill any of them, that I myself had heard her say she was planning to commit suicide, and now she's probably long since done it. Maybe they'll find her body soon. (The word for suicide—*samoubistvo*—isn't in the soldier's dictionary either. I got Andrei to teach it to me.)

Little by little the tension eases. I go so far as to portray the postmaster and his wife in a comic light, as a pair of silly old fools who don't have a clue about anything. In the end the postmaster turns back from the wall, threads of saliva dribbling from his open mouth, just like a baby. The woman is silent, her bright old-lady eyes darting wildly between the Russians and me. Finally they are both allowed to leave, unscathed.

The Russians instruct me to inform all the civilians in the building that if another weapon is found the entire place will be burned to the ground, according to martial law. And they swear to find the girl and liquidate her.

My merry vodka drinkers are completely changed—beyond recognition! They give not the slightest indication of all the times they've sat at our little round table and drunk to my health. Their happy singing doesn't mean a thing, evidently; work is work and drink is drink—at least for these three. I better make a note of that and be careful with them.

Afterward I am quite pleased with myself, but also scared. Intervening like that is a good way to attract attention, and sticking out like a sore thumb won't do me a bit of good. I have to admit that I'm afraid; I'd like to stay hidden. As I was leaving, the German who'd fetched me asked me to translate a Russian phrase he'd heard many times: "*Gitler durak.*" I told him what it means: "Hitler is a fool." The Russians say it all the time, triumphantly, as if it were their own discovery.

Wednesday, May 2, 1945,
and the rest of Tuesday

I spent half of Tuesday afternoon sitting by Herr Pauli's bed, updating my account. To play it safe I've doctored the last few pages of this notebook to look like a German-Russian vocabulary, which I can always show to any Russian who comes bursting in and wants to see what I'm writing. I actually had to do this on one occasion and was promptly rewarded with praise and a pat on the shoulder.

Toward evening we heard some commotion, someone kicking and pounding the front door. I opened it a crack, keeping the chain on, and caught a glimpse of something white—the baker from Tuesday morning, in his military issue smock. He wanted to come in. I didn't want him to and acted as if Anatol were inside.

Then he asked me for some other girl, any girl, an address, a hint as to where he might find one—he said he'd give her flour for it, much flour, and me, too, for mediating. I don't know of any girl, I don't want to know any. He got pushy, forced his foot in the door, started tearing at the chain. With difficulty I managed to push him out and slam the door.

Yes, girls are a commodity increasingly in short supply. Now everyone's ready when the men go on the hunt for women, so they lock up their girls, hide them in the crawl spaces, pack them off to secure apartments. At the pump, people whisper about a woman doctor who's fixed up a room in the air-raid shelter as a quarantine hospital, with big signs in German and Russian warning of typhus. But the patients are just very young girls from the neighboring apartment buildings, the quarantine is a ruse the doctor came up with to preserve their virginity.

A little later we heard more noise. Two men we hadn't seen before had managed to get into the empty apartment next door. The wall separating the apartment from ours was damaged in one of the last air raids, so that there's a hole about six feet up, nearly a foot wide. The men next door must have shoved a table against the wall right under the hole; they started shouting through the chink that we'd better open our door at once or they'd shoot us. (Apparently they didn't realize our back door was wide open.) One of the men shined his flashlight into our hall; the other leveled his automatic. But we know they're never quite that trigger-happy—especially when they're as sober and quick-tongued as these two seemed to be. So I put on a silly act, attempting to be funny in Russian. Anyway, they were just boys, not a hair on their chins. I cajoled them and even lectured them about the *ukaz* of Great Comrade Stalin. Finally they got down from their shooting gallery, kicked our front door a bit with their boots, and left, so we breathed a sigh of relief. It's somewhat reassuring to know that if need be I can run upstairs and call one of Anatol's men to help. By now most of them know that we're Anatol's private game preserve.

Even so, the widow started feeling more and more uneasy, especially when evening came and none of our usual guests showed up. Taking advantage of a calm moment in the stairwell, she darted upstairs to establish contact with the other residents. Ten minutes later she was back. "Please come up to Frau Wendt's. There are some very nice Russians. It's downright pleasant."

Frau Wendt is the woman with the weeping eczema—on her own, around fifty, the one who tied her wedding ring to her panties. It turns out that she's moved in with the former housekeeper for our westward-departed landlord, another example of the rampant regrouping, random alliances forming out of fear and need. Their small kitchen was stuffy and full of tobacco smoke. In the candlelight I could make out both women and three Russians. The table in front of them was piled with canned goods, most without labels, presumably German provisions now turned Russian booty. One of the Russians immediately handed the widow one of the tins.

The women asked me not to speak any Russian, so I just played stupid. None of these Russians knew me. One, named Seryozha, squeezed right up to me and put his arm around my hip. Whereupon one of the others intervened and said, in a gentle voice, "Brother, please, none of that." And Seryozha, caught in the act, moved away.

I'm amazed. The man who spoke is young, with a handsome face, and dark, regular features. His eyes are bright. His hands are white and slender. He looks at me seriously and says in clumsy German, "*Nicht haben Angst.*" Not to be afraid.

Frau Wendt whispers to the widow and me that this Russian is named Stepan. He lost his wife and two children in a German air raid on Kiev, but he's forgiven us all and is practically a saint.

Next the third Russian, who's small and pockmarked, shoves me a can of meat that he's opened with his pocketknife. He hands me the knife and gestures for me to eat. I spear a few large, fatty pieces and stick them in my mouth—I'm hungry. All three Russians look at me approvingly. Then Frau Wendt opens her kitchen cupboard and shows us row after row of canned goods, all brought by the three men. It really is pleasant here. At the same time neither of the two women could be called attractive: Frau Wendt has her eczema, and the ex-housekeeper is like a mouse—worried, withered, and bespectacled. Enough to give a rapist second thoughts. Heaven only knows why these men have set up here, dragging all those cans of food.

I'd be happy to stay longer: Stepan positively radiates protection. I gaze at him open-mouthed and in my mind rename him Alyosha, from *The Brothers Karamazov*. But the widow's getting restless; she's concerned about Herr Pauli, all alone in his bed, although it's clear that our men—especially those who are sick and bedridden—have nothing to fear from the Russians. It's impossible to imagine one of these soldiers swinging his hips and approaching a man with a whispered, "Let's go." They're all hopelessly normal.

Seryozha takes the candle and escorts us to the door, pious as a lamb under Stepan's eye, risking no more than a gentle pinch on my upper arm as we leave.

We trot downstairs, each with our own can of meat. We hear happy music coming from our apartment and find things there in high gear. Practically all of Anatol's contingent are camped out in the living room, having let themselves in through the eternally open back door. Somewhere they've come up with an accordion and are taking turns. They all try their hand at playing, but none of them really knows how, and the results are as expected. Even so they're laughing and enjoying themselves: after all, it's May Day and they want to celebrate. No one knows where Anatol is. They say he's out on business, he has a lot to take care of.

We go into Herr Pauli's bedroom—and find Russians there as well: the sullen lieutenant with his hiking pole covered in badges and someone else he's evidently brought along, whom he introduces offhandedly as Major ————ovich So-and-So. (They have a way of whispering and mumbling both their patronymics and their last names: they want to keep their identities secret, so they never say more than a typical-sounding first name and their rank, which you can figure out anyway if you know what to look for.)

I stare at the blond lieutenant, full of loathing, and wish him elsewhere. He acts as if he doesn't know me—distant and formal and flawlessly polite. The major he's brought along is even more polite, leaping to his feet when we enter, bowing as if at a dance lesson, greeting each of us individually. Tall and slender, dark hair, clean uniform. One of his legs drags a little. After a moment I notice a third person in the room, another new face. He has been sitting motionless by the window; now the major calls him over and he steps our way, blinking in the candlelight—an Asian with a thick jaw and narrow, swollen eyes. They introduce him as the major's orderly, and then the man immediately withdraws to his corner by the window, where he turns up the collar of his gray woolen coat to help against the wind blowing in from outside.

Now four of us are sitting around Pauli's bed: the widow, me, the surly blond lieutenant, and the major, who does all the talking. He asks me to translate his polite flourishes and carefully weighed words for Herr Pauli and the widow. He thinks they're married. As we carry on our exchange, the major and I size each other up furtively. I don't know what to make of the man, so I keep an eye on him. He offers some cigars that he's been carrying loose in his jacket pocket. Pauli thanks him, takes two, and lights one, puffing away, with help from the major. They smoke a while in peace and quiet; now and then the major holds the ashtray out for Herr Pauli, very politely. All of a sudden he jumps up and asks if he is disturbing us, in which case he'll leave right away, at once! And he makes a show of getting ready to leave. No, no, we beg to differ, he's not bothering us. He sits back down immediately and goes on smoking in silence. A perfect model of etiquette. Another completely new sample from the apparently inexhaustible collection the USSR has sent our way. What's more, he's visibly nervous; his hand with the cigar is shaking. Or maybe he has a fever—we've just learned that he's been wounded in the knee. He was in the same hospital as the lieutenant, which is how they know each other. (So the Russians are in the hospital as well. I'd like to know how they managed to squeeze in and where they sent our people, who as of last week had filled every bed in every available space.)

Meanwhile the glee club has taken its accordion and moved on out of our apartment. Things quiet down. I steal a peek at the lieutenant's watch. The hands are nearing eleven. The widow, Herr Pauli, and I swap glances, unsure what to expect from these guests.

Now the major gives an order to the Asian by the window, who reaches in his coat pocket and barely manages to pull out . . . a bona fide bottle of the best German champagne! He places it on the stand next to Pauli's bed, in the pool of candlelight. In no time the widow is off for glasses, and we clink and sip champagne while the major and the surly lieutenant carry on a quiet conversation that's evidently not meant for me. Finally the major faces me directly and asks, "What do you know about Fascism?" His voice is as stern and strict as a schoolmaster's.

"Fascism?" I stutter.

"Yes, please. Explain the origin of the word. Name the country where this political movement originated."

I think desperately for a moment, then blurt something about Italy, Mussolini, the ancient Romans, *fascio* as a bundle of rods, which I try to illustrate using the lieutenant's badge-covered stick . . . and all the while my hands and knees can't stop shaking, because I suddenly think I know what this major represents and what he's after. He wants to subject me to a political exam, ferret out my beliefs, my past—all in order to draft me into some Russian job, as an interpreter or army helper. Who knows? I see myself being dragged off and enslaved somewhere in some war-torn town. . . . Or are these GPU men hoping to recruit me as an informer? A hundred horrible thoughts flash in my mind. I can feel my hands turning to lead and dropping; I can hardly finish what I'm saying.

I must have blanched, because the widow looks at me, though she doesn't understand a word we're saying. She's obviously concerned, puzzled. Then I hear the major speaking to the blond lieutenant. He sounds satisfied: "Yes, she does have a decent knowledge of politics." And he raises his glass and drinks my health.

I breathe with relief, my heart stuck in my throat. Apparently I've passed the exam, which was only designed to test my basic knowledge. I finish my glass, which is refilled with the last of the champagne. The widow's eyes are drooping. It's time for the guests to leave.

Suddenly there's a new tone, an open proposition. The lieutenant sums it up in two sentences: "Here is the major. He wants to ask you, citizen, if you find him pleasant."

Out of the clouds and back to earth, I stare at the two men, dumbfounded. All of a sudden the major is fiddling with his cigar, carefully stubbing it out in the ashtray, as if he hadn't heard what the lieutenant asked on his behalf. It's so dark I can't make out the orderly, who's still sitting mutely by the window. No champagne for him.

Silence. The widow looks at me, lifting her shoulders inquiringly. Then the lieutenant, toneless, calm: "Do you find the major pleasant? Can you love him?"

Love? That damned word, I can't hear it anymore. I'm so shaken, so disheartened that I don't know what to say or what to do. After all, the lieutenant is part of Anatol's circle, so he knows about the taboo. Does this mean Anatol is no longer around? Could this major be his successor in the field? And does he think that means he can inherit me as well? He can't be thinking that— he's just told us that he's been staying in the hospital, that he had a bed there.

I stand up and say, "No. I don't understand."

The lieutenant follows me through the room, limping on his cane, while the major goes on sitting by Pauli's bedside, seemingly detached, looking right past the two Germans frozen there in silence, helpless and scared.

I murmur to the lieutenant, "And Anatol? What about Anatol?"

"What Anatol?" he shouts, coarsely, loudly. "What do you mean Anatol? The man's long gone. He's been transferred to staff headquarters."

Anatol gone? Just like that, without a word? Is it true? But the lieutenant sounds so certain, so superior, so scornful.

My head is spinning. Now the major gets up as well, says goodbye to the widow and Herr Pauli with great ceremony; I hear him thanking them repeatedly for their hospitality. Neither Pauli nor the widow has the faintest idea of the procuring being conducted. And I don't dare speak to them in German, right in front of the other two. I know from experience that the Russians don't like that—they immediately suspect conspiracy, treason.

The major heads toward the door, bowing to all of us. The Asian comes waddling over from the window. I hold my candle up to light the way out for all three. The major traipses very slowly through the hall, his right leg dragging slightly; he's clearly doing his best to minimize the limping. The lieutenant shoves me with his elbow, asks rudely, "Well? You mean you're still thinking about it?" Then there's a short discussion between him and the major about where to spend the night, whether in the hospital or . . . And once again the lieutenant asks me, coldly but politely, "Could we possibly spend the night here? All three of us?" And he points to the major and to the Asian standing beside them half asleep.

All three? Yes, why not? That way we have protection for the night, so I lead the three of them to the back room, next to the kitchen. There's a broad couch there with several woolen blankets. The lieutenant and the Asian push past me into the room. The lieutenant quickly pulls the door shut. Before it closes I see him shining a flashlight.

I'm standing in the kitchen, candle in hand. The major is standing next to me, in silence. He politely asks me where the bathroom is. I show him the door and hand him the candle. While I wait for him by the kitchen window, looking out into the dark, the door to the back room opens again. The surly blond lieutenant, already in his undershirt, hisses at me, "About us— yesterday—nobody needs to know about that." And then he's gone. I have to think a moment. What does he mean, "about us"? Then I remember the previous night: the dogs' love, his spitting next to my bed. It seems an eternity ago, repressed, nearly forgotten. I've lost all concept of time. A day is like a week, a gaping abyss between two nights.

The major is back; he goes with me into my room. By now Pauli and the widow in the next room will have realized what's going on. I can hear their muffled voices through the wall. The major pulls a tall new candle out of one of his bags, drips some wax onto an ashtray, secures the candlestick, and places it on the little table next to my bed. He asks quietly, still holding his cap, "May I stay here?"

I wave my hands and shrug my shoulders in signs of helplessness.

At that he lowers his eyes and says, "You should forget the first lieutenant. By tomorrow he'll be far away. That's what I've heard."

"And you?"

"Me? Oh I'll be here a long time, a very long time. At least another week, maybe even longer." He points to his leg. "There's a fragment inside. I'm being treated."

I actually feel sorry for him, the way he's standing there. I ask him to sit down, take a seat. He answers awkwardly, "You must be tired. It's so late. Perhaps you'd like to lie down?" And he moves over to the window of scraps and cardboard and acts as if he's looking outside—where you can no longer hear any sounds from the front, none at all. In a flash I take off my outer clothes, throw on an old robe that belongs to the widow, crawl into bed.

Then he comes closer, pushes a chair next to the bed. What is he after? More conversation, more etiquette manual, see under "Raping enemy demoiselles"? But no, the major wants to introduce himself; he takes all his papers out of his pockets, spreads them on the quilt, and moves the candle closer so that I can get a better look. This is the first Russian who's revealed himself that way, with all the details. I soon know his full name, date and place of birth, even how much he has in his bank account, because there's also a savings book from the city of Leningrad, with over 4,000 rubles. Then he gathers up his papers. He speaks a sophisticated Russian: as always I can tell by the fact that whole sentences go by without my understanding a word. He seems to be well read and quite musical, and he's clearly taking pains to behave like a gentleman even now. Suddenly he jumps up and asks, nervously, "Is my company not pleasing? Do you despise me? Tell me frankly!"

"No, no." No, not at all, you can go right on being the way you are. I just can't force myself into this role, to feel at ease so quickly. I have this repulsive sense of being passed from hand to hand; I feel humiliated and insulted, degraded into a sexual thing. And then once more the thought: "And what if it's true? What if Anatol really has disappeared? What if my taboo is gone, this wall I've taken such trouble to erect? Wouldn't it be good to create a new taboo, one that might last a little longer? To build a new wall of defense?"

The major takes off his belt and puts aside his jacket, all in slow motion, with sideways glances at me. I sit, wait, feel my palms sweating. I want to help him and I don't want to. Then suddenly he says, "Please, give me your hand."

I stare at him. More etiquette manual? Is he trying to grace me with a kiss on my hand? Or is he a palm reader? He takes my hand and clasps it firmly with both of his, then says, with pathetic eyes and trembling lips, "Forgive me. It's been so long since I had a woman."

He shouldn't have said that. Next thing I know I'm lying with my face in his lap sobbing and bawling and howling all the grief in my soul. I feel him stroking my hair. Then there's a noise at the door. We both look up. The door is ajar, the widow is standing there holding a candle, asking anxiously what the matter is. The major and I both wave her away. She undoubtedly sees that nothing bad is being done to me. I hear the door closing once again.

A little later, in the dark, I tell him how miserable and sore I am and ask him to be gentle. He is gentle and silently tender, is soon finished and lets me sleep.

That was my Tuesday, the first of May.

On to Wednesday. For the first time in all these nights of men I sleep into the morning, and when I wake up the major is still by my side. Evidently he doesn't have any duties; he can make his own assignments. We talk a bit, very friendly and rationally. Out of nowhere he confesses to me that he is not a Communist, not at all—he's a professional officer, trained at the military academy, and hates the young stool pigeons from the Komsomol. By which I understand him to mean that even higher-ranking officers have reason to be afraid of party watchdogs. I'm amazed at how openly he speaks to me. On the other hand, there are no witnesses. Then, just as abruptly, he wants to know if I really am healthy: "You understand, I mean, you understand what I'm saying." (The first "you" is formal; the second time he uses the familiar form—as a rule he mixes the two when he talks to me.) So I tell him the truth, that I've never had anything like that, but of course I can't be sure that I haven't caught something from one of the Russians who violated me. He shakes his head and sighs. "Oh, these hooligans!" (Pronounced *khuligan*, a loanword very common in Russian, used for scoundrels, louts, ruffians.)

He gets up, dresses, and calls for his orderly, who waddles in, still in his stocking feet, carrying his shoes. The lieutenant is nowhere to be seen; he is probably gone for the day. From the room next door I can hear the widow.

Outside, the May morning is chilly. Chains are clinking, horses neighing; the rooster has long since crowed. But no katyushas, no gunfire, nothing. The major limps around the room and stretches his leg, singing one song after the other in a beautiful voice, including the magical "Linger with me, my lovely one." Then he sits on the edge of the bed, pulls a little harmonica out of his pocket, and plays a march with amazing verve and skill. Meanwhile the Asian— who when I ask tells me he's from Uzbekistan—helps his superior put on his soft leather boots. Taking pains to spare the injured leg, he gazes adoringly at his musical major and sighs in foreign-accented Russian: "Ech, is so beautiful!"

Later, after both are gone, the widow hears in the stairwell that Berlin surrendered around 4:00 A.M.—someone heard it on a crystal set. "Peace"—so we think, and are happy. Until we find out there is still fighting going on north and south of the city.

Still Wednesday, the hours are creeping along. People are constantly interrupting me as I write. But no one has objected; the most I've heard was one soldier saying, "That's right. You all need to study hard and learn Russian."

A steady stream of Russians, liquor, kitchen work, fetching water. We hear there's a wooden beam lying around somewhere; I rush to get it before someone beats me to it. Two of Anatol's men come running out of the abandoned apartment they've commandeered for the past few days, carrying mattresses and bedcovers. Where are they moving to? Not a trace of Anatol himself. Evidently the lieutenant wasn't lying. And the major promised in parting that he would take good care of me, bring me something to eat. Fine with me. For days I've had misgivings about the butter Herr Pauli brought from the Volkssturm. This is definitely a different life from my hungry existence in the attic, where everything had been stripped bare and eaten. First we had the end of the German rations, then what I managed to steal—the loot from the police barracks, the potatoes. And the widow had a few stores of her own—potatoes, beans and peas, bacon. Next we had everything that Anatol and his men left in the way of bread, herring, pork rinds, canned meat (though the alcohol was always drained to the last drop). And the two cans of meat from the white hands of Stepan-Alyosha. A life of plenty. Actually, I haven't eaten this richly in years; it's been months since I was so full after eating. It can't go on like this. But for the moment I'm stuffing myself to build up my strength.

Outside it's cold and overcast. Today I stood at the pump for a long time in a fine rain. Little fires burning all around in the trampled gardens, men's voices singing to an accordion. A woman in front of me is wearing men's shoes. She has a scarf on her head, covering half her face; her eyes are swollen from crying. But for the first time since I've been standing in line for water things are calm. No katyushas. The sky is still smoldering yellow. The previous night had been full of fires. But there's no more gunfire in Berlin; things are quiet. We stand there in the pouring rain, speaking quietly and saying little. The pump creaks, the lever squeals, Russians fill canister after canister. We wait. The pathetic figure in front of me reports in a monotone that no, she hasn't been raped yet, she and a few neighbors managed to lock themselves in the basement, but now her husband has come back, from his unit, you understand . . . So she has to take care of him, hide him, find food and water for him; she can't just think about herself anymore. And a disheveled woman behind me is moaning about furniture: "My good couch, with the royal blue velvet. I had two matching armchairs—they broke them into pieces and used them for firewood!" And finally a scrawny man, all bones, with a face no bigger than a fist, tells us a story about a family in his building that hid their daughter under the chaise longue. They pulled the cover all the way down to the floor, and the Russians even sat on it without any idea the girl was lying underneath. I can't tell whether the story is fact or fiction. It's entirely possible. Our lives are all rumors and melodrama, one big kitschy novel.

I'm not in a position to hide, although I know of a hole in the attic I could crawl into. But I don't have anyone to bring me food and water. Once, when I was nine years old, on vacation at my grandparents' house, I hid in the attic with my cousin Klara. We climbed into a corner beneath the straw dolls in the rafters, which were warm from the sun, and had a secret conversation about where babies come from. Klara, who was younger than me but knew more, whispered something about women being cut open with big knives so the babies could get out. I can still feel the horror that crept up my throat, until finally I was saved by our grandmother's sedate voice calling us for a snack. I clambered down the stairs and breathed a sigh of relief when I saw my grandmother in her satin apron, uncut and intact, broad and round as always, her metal-rimmed spectacles perched on the tip of her nose. The house smelled of coffee and apple cake, and I'm sure the cake was dusted with powdered sugar, though in those days a pound of that cost several million paper marks. As I chewed away I forgot all about Klara's knives and my own fear. But these days I think children are right to be afraid of sexual things—there really are a lot of sharp knives.

The Russians at the pump don't spend much time sizing up us water carriers. They've already caught on that it's mostly old, gnarled women who are sent to the pump. When I'm there I, too, wrinkle my forehead, pull down the corners of my mouth, and squint in order to look as ancient and wretched as I can.

At first, before I started sticking out like a sore thumb, our Russian guests often asked me how old I was. If I told them I'd just turned thirty they would grin and say, "Aha, she's a sly one, pretending to be older than she really is." Then I'd show my ID, and they had no choice but to believe me. They can't really tell with us: they're used to their Russian women, who have lots of children and are quickly worn out; they can't read how old our bodies are—even if most of us look miserable compared with how we looked in peacetime.

A red-cheeked Russian walks down our line playing an accordion and calling out to us. "*Gitler kaputt, Goebbels kaputt. Stalin ist gut.*" He laughs and cackles one of their mother curses, slaps a comrade on the shoulder, and shouts in Russian, even though the people in line won't understand a thing, "Look at him! A Russian soldier. And he's marched from Moscow to Berlin!" They're all so proud of their victory they're bursting their buttons. Even they are amazed that they made it this far. We swallow it all, stand in line and wait.

I come home with two buckets full of water. A new commotion inside the apartment. Two soldiers we don't know are running through our rooms looking for a sewing machine. I show them our Singer in the kitchen. Ever since Petka the bristle-haired Romeo played catch with it the machine seems a bit worse for the wear. What do these two need a sewing machine for?

It turns out they have a package they want to send to Russia; they'd like to have it sewn up in a cloth cover—which of course should be done by hand. With great eloquence consisting mostly of repetition, I convince the boys that such advanced technology isn't up to the task, that this is more a job for grandmother's simple handiwork.

Finally they nod their round heads and agree. They're carrying a whole loaf of bread as payment. The widow thinks for a moment and decides to pass this princely commission to the bookselling wife, who is skilled at sewing and short on bread. She hurries over to fetch her from her triply secured apartment.

And the woman actually decides to come. She's mistrustful, hesitant . . . and at the same time eagerly eyeing the bread. She and her husband are living off beans and barley. She takes her place at the kitchen window and carefully sews white linen cloth around the bundle. The contents remain a mystery. It feels soft— probably clothes.

I try to imagine what the Russians think about all these things lying around unprotected and abandoned. There are deserted apartments in every building that are theirs for the taking. Basements with whatever is stowed in them. There's nothing in this city that isn't theirs if they want it—the problem is there's simply too much. They can no longer take it all in, this abundance; they nonchalantly grab the objects that catch their eye, then lose them or pass them on; they haul things away and then discard them as soon as they become a burden. This is the first time I've seen them take the trouble to really pack up and mail some of the plunder. For the most part they have no ability to assess the value of things. They snatch the first thing they see and have no concept of quality or price—why should they? They've always just worn what they've been allotted; they don't know how to judge and choose, how to figure out what's good, what's expensive. When they steal bedding, for instance, they're just looking for something to lie down on right away. They can't tell eiderdown from shoddy. And what they value most of all is liquor.

While she sews, the bookseller passes on what she knows. Yes, eighteen-year-old Stinchen is still being kept by her mother in the crawl space, lately during the day as well, ever since two Russians came back with the designated water carriers, burst into the apartment, brandished their pistols, and shot a hole in the linoleum floor. The girl looks pasty. No wonder. But at least she's still intact. The bookseller also tells about some new residents, two young sisters, one a war widow with a three-year-old son. They moved into one of the empty apartments, where they carry on with the soldiers, sometimes by day, sometimes by night; rumor has it things are very merry there. We also learn that a woman across the street jumped out a fourth-story window when some Ivans were after her. She's buried in the little yard in front of the cinema. A number of people have apparently been buried there. I can't say, since I take a different path to get my water. And that's the only place you go to outside these days.

So the bookseller stitches away and recounts what she knows. Rumor—the goddess Fama. I've always pictured her as an old woman all shrouded up and murmuring away. Gossip. We feed on it. In the old days people got all their news through hearsay and word of mouth. It's impossible to overestimate how this affected ancient cultures, how unclear and uncertain their view of the world must have been—spooky, nightmarish, a swamp of murmured horrors and fears, of malicious men and resentful gods. These days, too, there are times when I feel I can't be sure of anything, that nothing is true, that Adolf may have long ago escaped by submarine to Spain and that Franco is putting him up in a castle where he's sketching plans for Truman about getting the Russians back to Russia. But one thing is beyond doubt—the deep-down feeling of defeat, the certainty of our being at the mercy of the victors.

The two Russians come back, are very pleased with the sewing, take the package, and give the woman her fresh bread. I talk with them and find out that neither one is actually an ethnic Russian. One comes from around Kuban and is of German descent; the other is a Pole from Lvov. The German is named Adams, his ancestors came from the Palatinate two hundred years ago. The few German words he produces are in that local dialect, for example, "*Es hot gebrennt*"—it burned—for "Es hat gebrannt." The Pole is strikingly handsome, with black hair and blue eyes, quick and lively. He breaks up a crate for our firewood and exchanges a few words with the widow, who as a child used to visit relatives on an estate in East Prussia, where she picked up a few phrases from the Polish field hands. He offers to go with me to get the water.

I accept, though reluctantly. During my first trip this morning I discovered a poster by the door proclaiming that effective immediately Russians are no longer allowed to enter German homes or to fraternize with German civilians.

We set off. I'm glad because this way I'll save at least an hour of standing in line, since if a Russian does the pumping for me I'll have priority. But no sooner are we outside than an officer calls out after my Pole, "Hey, you! What are you doing, going with a German?" The Pole winks at me, hangs back, and meets up with me at the pump, where he serves himself ahead of everyone else. The people in line stare at me with bitterness and contempt. But no one says a word.

The Pole has a violent temper. On the way home he picks a fight with some soldier over nothing, snorting and roaring and swinging his fists. Then a spasm runs through his entire body, and he calms down, catches up with me, and points to the back of his head, explaining that he took a bullet there during the fighting at Stalingrad. Ever since then he's been prone to these rages and violent fits. He often has no idea what he does in his fury; he never used to be like that. I look at him, uneasy, and hurry ahead with my two buckets. He really does have the thick copper Stalingrad medal, hanging from a colorful ribbon wrapped in cellophane. I'm happy when we get to our building and he slips away. Clearly the new order won't take effect as long as their soldiers are billeted in abandoned apartments right next to our own.

Thursday, May 3,
with the rest of Wednesday

Something comic: While I was at the pump with the Pole, the widow had a visit from Petka, my ex-rapist with the blond bristle, the man who wrecked our sewing machine. But he must have forgotten all about this drunken exploit; the widow says he was exceedingly friendly. He showed up lugging a beautiful yellow leather, Petka-sized trunk that another man would have had trouble lifting. Spreading out the contents—mostly clothes—he indicated to the widow that she could take whatever she wanted, that everything was meant for her—while "nothing, nothing, nothing" was to go to me, as he made clear. But that was more for show than anything else. After all, what was to prevent the widow from giving me whatever she liked the minute he was gone? He had probably wanted to play Santa Claus for me—one final, hasty attempt to snatch some more of what he calls love, because he let the widow know that his whole troop was moving on and actually said farewell—"*Do svidanya.*"

With a good deal of self-restraint, the widow declined Petka's largesse and sent him on his way, together with his trunk. Not that she'd been plagued by moral scruples: "Why should I be? After all, they carried off my trunk, too, didn't they?" And that from a woman of proper bourgeois breeding, from a good German home. No, her reservations were of a purely practical nature: "I can't wear those things. The trunk was obviously taken from one of the neighboring buildings. If I went out with those clothes on I'd risk running into their rightful owner." So she limited her take to two pairs of shoes—she couldn't resist, they were exactly her size. Brown street shoes, nondescript and easy to disguise with a little black polish, according to the widow. She wanted to give one of the pairs to me; goodness knows I could use them, since the only shoes I have are the ones I'm wearing. Unfortunately they're too small.

The afternoon passed quietly. We didn't see any of our acquaintances, not Anatol or Petka, Grisha, Vanya, Yasha, or Andrei the schoolteacher. The major, however, showed up promptly at sunset, along with his chubby Uzbek shadow and someone else—thank God not the surly lieutenant with the hiking pole. No, this time it was a little red-cheeked boy in a blue sailor's suit, eighteen years old, Soviet navy. Apparently they've taken Berlin by sea as well. We certainly have enough lakes around. The sailor looks like a schoolboy; he smiles innocently from ear to ear as he tells me quietly he has a favor to ask.

Please, go ahead! I call him over to the window, through which we can still smell the stench of burning. And then the little sailor asks politely and very like a child whether I would be so kind as to find a girl for him, a nice clean girl, respectable and kind. He'd bring her food, too.

I stare at the boy, trying not to laugh out loud. Isn't that the limit—now they're demanding that their sexual spoils be tidy and well behaved and have a noble character to boot! Next thing they'll be asking women to present a police affidavit testifying to their clean record before they're allowed to bed down with the victors! But this one just gazes at me with hopeful eyes and looks so tender-skinned, so much like mama's little boy, that I can't be mad at him. So I shake my head with the proper regret and explain to him that I haven't been living in the building very long, that I hardly know a soul, and that, sad to say, I don't know where he might find such a nice girl. He takes it all in, visibly disappointed. I have an urge to check behind his ears to see if he's still wet. But I know that even the most seemingly gentle Russian can turn into a savage beast if you rub him the wrong way or offend his self-esteem. I just want to know why they keep expecting me to play matchmaker. Probably because I'm the only one around who understands them when they say what they're after.

My sailor boy held out his little paw to thank me and then took off. But why are these youngsters so eager in their pursuit of anything female? At home they'd probably wait a little longer, though it's true that most of them marry earlier than our men. They probably want to prove themselves to their older comrades, like sixteen-year-old Vanya, the stairwell rapist, to show that they're real men, too.

Anyway, the unbridled raping sprees of the first few days are over. The spoils are now in short supply. I hear that other women have done the same thing I have, that they're now spoken for and therefore taboo. The widow has more details concerning the two drink-and-be-merry sisters: evidently they're for officers only, who don't take kindly to low-ranking poachers trespassing on their private preserve. As a rule, those who don't have marching orders in their pockets look for a more permanent arrangement, something exclusive, and they're prepared to pay. They've realized how bad off we are when it comes to food. And the language of bread and bacon and herring—their principal gifts—is internationally understood.

As for me, the major has brought all sorts of things; I can't complain. First he brought a pack of candles under his coat. Then more cigars for Pauli. Next the Uzbek showed up, heavily loaded down, and started pulling out one thing after another: a can of milk, a tin of meat, a side of bacon covered with salt, and a lump of butter wrapped in cloth—at least three pounds of it, all smeared with tiny wool fibers that the widow picked out right away. Then, when we were sure nothing more was coming, he fished out a pillowcase filled with sugar, probably five pounds' worth! Princely wedding gifts indeed. Herr Pauli and the widow were astounded.

The widow dashed off to the kitchen cupboard to squirrel away the presents. Herr Pauli and the major had a friendly smoke, and I sat there brooding. This is a new situation. By no means could it be said that the major is raping me. One cold word and he'd probably go his way and never come back. So I am placing myself at his service of my own accord. Am I doing it because I like him or out of a need for love? God forbid! For the moment I've had it up to here with men and their male desire; I can't imagine ever longing for any of that again. Am I doing it for bacon, butter, sugar, candles, canned meat? To some extent I'm sure I am. I didn't like having to sponge off the widow. I'm happy to be able to give her something of mine— through the major, of course. That way I feel more independent, can eat with a clearer conscience. In addition, I like the major, and the less he wants from me as a man, the more I like him as a person. And he won't be wanting much, I can tell. His face is pale. His knee wound is causing him trouble. He's probably not so much after sexual contact as human companionship, female company—and I'm more than willing to give him that. For out of all the male beasts I've seen these past few days he's the most bearable, the best of the lot. Moreover, I can control him, something I didn't dare do with Anatol, not that easily, though Anatol was extremely good-natured with me. But he was so avid, such a bull, so strong! Without meaning to he might give me a little box on the ear . . . and I'd end up spitting out a tooth—just like that, from sheer excess of strength, sheer bearishness. But I can actually talk with the major. Which still isn't an answer to the question of whether I should now call myself a whore, since I am essentially living off my body, trading it for something to eat.

On the other hand, writing this makes me wonder why I'm being so moralistic and acting as if prostitution were so much beneath my dignity. After all, it's an old, venerable line of work, practiced in the highest social circles. Actually, I've had only one conversation with a bona fide member of the profession. It was on a ship in the Mediterranean, not far off the coast of Africa; I had gotten up very early and was wandering the deck as the sailors were scrubbing the planks. Another woman was up as well, someone I didn't recognize; she was plump, modestly dressed, and smoking a cigarette. I joined her at the railing and started a conversation. She knew a little English and addressed me as "Miss." Smiling, she offered me a cigarette. Later the head steward informed me in a dramatic whisper that the woman was a "bad person," that they'd had to take her along but only let her on deck early in the morning, before the passengers were usually up. I never saw her again, but I can still see her plump, friendly female face. What is that supposed to mean, anyway—a bad person?

But morality aside, could I actually slip into that profession and still be pleased with myself? No, never. It goes against my nature, it wounds my self-esteem, destroys my pride—and makes me physically miserable. So there's no need to worry. I'll be overjoyed to get out of this line of work, if that's what I have to call my present activity, as soon as I can earn my bread in some more pleasant way better suited to my pride.

Around 10:00 P.M. the major deposits his Uzbek in the room behind the kitchen. Then once again a belt rattles against the bedpost, a revolver dangles down, a soldier's cap crowns the post. But the candle goes on burning, and we talk at length. That is, the major talks, telling me about his family and showing me some small snapshots he carries in his wallet. There's one of his mother, who has wild, slanting black eyes against a white head of hair. She comes from the south of the country, where the Tatars settled ages ago; she married an ash-blond Siberian. Judging by appearance, the major takes after his mother, but now I realize that his general demeanor comes from this mix of northern and southern temperaments—his mercurial character, the alternation of speed and gravity, of fire and melancholy, the lyrical upswings and the sudden dark moods that follow. He was married but divorced a long time ago—he himself admits he was a difficult partner. No children, which is unusual for a Russian. I know this because they always ask if I have any, then shake their heads in wonder, amazed that there are so few children here and so many childless women. They also have a hard time accepting the fact that the widow has no children.

The major shows me one more photo, of a good-looking girl with scrupulously parted hair, the daughter of a Polish professor in whose house the major was billeted last winter.

He starts to grill me about my own situation, but I answer evasively. I don't want to talk about that. Then he wants to know about my schooling and is full of respect when I tell him about the *Gymnasium* and the languages I speak and my travels across Europe. "You have good qualifications," he says, appreciatively. Then all of a sudden he wonders why German girls are all so slender, with no fat—had we really had that little to eat? And after that he starts going on about what it would be like if he took me back to Russia, if I were his wife, if I could meet his parents. He promises to fatten me up with chicken and cream; they used to live very well at his home before the war . . . I let him go on fantasizing. It's clear how impressed he is by my "education," though admittedly his Russian standards are pretty modest. My schooling makes me desirable in his eyes. That's a far cry from our German men, for whom being well read does little to enhance a woman's appeal, at least in my experience. In fact, my instinct has always been to play down my intelligence for them, to make a pretense of ignorance—or at least to keep quiet until I know them better. A German man always wants to be smarter, always wants to be in a position to teach his little woman. But that's something Soviet men don't know about—the idea of the little woman tending her cozy home. In the Soviet Union, education is highly valued: it's so rare, so sought after, and so much in demand that it has a special aura, particularly with the authorities. It also brings special pay, which is what the major is getting at when he explains to me that I would have no difficulty finding a "qualified job" in his homeland. Thank you very much, I know you mean well, but I've had my fill of this Russian brand of schooling. Too many night classes. And as soon as they're finally over I intend to reclaim the evenings for myself.

Once again he's singing, quietly, melodically. I enjoy hearing it. He's upstanding, frank, and clean. But he's also distant and alien and so unfinished. Whereas we Westerners are old and experienced and tremendously clever—and now no more than dirt beneath their boots.

All I remember about the night is that I slept deeply and soundly, that I even had nice dreams, and that it took me a long time to ferret the Russian word for "dream" out of the major—I spent much of the morning trying to convey the concept some other way: "movies in the head," "pictures when your eyes are closed," "not real things in sleep." Another word missing from my soldier's dictionary.

At six in the morning the major knocked on the door of the back room for the Uzbek, but there was no reply. He called me over, anxious and upset, worried that something might have happened to the Asian, that he might have fainted or been attacked or even murdered. We both rattled the handle and knocked on the wooden panel. Nothing, not a sound, but it was clear that the key was still in the door. No one, not even the Uzbek, could sleep that soundly. I ran into the front room, shook the widow awake, and whispered our concerns in her ear.

"Come on," she yawned. "He just wants to stay here alone and then try his luck with you himself."

Herr Pauli makes frequent mention of the widow's female intuition and "feminine wiles." But in this case I don't think she's right, and I just laugh at the idea.

Finally the major leaves, after repeated glances at his watch. (A Russian make, as he proved to me when we first met, by showing me the manufacturer's mark.)

Scarcely is he out the door but who appears in the hall, well rested and smartly dressed but Mr. Uzbek himself!

He moves in my direction, looking at me with his swollen little eyes, now strangely clouded over, and pulls a pair of silk stockings from his coat pocket, still in their paper wrapping. He hands them to me, saying in broken Russian, "You want? I give to you. You understand?"

Clear as day, my chubby dear! I fling the front door wide open and show him out. "And now be gone," I say, in German. He understands and saunters off, giving me a last reproachful look as he stuffs the stockings back in his pocket.

One-nothing for female intuition!

At night, between Thursday, May 3,
and Friday, May 4

A little after three in the morning, still dark. I'm all alone in bed, writing by candlelight—a luxury I can afford because the major has provided us with an ample supply of candles.

All through Thursday our apartment was bustling with activity. Three of Anatol's men showed up without warning. They sat around the table chewing the fat, raucous as ever, smoked, spat on the floor, and mucked around with the gramophone. They couldn't get enough of the C&A Textile Company advertising jingle. When I asked—in a panic—about Anatol, they shrugged their shoulders but hinted that he was likely to be back. Before I forget: the regimental baker reappeared wearing his white smock and repeated his stock question: didn't I know of a girl for him? He'd give us flour, much flour.

No, I don't know of a girl for the baker. The drink-and-be-merry sisters are clearly spoken for by the officers. Stinchen is safely hidden away. Lately I haven't heard or seen a thing about either of the concierge's daughters; I assume they've found shelter somewhere. One of the two bakery salesgirls has left us and is said to be hiding in another basement. The other is being kept out of sight in the small room behind the shop—so the widow has learned—where they've blocked the door with a large chest and covered the window with Venetian blinds. It must be pretty dark and gloomy for her. In theory that leaves the young woman who looks like a young man—twenty-four years old and lesbian. From what we've heard she's managed to escape the Ivans up to now. She goes around in a gray suit with a belt and tie, and a man's hat pulled down over her face. As it is, she's always worn her hair short in back. So she slips right past the Russians, who think she's a man; they aren't familiar with such borderline types. She even goes for water and stands in line at the pump, smoking a cigarette.

Pauli keeps cracking jokes about her, how he hopes she gets a proper reschooling, how it would be a good deed to send some of the boys her way, Petka, for instance, with his lumberjack paws. Slowly but surely we're starting to view all the raping with a sense of humor—gallows humor.

We have ample grounds for doing so, too, as the woman with the scabby eczema discovered this morning, contrary to my prediction. She was on her way upstairs to visit some neighbors when two men jumped her and dragged her into one of the abandoned apartments. There she had to take it twice, or really one and a half times, as she explained rather enigmatically. She told us that one of the men pointed to her cheek and asked if she had syphilis; the silly girl was so shocked at the idea that she just shook her head and shouted no. A little later she staggered into our apartment. It took a few minutes before she could speak, we revived her with a coffee cup full of Burgundy. Finally she recovered, then grinned at us and said, "So that's what I've spent seven years waiting for." (That's how long she's been separated from her husband.) She shuddered as she told us about the apartment they dragged her into: "Does that place stink! They do their business anywhere and everywhere!" Despite this she's diligently learning Russian. She's gotten hold of a little dictionary and has been writing out words. Now she wants me to teach her the proper pronunciation. Her eczema is right in front of me. She's smeared it with some kind of salve; it looks like a piece of rotten cauliflower. But these days I've become a good deal less squeamish than I used to be.

We, too, consider the abandoned apartments fair game. We take whatever we need and steal whatever we can eat. I went to the apartment next door (where they've been using the kitchen sink as a toilet, among other things) and walked off with an armful of briquettes, a hammer, and two jars of cherry preserves. We're living well and keeping the drone Pauli well fed on his bed of pain, to the point where his cheeks are getting chubby.

Toward evening, out of nowhere, Anatol bursts into our room, unexpected and practically forgotten. I'm terrified, my heart leaps into my throat. But Anatol laughs, puts his arm around me, doesn't appear to know anything about any major. It seems he really has been transferred to staff headquarters, since he's so well informed. He tells us that the center of Berlin is in ruins, that Soviet flags are fluttering over the wreck of the Reichstag and on the Brandenburg Gate. He's been everywhere. Although he doesn't have any information about Adolf, he confirms that Goebbels killed himself along with his wife and all their children. Anatol heads to the gramophone, but no sooner does he touch the cover with his strong hands . . . than it breaks into five pieces, leaving him standing there holding them, bewildered.

Confused images, scraps—it's all mixed up in my brain, I can't keep it straight anymore. Another evening with lots of vodka, another night. Anxiously I keep one ear cocked, listening for the door, starting each time I hear a noise, a footstep. I am afraid the major might show up, but he doesn't. Maybe the surly lieutenant told him that Anatol was back; after all, the lieutenant also knows Anatol and his entourage. In any event, Anatol has heard a rumor about the major and wants to know whether I've . . . I brushed off his question, saying that we just talked about politics, and Anatol is satisfied, or at least he pretends to be. For his part, he assures me that he hasn't touched any girl in Berlin but me. Then he pulls out some mail from home. Fourteen letters, thirteen of them addressed by women. He smiles bashfully but acts as if the reason were completely obvious: "What can I say, they all love me."

Anatol was careless enough to let me know that he had to leave by three o'clock in the morning to get back to his new billet in the center of the city and that he probably wouldn't be coming back, so I tried to deprive him of as much time in bed as I could. I fussed over his letters one by one, asking as many questions as I could think of, getting him to tell me things, to explain the map of Berlin, show me the progress of the front. I encouraged his men to drink and play records, asked them to sing, which they were happy to do, until Anatol kicked them out. In bed I stalled some more and finally told him, after he'd gotten his way once, that that was it for the moment, I was tired and exhausted and needed to rest. I gave him a sermon, told him I was sure he was no "hooligan" but a considerate, refined man of tender feelings. He accepted it, though more than a little reluctantly, with occasional relapses into bullishness, which I managed to put a stop to. Naturally I didn't sleep a wink. Even so it finally turned three, and Anatol had to leave. A friendly parting from the hot stallion, but then relief, a chance to stretch my legs. I stayed awake a while, since I had this idiotic feeling that I was being spied on, that everything I did was being reported, and that the major would show up any second to take over. But so far no one has come. Now the rooster is crowing outside and I want to sleep.

Looking back on Friday, May 4
Recorded on Saturday, May 5

The major showed up around 11:00 A.M. He'd gathered that Anatol was back in the area and wanted to know if I had . . . I said no, that Anatol had just brought his men over for fun and drink but that he'd had hurry back into town. The major swallowed it. I felt rotten. Sooner or later they're going to bump into each other. What am I supposed to do? I'm nothing but booty— prey that has to stand back and let the hunters decide what to do with their game and how to parcel out. Still, I very much hope that Anatol won't be coming back.

This time the major brought all sorts of sweets, Luftwaffe provisions, concentrated foodstuffs. We ate some for dessert, just the three of us, because the major couldn't stay long. He didn't know whether to laugh or get angry when I told him about his Uzbek and the offer of stockings. Finally he decided to laugh. He promised to return in the evening. There was an edge to his voice, and he gave me a sharp look. Now I'm not so sure that I can control him. I have to watch myself and not forget that they're our masters.

Herr Pauli and I are eating like there's no tomorrow, much to the annoyance of the widow. We spread our butter finger-thick, are extravagant with the sugar, want our potatoes browned in fat. Meanwhile the widow is counting every one of those potatoes. And she's not entirely wrong to do so. Our small stockpile is dwindling. We probably have one more basketful of potatoes in the basement, but we can't get to it. A group of residents took advantage of the quiet hours between five and seven in the morning and barricaded the entrance with a mountain of rubble, chairs, spring mattresses, chests, and wooden beams—all lashed down with wire and rope. It would take hours to undo, and that's the whole point. No plunderer would have the patience. We won't dismantle it until "afterward," though no one can say when that will be.

What a crazy day! Anatol turned up after all, in the afternoon, this time on the passenger seat of a motorcycle. He showed me the bike, which was waiting downstairs along with the driver. He claimed that this really was his last visit, that he was being transferred out of Berlin along with the general staff. Where to? He wouldn't say. Was it to a German city? He just shrugged his shoulders and grinned. It's all the same to me; I only want to know for sure if he's going to be far away. The widow's greeting was amicable but measured. She sees things in terms of the larder and prefers the major, who leaves more of a mark on her cupboard shelves.

I sit with Anatol on the edge of the bed and have him tell me all about "his" motorcycle—he's very proud of it. The door is blocked by the usual chair. But suddenly it's pushed open, and Anatol looks up, annoyed. There's the widow, all red in the face, her hair disheveled. She squeezes inside, pursued by a Russian. I recognize him as the handsome Pole from Lvov, the one with the head wound from Stalingrad and the special talent for getting enraged. He looks like he's on the verge of having a fit right now. He immediately starts shouting, appealing to me as well as Anatol as referees: he's young, what's good for others is good for him, too, it's been a long time since he had a woman, the widow's husband (meaning Herr Pauli, who's having his afternoon nap in the next room) doesn't need to know anything—it won't take long at all! His eyes flash, he waves his fists, his hair is flying. He seems utterly convinced that the widow is his by right—her bits of field-hand Polish must have lodged in his ear and struck a chord in his heart. He even tries some on her now, tosses a few Polish words her way, all the while greatly agitated. The widow stands there wiping away the tears that are streaming down her face.

Anatol looks at me, then at the widow. It's clear he doesn't want to have anything to do with this. He turns to me, saying it isn't such a big deal, I should talk to the widow, everything will soon be over, she shouldn't make trouble for herself. Then back to the Pole, waving him away: Kindly leave me out of it, I'm in a hurry, I have to go soon. And he makes as if to shove the chair back against the door. I whisper a few quick words to the widow, remind her of the head wound, the Pole's tantrums. The man is capable of doing anything, goes crazy if he doesn't get his way. . . . Anatol will soon be gone and won't be able to help . . . or does she want to wake Herr Pauli, so he can take care of the frenzied man from Lvov? She dismisses that idea: No, what for? And she cries. The Pole, once again calm, strokes her. Then they both disappear.

A quarter of an hour later the motorcycle rattles off, with Anatol on the passenger seat. He looks back up at the apartment, sees me by the window, and gives a lively wave. Then the bike vanishes around the corner.

The widow was angry and didn't speak to me the whole afternoon. In the evening, though, she told me what happened. Apparently the young devil turned out to be so tame and docile he was downright boring by the time he let her go. It seems he left her with a compliment. At first she didn't want to reveal it, but finally she told us: "Ukrainian woman—like this. You—like this." The first "like this" he illustrated with a circle formed by both his thumbs and forefingers, the second "like this" with a single thumb and forefinger.

What else did the day bring? Another stair victim, once again an older woman, about sixty; the younger ones don't dare venture into the stairwell by day. This time it was one of the three dressmakers, the black-pudding sisters. They'd heard that Anatol's men had vacated their apartment, so they made their way into the abandoned rooms, escorted by our deserter. Together they fished a sewing machine out of the trash and general clutter and lugged it up two flights of stairs. Then one of the aunties went back down by herself, to salvage some other sewing equipment—and ran right into the hands of a Russian. When the widow spoke with her it was nearly evening and the dressmaker was still sobbing on the sofa in the booksellers' apartment, surrounded by a whole bevy of women, moaning and groaning.

They got hold of the concierge's younger daughter as well, her mother told me today at the pump. At first the whole family— mother, two daughters, and the three-year-old grandson—had stayed hidden in the basement next door, which was well secured. But once people started saying that things were a little better with the Russians, the girls went back to their apartment on the first floor to cook and do their wash. That's where two drunken, singing heroes caught them by surprise. According to the mother, they left the older sister alone. I've seen the girl in the meantime and I can understand why: she looks clinically emaciated, and her face is so small, her cheeks so hollow, that the outline of her skull shows through. Her mother whispered to me that the younger daughter had barricaded herself with cotton wool, though there was no real reason to, but the girls had heard that the Russians don't like women at that time of month. It didn't help. The men just howled with laughter as they tossed the stuff around the room and then took the sixteen-year-old on the chaise longue in the kitchen. "She's doing well so far," her mother said, herself amazed. Even so, just to be safe, she took her daughter up to the booksellers', where the widow says she's been boasting to everyone how the Russians went straight for her without giving her older sister even a second glance.

One more person came to say good-bye: Andrei, the schoolteacher from Anatol's group with the icy blue eyes. He sat with me a while at the table, talked about politics in his quiet, composed voice, gave me a lecture full of words like *sotsialisticheski, kapitalisticheski, ekonomicheski*. I listened quietly, mending my one and only towel and patching my violated garter. We're starting to see a semblance of order again.

That evening we sat by Herr Pauli's bed—the widow, the deserter's wife, and me—by candlelight. We gave the deserter's wife one of our candles; she let us have a box of matches. The major showed up right on time, along with his chubby Uzbek shadow. He played on his little harmonica—a plundered German Hohner—wildly and full of fire. He even wound up asking his orderly to help him out of his soft leather boots and danced a Krakowiak in his socks, swinging his hips gracefully and lithely, fully aware of his talent, too. Then he danced a tango with the widow, while the rest of us sang a popular hit. After that he played some more, this time from *Rigoletto* and *Il Trovatore*—it's amazing the music he can get out of that tiny mouth organ. His Uzbek didn't take his pitch-black Mongol eyes off him for a second, and every now and then he'd voice his admiration in childlike, awkward Russian: "Oh, he is good. No one else like that." Finally the Uzbek let the major talk him into singing a Uzbek song, very nasal, very strange. After endless begging he also agreed to dance on his chunky legs. The deserter's wife, a tough Berlin woman, drank the major's wine and received his ceremonial bows. While he was dancing with the widow our guest whispered to me, "Well, for him I could flat out forget myself!"

The major stayed. A difficult night. His knee had swollen up from all the dancing and caused him a lot of pain. He groaned every time he moved. I scarcely dared stir. He left me alone completely. I slept deeply.

Saturday, May 5, 1945

The May sky is dreary today. The cold doesn't want to go away. I sit hunched on the stool in front of our stove, which is barely kept burning with all sorts of Nazi literature. Assuming everyone is doing the same thing—and they are—*Mein Kampf* will go back to being a rare book, a collector's item.

I just polished off a pan of cracklings and am giving myself a thick spread of butter, while the widow paints a black picture of my future. I pay no attention to her. I don't care about tomorrow. I just want to live as well as I can for now, otherwise I'll collapse like a wet rag, given our recent way of life. My face in the mirror is round again.

Today the three of us discussed the future. In his mind Herr Pauli is already settling back at his desk at the metal works; he forecasts a huge upturn in the economy with the help of our conquerors. The widow wonders whether she could land a job there herself, as a cook in the factory cafeteria; she's pessimistic

about the modest annuity from her deceased husband's insur-
ance and is afraid she'll have to look for work. And me? Well, at
least I've studied a number of things; I'm sure I'll find something. I'm not afraid. I'll just sail blindly ahead, trusting my little
ship to the currents of the times; up to now it's always managed
to carry me to green shores. But our country is despondent, our
people are in pain. We've been led by criminals and gamblers,
and we've let them lead us, like sheep to the slaughter. And now
the people are miserable, smoldering with hate. "No tree is high
enough for him," I heard someone say of Adolf this morning at
the pump.

A number of men showed up in the afternoon, German men
this time, from our own building. It felt very strange, once again
being around men you don't have the slightest reason to fear, men
you don't have to constantly gauge or be on guard against or keep
an eye on. They recounted the saga of the bookseller that is now
echoing throughout the building, the tale of how this Bavarian, a
gnarled stump of a man, really and truly yelled at a Russian. It all
happened right outside the couple's door, when an Ivan grabbed
the bookseller's wife as she was coming back with water. (She
won't let her husband go to the pump because he was in the party.)
The woman shrieked, and her husband came running out of the
apartment, making straight for the Ivan and shouting, "You
damned bastard! You prick!" As the saga has it, the Russian piped
down, shriveled up, and backed off. So it can be done after all.
The Russian's barbarian-animal instinct must have told him that
the bookseller was capable of anything at that moment, that his
rage had blinded him to all consequences—so the soldier simply
relinquished his booty.

It's the first time I've heard of one of our men responding with
that kind of red-eyed wrath. Most of them are reasonable—they

react with their heads, they're worried about saving their own skins, and their wives fully support them in this. No man loses face for relinquishing a woman to the victors, be it his wife or his neighbor's. On the contrary, they would be censured if they provoked the Russians by resisting. But that still leaves something unresolved. I'm convinced that this particular woman will never forget her husband's fit of courage, or perhaps you could say it was love. And you can hear the respect in the way the men tell the story, too.

But they didn't come just for conversation; they make themselves useful. They'd brought a few boards, which they sawed to size on the kitchen table and nailed up diagonally across the jambs of the back door. They had to work quickly so as not to get caught by some Russian. As payment we handed out cigars from the ample supply the major brought yesterday. We really are quite rich.

After the entire doorframe was boarded up, a Russian appeared on the back stairs. He kicked hard at the boards, tried to break in, but without success. That was a relief. Now we won't have strangers barging in night and day. Of course, they also come to the front door, but that has a good lock and is made of solid wood. As it is, most of the people who know us call up from outside, just to reassure us: "*Zdyes'* Andrei," for example, means that it's Andrei. And the major and I have worked out a special knock.

A touching story: around noon we have a visit from Fräulein Behn, our fearless lead mare from the basement. She's now lodging with young Frau Lehmann, whose husband is missing in the East, and helping out with her two children. To date, neither the young mother nor Fräulein Behn has been raped . . . although both are quite nice-looking. It turns out the small children are their great protection. They understood this from the first night of Russians, when two rough men showed up shouting and pounding their rifle butts, and demanded to be let in. When Fräulein Behn started to open the door they just pushed her into the room . . . then stopped in front of the crib where the baby and four-year-old Lutz were sleeping together. One of them said in flabbergasted German, "Small child?" They both stared at the crib a while— and then stole away on tiptoe.

Fräulein Behn asks me to come up for a couple minutes; they have two Russian visitors, one older, one young. They've been there once before and today they've brought some chocolate for the children. The women would like to speak with them, so they've asked me to play interpreter.

Soon we're all sitting across from one another: the two soldiers, Fräulein Behn, Frau Lehmann, with Lutz clinging to her knee, and me. The baby is right there in her stroller. The older Russian asks me to translate: "What a beautiful little girl! A real beauty!" And he winds his index finger into one of the baby's copper curls. Then he asks me to tell the two women that he also has two children, two boys, who are living with their grandmother in the country. He fishes a photo out of his battered cardboard wallet: two crew-cut heads on paper that's turned a darkish brown. He hasn't seen them since 1941. I've figured out that the concept of home leave is foreign to nearly all the Russians. Most of them have been separated from their families since the beginning of the war; that's nearly four years. I assume that this is because most of the war has been fought in their country, and with the civilian population being transferred back and forth no one knows for sure where his family is at any given moment. On top of that, there's the enormous distances and the pitiful condition of the roads. It's also possible that, at least in the first years of the German advance, the authorities were afraid their people might desert or go over to the other side. Whatever the case, these men were never entitled to home leave like ours were. I explain this to the two women, and Frau Lehmann says, full of understanding, "Well, that excuses some things."

The second Russian guest is a young boy of seventeen, a former partisan who joined up with the westward advancing troops. He looks at me, brow deeply furrowed, and asks me to translate that in his village German soldiers stabbed some children to death and took others by the feet and bashed their heads against a wall. Before I translate, I ask, "Did you hear that? Or see it yourself?" He gazes off and says in a stern voice, "I saw it twice myself." I translate.

"I don't believe it," answers Frau Lehmann. "Our soldiers? My husband? Never!" Fräulein Behn tells me to ask the Russian whether the soldiers in question had "a bird here" (on their caps) or "a bird there" (on their arms)—in other words, whether they were Wehrmacht or SS. The Russian understands the question right away—the villagers probably learned to make that distinction. But even if it was SS men in this case and similar ones, our conquerors will consider them part of the "nation" and charge us all accordingly. Talk like this is already making the rounds; today at the pump I heard several people say, "Our boys probably weren't much different over there."

Silence. We all stare into space. A shadow has fallen in the room. The baby pays no attention—she bites the foreign finger, cooing and squealing. I feel a lump rising in my throat. She seems like a miracle to me, pink and white with copper curls, flowering here in this desolate, half-looted room, among us adult human beings so mired in filth. And suddenly I realize why the warriors are drawn to the little baby.

First for the rest of Saturday. Once again the major showed up around 8:00 P.M. with his Asian orderly, who reached into his bottomless pockets and this time pulled out two turbots—by no means large, but fresh. The widow breaded and baked the delicious fish, which we then all shared. Even the Uzbek was given a piece in his corner window, which he always makes a beeline for, just like a loyal dog. A very tasty meal indeed.

Did the major stay the night? I wouldn't have dared undress on my own, wouldn't have dared go to sleep in the room alone, I know that. Even though our back door is now boarded up, even though the war is no longer raging outside, there's still a strong dose of fear in all of us. Fear of people who are roaring drunk or in a fury. The major is our protection. Today he was limping; his knee is still swollen. The widow, who has gentle hands for that kind of work, made him a compress before he joined me in bed. He's confessed to me the funny nickname his mother used to call him, and he translated my own name into Russian, using an affectionate diminutive. So I guess we're friends. Nevertheless I keep telling myself to be on guard and to talk as little as possible.

In the morning, alone again, we sat around Herr Pauli's bed, ate a solid breakfast, and listened to what was going on outside. Finally the widow ventured into the stairwell and ran upstairs to the booksellers', where a dozen neighbors are still rooming together. When she came back she said, "Here, give me the rest of the Vaseline." She was swallowing hard and her eyes were full of tears.

She'd heard that the liquor distiller had returned to his wife, in the night under cover of darkness, creeping and crawling through the front line, right past the troops, together with Elvira, the redhead who'd been helping him man his post in the distillery, though why I can't say. Was it a joint defense of the liquor bottles? There must be something rooted in us, some instinct that makes us sink our claws into our possessions when threat looms near.

Together the widow and I went up to the apartment on the fifth floor. It turns out that the distiller's buxom wife, the one from the basement who'd been honored with the first Russian advances, has been living unmolested in her fifth-story apartment ever since—just a minute while I do the calculations—for over a week. Equipped with a tub full of water and a decent stock of provisions, she's been left entirely to herself. I can believe it, too. Although it took us a while to figure it out, the fact is that the Russians dislike climbing stairs. Most of them are farm boys, used to living close to the earth in homes with only a single floor, so that they're not very experienced stair climbers. Moreover, they probably feel too cut off when they're so high up, that four flights of stairs is too long a retreat. As a result they hardly ever dare go that far up.

We tiptoe into the apartment, as if entering a sickroom. The redhead is sitting on a kitchen chair, staring off into the distance. Her feet are in a bucket of water. She's soaking her toes, which are battered and bloody, according to the distiller. His own feet look just as bad. They both passed through the front line in their stocking feet, through streets full of rubble and ruin. The Russians had taken their shoes.

The redhead is in her slip, with a blouse draped over her, probably from the man's wife—it's way too big. She sits there groaning as she moves her toes, while the man tells us how his distillery was in the middle of the fighting for two whole days, how first

German, then Russian soldiers had regaled themselves with what was left of the alcohol. As they were rummaging for liquor the Russians finally found Elvira and him behind a wooden partition, along with another woman, an employee who'd sought shelter there as well. Here the man shrugs his shoulders, doesn't want to say any more, walks out of the kitchen.

"They lined up," his wife whispers to us, while the redhead stays silent. "Each took his turn. She says there were at least twenty, but she doesn't know exactly. She had to bear the brunt of it herself. The other woman wasn't well."

I stare at Elvira. Her swollen mouth is sticking out of her pale face like a blue plum. "Show them," says the distiller's wife. Without a word the redhead opens her blouse and shows us her breasts, all bruised and bitten. I can barely write this; just thinking about it makes me gag all over again.

We left the rest of the Vaseline. There was nothing to say, so we didn't try. But Elvira started talking on her own, although we could barely understand, her lips were so swollen. "I prayed while it was happening," she said, or words to that effect. "I kept on praying: Dear God, thank you for the fact that I am drunk." Because before the boys lined up they plied her with whatever they'd found, and they kept giving her drinks in between. And for all of this we thank the Führer.

Apart from that there was much to do in the afternoon, a lot of wiping and washing: the time passed. I was astonished to suddenly see the major standing in the room; the widow had let him in. This time he'd brought a brand-new pack of cards, which he laid out on Pauli's quilt. Apparently the two men have found a game they both play. I don't have the faintest idea what it is, so I've slipped off to the kitchen, where I'm quickly writing this down. The major has even brought some "play money"—German coins,

three- and five-mark pieces, which were withdrawn from circulation ages ago. How on earth did he get them? I don't dare ask. He
didn't bring anything to drink, for which he apologizes to each of
us. No matter, today he's our guest—we inherited a bottle of
liquor from the distiller.

Monday, May 7, 1945

It's still cool, but clearing, a little ray of sunlight. Another restless
night—the major woke several times and kept me up with his
groaning. Supposedly his knee is getting better, but it hurts when
he bumps it. Despite that he didn't let me rest much. Among other
things he talked about the drink-and-be-merry sisters, who moved
into the abandoned apartment on the ground floor. Apparently
they're very popular with the Russian officers, who call them Anya
and Liza. I saw one of them on the stairs: very pretty, dressed in
black and white, tall and delicate. As he reported their goings-on,
the major looked uncomfortable and slightly embarrassed. He
himself had been invited into the apartment that morning, in
broad daylight—and found the girls in bed with two men. Laughing, they asked him to join in—an offer that continued to shock
the proper middle-class major as he was telling me the story. Apparently a prime attraction for the soldiers is one sister's very cute
three-year-old son, who can already babble a few words of Russian, according to the major, and whom the male guests pamper
as best they can.

Moving right along—the new day. It's so strange living without

papers or calendars, clocks or monthly accounting. A timeless
time that slips by like water, its passing measured only by the com-
ings and goings of the men in their foreign uniforms.

Occasionally I'm amazed at how determined I am to capture
this timeless time. This is actually my second attempt to carry on a
conversation with myself in writing. My first was as a schoolgirl;
we were fifteen or sixteen, wore wine-red school berets, and talked
endlessly about God and the world (sometimes about boys as well,
but very condescendingly). In the middle of the school year our
history teacher had a stroke and was replaced with someone who
had just finished her training, a snub-nosed novice who exploded
into our class. She brazenly contradicted our patriotic history
book by calling Frederick the Great an adventurer, a gambler, and
praised Friedrich Ebert, the Social Democrat, whom our old
teacher had enjoyed deriding as a mere "saddler's apprentice."
After making these audacious declarations she would flash her
black eyes, lift her hands, and appeal to us, "Girls, you better go
and change the world. It needs it!"

We liked that. Because we didn't think much of the world of
1930, either. In fact, we emphatically rejected it. Everything was
so muddled, so full of barriers and obstacles. Unemployment was
in the millions, and we were constantly told that practically all the
professions we aspired to had no prospects, that the world wasn't
waiting for us in any way.

By chance elections to the Reichstag were being held then.
The ten or fifteen largest parties convened assemblies every evening, and we would march over in little groups, spurred on by our
teacher. We worked our way from the National Socialists through
the Centrists and the Democrats to the Social Democrats and
Communists, raising our arms in the Hitler salute with the Nazis
and letting ourselves be addressed as "comrade" by the Commu-

nists. That's when I started my first diary, out of a desire to form my own opinion. For nine days, I believe, I faithfully wrote down the gist of what the speakers had said—along with my youthful rebuttals. On the tenth day I gave up, although my notebook still had many blank pages left. I couldn't find my way out of the political underbrush. It was the same for my friends. Each party, we felt, was partly right. But they all engaged in disreputable tactics—horse trading, we called it—the haggling, the lobbying, the cudgeling for power. No party seemed clean. None of them stuck uncompromisingly to their principles. Today I think we probably should have founded a party of sixteen-year-olds, just to satisfy our moral demands. Whatever grows older, grows dirtier.

Monday around noon we had a visitor. Not from the building and not from next door but from distant Wilmersdorf, a district in the west of the city, two hours from here by foot. A girl named Frieda, whom the widow had heard of but never met.

Thereby hangs a tale, which begins with the widow's nephew, who once upon a time was a medical student. One night he was assigned to air-raid duty at his university. A young female medical student was assigned as well, and their joint watch produced a pregnancy and a shotgun wedding. The bride was nineteen and the groom twenty-one. Then the war machine snatched him and sent him off to the front, and no one knows where he is. His wife, however, who is now in her eighth month, moved in with a girlfriend, the Frieda now sitting on our kitchen chair and bringing us news from the outside world.

The widow's first question: "And you, did they also . . . ?"

No, Frieda is still unscathed—well not entirely: some Russian pushed her against the wall of the basement but had to run off and fight before he could take his full pleasure. It seems the soldiers reached the block where the two girls are living shortly before the surrender, and galloped through without setting up camp. The expectant mother had tapped her belly and said, "Baby," and they didn't touch her.

Frieda delivers her report and turns to us with blank, shiny eyes. I know that look. I saw it far too often in my mirror, back when I was living off nettles and porridge. And that's the predicament the two women are in now, which is why Frieda took it on herself to make the long, arduous journey here, through streets she says were completely silent and deserted. She asks if she could have some food for the widow's niece by marriage, and the child who is on the way. She tells us that the young woman spends the whole day flat on her back and gets dizzy at the slightest attempt to stand up. A nurse who looks after her occasionally explained that when a mother isn't getting proper nourishment the fetus sponges off her body, draining her calcium and blood and muscle tissue.

Together the widow and I look for what we feel we can give: some of the major's butter and sugar, a can of milk, a loaf of bread, a piece of bacon. Frieda is ecstatic. She herself looks pitiful; her legs are like sticks and her knees jut out like gnarled bumps. Even so she's quite cheerful and not afraid of the two-hour trip home. For our part, we're happy to have this envoy from the distant district. We ask her to describe in detail the route she took, to tell us what she saw. We pet her and beam at this calflike, half-starved eighteen-year-old, who mentions that she once wanted to teach gymnastics. Well, there won't be much demand for that any more, not here, not for the foreseeable future. People are happy not to have to make any extraneous movements—or at least the others are, the people going hungry. Right now this doesn't apply to me, I still have my strength. The widow hits a sore point when she suggests to Frieda, "Well, my child, couldn't you find some halfway-nice Russian and give him a pretty smile? So that he'd bring you girls a little something to eat?"

Frieda gives a silly kind of smile, and says that there are hardly any Russians left on her block, otherwise . . . And she packs up the presents and stashes them in the shopping bag she brought along.

Her visit really bucked us up. So we're not entirely cut off from the world—we, too, could risk hiking across town to see friends and acquaintances. Since Frieda came we've been planning and scheming, wondering whether we should take our chances. Herr Pauli is against the idea. He sees us both being nabbed and sent off somewhere to do forced labor, possibly to Siberia. We think of Frieda, who actually managed to do it, and keep on planning.

Moving along. It's late afternoon as I write this and I've just returned from my first big trip. It came about very unexpectedly. I was sitting at the window seat, even though you hardly see anyone on the street now except Russians and people getting water. And lo and behold, a Russian comes bicycling right up to our door . . . it's the major.

I race downstairs. He has a sparkling new German men's bicycle. I beg and plead: "Could I take it for a ride? Just for five minutes?" The major stands on the curb, shakes his head. He's not sure what to do; he's afraid that someone might steal the bike from me. At last I persuade him.

Sunshine. The weather turns warm in the twinkling of an eye. I pedal as fast as I can. The wind roars in my ears. I'm speeding because it makes me happy after being so miserably cooped up all the time—and also because I want to prevent anyone from stealing the bike. I race past blackened ruins. In this part of town the war ended one day earlier than where we are. You can see civilians sweeping the streets. Two women are pushing and pulling a mobile operating unit, probably recovered from the rubble, its sterile lamps ablaze. An old woman is lying on top under a woolen blanket; her face is white but she's still alive.

The farther south I ride the further the war recedes. Here you can even see whole groups of Germans standing around and chatting. People don't dare do that where we live. There are even children outside, hollow-cheeked and unusually quiet. Women and men are digging around in the gardens. There are only a few isolated Russians. A Volkssturm barricade is still piled up in front of the tunnel. I dismount and push my bike through a gap in the barricade. Beyond the tunnel, on the lawn in front of the S-Bahn station, there is a knee-high mound strewn with greenery and marked with three wooden posts painted bright red and affixed with small handwritten plaques—edged paper under glass. I read three Russian names and the dates of their deaths: April 26 and 27, 1945.

I stand there a long time. As far as I can remember this is the first Russian grave I've seen so close. During my travels there I caught only fleeting glimpses of graveyards, weathered plaques, bent crosses, the oppressive neglect of poor village life. Our papers were always reporting on how the Russians hide their war dead as a disgrace, how they bury them in mass unmarked graves and stamp down on the earth to render the spot invisible. This can't be true. These posts and plaques are obviously standard-issue supply. They're mass-produced according to a pattern, with a white star on top—coarse, cheap, and thoroughly ugly, but at the same time utterly conspicuous, glaring red, garish, and impossible to miss. They must put them up in their country, too. Which means that they, too, practice their own cult of graves, their own hero veneration, although their ideology officially rejects any resurrection of the flesh. If the plaques were there just to mark the grave for future reburial, a simple sign with the name or number would suffice. They could save themselves a lot of red paint and star cutting. But no, they envelop their dead soldiers in an aura of red and sacrifice both work and good wood to provide them with an aureole, however paltry it may be.

I pedal on as fast as I can and soon see the former manor house where my firm was last housed. I wonder about the family on the ground floor, if the little baby made it through the milkless time?

No children, no young mother—none of them are there. Finally, after much knocking and shouting, an elderly man appears, unshaven and wearing an undershirt. It takes me a while to recognize him as the authorized representative of our former publishing house, someone who was always immaculately groomed from cuff to collar—now in a dirty state of decline. He recognizes me but doesn't show the least bit of feeling. Grumpily he tells me how he and his wife snuck over here when their apartment was hit on the last day of the war. The place was deserted, all the furniture carried off, whether by Germans or Russians, he can't say— presumably both. Inside, the building is ransacked, wrecked, and reeks of human excrement and urine. Even so, there's still a mountain of coal in the basement. I scrounge around for an empty carton and pack it full of briquettes, much to the man's displeasure, but the coal is no more his than it is mine. The idea of helping me doesn't occur to him. With effort I haul the box over to the bike and tie it onto the luggage rack with my belt and a bit of string I find lying around.

Back home, on the double. I race up the street, this time past endless rows of soldiers hunched on the curb. Typical front-line men, tired, grimy, dusty, with stubbly chins and dirty faces. I've never seen Russians like this before. It dawns on me that we've been dealing with elite troops: artillery, signal corps, freshly washed and clean-shaven. The lowliest types we've seen are the supply-train men, who might have smelled of horses but weren't nearly as battleworn and war-weary as these soldiers, who are far too exhausted to pay attention to me or my bike. They barely glance up; it's clear they're at the end of a forced march.

Quickly, quickly, there's our corner. The old police barracks is swarming with automobiles that hum with a deep, satisfied drone—they smell of real gasoline. German cars never smelled like that.

Gasping for breath, I proudly carry the bike upstairs, along with my load of coal. This time it's the major who comes running down toward me. He's all agitated, imagining his bike stolen and me who knows where. Meanwhile the Uzbek has drifted in as well. Right away the widow sends him to the pump with two buckets to get water for us. He trots off good-naturedly: he's become like part of the family.

I'm sun-drunk and exhilarated from riding fast. I feel more cheerful than I have in weeks, practically elated. On top of that the major has brought some Tokay wine—5 puttonyos. We drink it; I feel good, cozy as a cat.

The major stayed till 5:00 P.M; after he left I felt rotten. I cried.

(Weeks later, scribbled in the margin, to be used by novelists: "For three heartbeats her body became one with the unfamiliar body on top of her. Her nails dug into the stranger's hair, she heard the cries coming from her own throat and the stranger's voice whispering words she couldn't understand. Fifteen minutes later she was all alone. The sunlight fell through the shattered panes in broad swaths. She stretched, enjoying the heaviness in her limbs, and brushed the tousled bangs back from her forehead. Suddenly she felt, with uncanny precision, a different hand burrowing into her hair, the hand of her lover, perhaps long dead. She felt something swelling, churning, erupting inside her. Tears came streaming out of her eyes. She tossed about, beat her fists against the cushions, bit her hands and arms until they bloomed red and blue with tiny tooth marks. She howled into the pillow and wanted to die.")

Tuesday, May 8, 1945, with the rest of Monday

Evening came and we were all alone—Herr Pauli, the widow, and I. The sun went down red—a repugnant image that reminded me of all the fires I'd seen over the past few years. The widow and I went to the little pond for some dirty washing water. (For drinking water a German still has to count on an hour's wait.)

It might have been eight o'clock—we're living without a clock because the one wrapped in a towel and hidden in the back of the chest keeps stopping. Things are quiet around the pond. The murky water is littered with bits of wood, old rags, and green park benches. We fill our buckets and trudge back, letting the cloudy liquid inside the third one slosh away as we carry it between us. Beside the rotting steps that lead up the grassy slope we see something, a shape on the ground—a person, a man, lying on his back in the grass, knees bent and pointing upward.

Is he sleeping? Yes, and very soundly, too: the man is dead. We both stand there gaping. His mouth is hanging open so wide you could stick your whole hand inside. His lips are blue, his nostrils waxen, caved in. He looks to be about fifty, clean-shaven, bald. Very proper appearance—a light gray suit with hand-knit gray socks and old-fashioned lace-up shoes that are polished and shiny. I touch his hands, which are splayed out on the lawn next to him;

his fingers are crooked into claws, facing up. They feel lukewarm, far from the cold of rigor mortis. But that doesn't mean anything since he's been lying in the sun. There's no pulse; the man is definitely dead. His body hasn't been looted, though: there's a silver pin in his tie. We wonder whether we should check his vest for papers in case there are relatives to notify. It's a creepy feeling, disturbing. We look around for people, but there's no one in sight. I bound a few steps down the street and see a couple standing in a doorway, a young woman and a young man, and ask them both to please come with me, there's a body lying over there. Reluctantly they follow me, pause beside the dead man a moment, don't touch a thing. Finally they leave without a word. We stand there a little longer, at a loss, and then we leave as well. Our hearts are heavy. Nevertheless my eyes automatically register every little piece of wood, and, just as mechanically, my hands stash them in the bag we've brought expressly for that purpose.

Just outside the door to our building we run into our old friend Curtainman Schmidt, together with our deserter. I'm astounded that these two have dared venture out onto the street. We tell them about the dead man, the widow imitating the position of his mouth. "Stroke," mumbles the ex-soldier. Should we all go have another look?

"I wouldn't," says Curtainman Schmidt. "Next thing there'll be something missing from his pockets and everyone'll claim it was us." And then he says something that makes even us immediately forget about the dead man: "The Russians have all left." While we were getting water from the pond they moved out of our building and out of the block and drove off in their trucks. Curtainman Schmidt describes how well upholstered the trucks were, with mattress parts and sofa cushions from the abandoned apartments.

They're gone! They're all gone! We can hardly believe it. Out of some involuntary reflex we look up the street, as if trucks had to be arriving any minute with new troops. But there is only silence—an eerie silence. No horses, no neighing, no roosters. Nothing left but horse manure, which the concierge's younger daughter is already sweeping out of the hall. I look at the sixteen-year-old girl, up to now the only person I know who lost her virginity to the Russians. She has the same dumb, self-satisfied look she always had. I try to imagine how it would have been if my first experience had come in this way. But I stop myself—it's unimaginable. One thing is for sure: if this were peacetime and a girl had been raped by some vagrant, there'd be the whole peacetime hoopla of reporting the crime, taking the statement, questioning witnesses, arrest and confrontation, news reports and neighborhood gossip—and the girl would have reacted differently, would have suffered a different kind of shock. But here we're dealing with a collective experience, something foreseen and feared many times in advance that happened to women right and left, all somehow part of the bargain. And this mass rape is something we are overcoming collectively as well. All the women help each other by speaking about it, airing their pain, and allowing others to air theirs and spit out what they've suffered. Which of course doesn't mean that creatures more delicate than this cheeky little Berlin girl won't fall apart or suffer for the rest of their lives.

For the first time since April 27 we were able to actually lock the door to our building. And with that, unless new troops are housed here, we begin a new life.

All the same at around 9:00 P.M. someone called up for me. It was the Uzbek repeating my name over and over in his labored voice (actually the Russified version of my name that the major bestowed on me). When I looked out, I saw him cursing and making threatening gestures at me and pointing at the locked door with great indignation. Well, my chubby friend, that won't help you one bit. But I let him in, the major close at his heels, limping badly. It's clear that the bicycling hasn't helped his condition. Once again the widow fixed some compresses. His knee looks hugely swollen and dangerously red. I can't imagine how anyone could bike, dance, or climb stairs with that. They're sturdy as horses. We can't keep up.

A bad night with the feverish major. His hands were hot, his eyes bleary; he couldn't sleep and kept me awake. Finally the new day dawned.

I escorted the major and his man downstairs and unlocked the door, which once again belongs to us. Afterward we had a revolting job: the Uzbek evidently has some kind of dysentery and sprayed the toilet, the wall, and the floor tiles. I wiped it up with issues of a Nazi professional journal for pharmacists and cleaned things as well as I could, using nearly all the water we brought from the pond yesterday evening. If only Herr Pauli knew, with his constant grooming, and his sissy manicures and pedicures!

On to Tuesday. Around 9:00 A.M. the secret knock, which we still use even though there are no longer any Russians in the house. It's Frau Wendt, with the eczema; she's heard a rumor that peace has been declared. The last, uncoordinated German defense has been broken in the south and north. We have surrendered.

The widow and I breathe more easily. Good thing it happened so quickly. Herr Pauli is still cursing about the Volkssturm, all those people senselessly sent to die at the last moment, old, tired men just left there to bleed to death, helpless, with not even a rag to dress their wounds. Fractured bones jabbing out of civilian trousers, snow-white bodies heaped on stretchers and bleeding in a steady drip, every trench and passageway blotted with slippery, lukewarm puddles of blood. No doubt about it: Pauli has been through a rough time. Which is why I think the neuralgia that's kept him chained to his bed for over a week is half-psychosomatic—it's a refuge, a retreat. He's not the only man in the building with that kind of refuge. There's the bookseller, for instance, with his Nazi party affiliation, and the deserter with his desertion, and any number of others with this or that Nazi past that makes them fear deportation or something else—they all have some excuse when it comes to fetching water or venturing out to perform some other task. And the women do their best to hide their men and protect them from the angry enemy. After all, what more can the Russians do to us? They've already done everything.

So we put on our harness and pull. That's logical enough. Nevertheless there's something about this that bothers me. I often find myself thinking about the fuss I used to make over the men on leave, how I pampered them, how much respect I showed them. And some of them had come from cities like Paris or Oslo, which were farther from the front than Berlin, where we were under constant bombardment. Or else they'd been in places where there was absolute peace, like Prague or Luxemburg, But even when they were coming from the front, until 1943 they always looked neat and well fed, unlike most of us today. And they loved to tell their stories, which always involved exploits that showed them in a good light. We, on the other hand, will have to keep politely mum; each one of us will have to act as if she in particular was spared. Otherwise no man is going to want to touch us anymore. If at least we had a little decent soap! I have this constant craving to give my skin a thorough scrub—I'm convinced that would make me feel a little cleaner in my soul as well.

A good conversation in the afternoon that I want to record as precisely as I can. I still have to mull it over. The hunchbacked chemist from the soft drink plant showed up again. I'd practically forgotten about him, although we often exchanged a few words down in the air-raid basement. Until recently he'd survived in a neighboring basement, but where he nevertheless heard all the latest news—particularly about women raped while getting water. One of the victims, a very shortsighted woman, lost her glasses in the struggle, so that she now staggers about completely helpless.

It turns out that the chemist is a "comrade," meaning he was a member of the Communist Party until 1933. He once even spent three weeks with an Intourist group traveling through the Soviet Union, and he understands a few words of Russian—none of which he admitted to me in the basement, any more than I told him about my own travels and language skills. The Third Reich cured us of that kind of hasty confidence. Still, I have to wonder: "So why didn't you stand up and identify yourself to the Russians as a sympathizer?"

He looks at me, embarrassed. "I would have," he claims. "I just wanted to let the first wild days pass." And then he adds, "In the next day or so I'll go down and report at the town hall. As soon as there are authorities in place I'll out myself at their disposal."

My own sense, which I didn't share with him, is that the reason he didn't come forward is because of his hunchback. With so much male fury seething all around, he would have felt doubly bitter about his deformity, which would have made him seem pitiful, half a man in the eyes of those strong barbarians. His head is set deep between his shoulders, he moves with difficulty. But his eyes are bright and intelligent, and he is very articulate.

"So have you lost a little of your enthusiasm?" I ask him. "Are you disappointed in your comrades?"

"Hardly," he says. "We shouldn't look at what's happened too personally, we shouldn't be too narrow in our perspective. It's a case of urges and instincts having been unleashed. A thirst for revenge, too. After all, we did a few things to them over in their country. Now it's time for change and introspection, for us as well as for them. Our old West is a world of yesterday. A new world is being born, the world of tomorrow, and it's a painful birth. The Slavic nations are stepping onto the stage of world history, they're young, full of unspent energy. The countries of Europe will blast open their borders and merge into larger regions. Just as Napoleon swept away all the little kingdoms and tiny fiefdoms, the victorious superpowers will do away with the nations and countries."

"So," I said, "you believe that Germany will become a part of the Soviet Union, a Soviet republic?"

"That would be nice."

"Then they'll take away our homeland and scatter us far and wide to destroy our sense of nationhood."

"It's quite possible that we Germans living today are really just a sacrifice, a kind of fertilizer, a means of transition. Maybe our best use is as skilled teachers. But no matter what the case I think it's up to each of us to make our lives as meaningful as we can even under these circumstances. No matter where we end up, we take ourselves."

"Even if it's to Siberia?"

"I have enough faith in myself that with a measure of good will I would be able to create a meaningful life even in Siberia."

He certainly would, too, judging from his past performance: a hunchback, he still managed to hold a good job, as the head chemist of a large soft drink and mineral water plant. But is he physically up to what the future might demand of us? Are the rest of us up to it? He shrugs.

At times I think I could survive anything on earth, as long as it came from without and not from some devious trick of my own heart. I feel so burned up, I can't imagine what could possibly move me today or excite me tomorrow. So if one has to go on living, it might just as well be in some icy wasteland. The chemist and I shook hands, both feeling recharged by the conversation.

At the moment, though, I'm completely surrounded by anxiously guarded bourgeois propriety. The widow once again feels herself mistress of her rooms. She wipes and scrubs and buffs, hands me a comb with a few missing teeth so I can comb out the fringes of the rugs. She's busy in the kitchen with sand and baking soda, moaning about her Meissen figurine that lost its nose and a hand in the various lootings of the basement, whining about not being able to remember where she hid the pearl tie pin that belonged to her late husband. Sometimes she sits deep in thought and suddenly blurts out, "Maybe I put it in my sewing box." Then she starts tossing out spools of thread and old buttons . . . and still doesn't find the pearl tie pin. Other than that, though, she's very capable and ingenious and unafraid of anything. She's much better at breaking up crates than I am, something she learned from watching the Pole from Lvov, whose uncontrollable temper made him particularly talented at it. (Incidentally, by now the whole house has learned the difference between "Ukrainian woman—like this" and "You—like this.")

Today the sun is out. Endless fetching of water. We washed our sheets, so my bed is freshly made—a much needed change after all those booted guests.

A press of people down at the baker's—through our shattered windows we can hear them making noise and chatting. Actually there's no real bread today, only numbers for tomorrow's bread, or for the day after. Everything depends on flour and coal, which the baker is waiting for. Still, using a few leftover briquettes he did manage to bake a few loaves, just for the building, and I was given a generous share. The baker hasn't forgotten that I stood up for his wife when the boys were going after her. His salesgirl, Erna, the one who survived intact in the little room blocked off by the chest, brought the loaves to our apartment. In fact, the whole building chipped in a little to get this bread made. A number of the men, led by Fräulein Behn, brought a small cartload of water buckets for the dough. And a few of the women "shoveled shit," as Frau Wendt so crudely put it. It seems the Russians used an upholstered bench in the shop as a latrine, pulling it a little ways out from the wall and perching on the back . . . So the bread is honestly earned.

The Russians have brought us an odd sort of money. The baker showed us a fifty-mark bill, a kind of military issue for Germany that we've never seen before. He got it from a Russian officer for a mere fourteen loaves of bread. The baker couldn't make change, but the Russian didn't seem to mind; evidently he had a briefcase stuffed with similar bills. The baker doesn't know what to do with the money. He would have given the Russian the bread anyway, but the man insisted on paying. Perhaps some semblance of good faith is coming back. I assume that we, too, will be given this money and that our own currency will be withdrawn and exchanged, probably for half the value.

Anyway, the prospect of bread is the first indication that the higher-ups are concerned for our welfare, doing something on our behalf. A second indication is hanging next to the front door of the building: a mimeographed notice signed by district mayor Dr. So-and-so ordering us to return all goods stolen from shops and offices—typewriters, office furniture, shop equipment, etc. After an initial period of amnesty, discovery of such stolen goods will be punishable under martial law. The notice further decrees that all weapons must be turned in. Apartment buildings where weapons are found will be punished collectively. And anyone residing in a building where a Russian comes to harm is subject to the death penalty. I can hardly imagine any of our men armed and lying in wait for Russians. At any rate, I haven't seen any men up to that these days. We Germans are not a nation of partisan fighters. We need leadership, orders, commands. Once I spent several days on a Soviet train, rocking across the countryside, and heard a Russian tell me: "Our German comrades won't storm a train station unless they've bought valid platform tickets first." Less sarcastically put, most Germans are horrified by unbridled lawlessness. Besides that, our men are now afraid. Reason tells them that they've been conquered, that any attempt to stir things up or make a fuss will only make things worse.

So the men in our building have begun eagerly tracking down weapons. They—all men, not a woman among them—comb one apartment after the next, They ask for weapons everywhere, but all they manage to dig up is one ancient firearm without a cock. This is the first time in ages I've heard German men speaking out loud or seen them moving with any vigor. They appear downright manly—or at least what we used to think of as manly. Now we have to come up with a new and better word, one that can serve in foul weather as well as fair.

Wednesday, May 9, 1945,
without the rest of Tuesday

Up to now I've always had to start with an update on the previous night. But this time there's nothing, absolutely nothing to say about last night except that I was able to spend it entirely by myself. Alone between my sheets for the first time since April 27. No major, no Uzbek. This state of affairs led to renewed existential worries on the part of the widow, who foresaw doom and destruction and no more butter. As far as she was concerned, the sooner the major showed up with new provisions, the better. I just laughed. He'll be back. I lay in my fresh bedding the whole night long—it felt so good to stretch out. I got a full night's sleep and woke up in fine spirits. Then I washed with warm water, courtesy of the widow, put on some clean clothes, and whistled a little to myself.

That's what I wrote at nine o'clock. Now it's eleven, and everything looks very different.

Some people equipped with heavy scoops called us down to the street, where we shoveled the pile of refuse on the corner, loading the rubble and horse manure onto a wheelbarrow. Then we carted it to a nearby rubble site: ancient plaster and scrap metal from the air raids had been covered with fresh debris from the recent artillery bombardment, which in turn was strewn with rags and cans and lots of empty bottles. I found two silver bromide postcards, made in Germany, with pictures of nudes embracing—all covered with thumbprints. I was reminded of the time I was in an office in Moscow and left some German and American newspapers lying about for a few minutes. When I picked them up and went back to reading I noticed some pages were torn—several ads for women's girdles and bras had been hastily ripped out. The Russians never see ads like that; their newspapers are utterly devoid of sex appeal. So in their eyes even a stupid ad that a man from the West would hardly give a second glance must seem like the most amazing pornography.

They're bound to be interested in that—all men are. But they can't get it at home. Maybe that's a mistake. If pictures like that were available, the men could fill their fantasies with all those idealized figures and wouldn't wind up throwing themselves on every woman in sight, no matter how old or ugly. I'll have to give this some more thought.

When I came back around 10:00 A.M. for a little ersatz coffee, I found the major in the apartment waiting for me, alone. He'd come to say good-bye. His knee isn't doing well, so he's been given two months' recuperation leave, which he's supposed to spend in a soldiers' home not far from Leningrad, where he's from. He's moving out this very day.

He's very serious, almost stern, keeping an iron grip on himself. Awkwardly he carefully spells out my address on a piece of paper; he wants to write, to stay in touch. I can't give him the photo he asks for because I don't have any. My entire photographed past—consisting of one album and a thick envelope—burned up during the bombing. And in the intervening weeks I haven't had a chance to get a new snapshot taken. The major looks at me for a long time, as if to photograph me with his eyes. Then he kisses me in the Russian style on both cheeks and marches out, limping, without looking back. I feel a little sad, a little empty. I think about his leather gloves, which I saw for the first time today. He was holding them elegantly in his left hand. They dropped on the floor once and he hurried to pick them up, but I could see they didn't match—one had seams on the back while the other didn't. The major was embarrassed and looked away. In that second I liked him very much.

Then it was back outside, since I had more shoveling to do. After that we were planning to look for wood. We need something for the stove; all the pea soup we've been eating uses up a lot of fuel. Which made me realize that no one will be bringing food, candles, and cigarettes anymore. I have to break the news to the widow gently, when she comes back from the pump. But I won't tell Pauli anything—let the widow take care of that.

My search for wood brings me to the patch of grass outside the cinema; it's the first time I've been there in two weeks. The place has become our block's local burial ground. There are three double graves among the rubble and the bomb craters—three married couples, all suicides. An old lady who is sitting on a stone and

chewing away at something tells me the details, with bitter satisfaction, all the while nodding her head. The grave on the right is
for a high-ranking Nazi political leader and his wife (revolver).
The middle grave, which is strewn with a few wilted lilacs, contains a lieutenant colonel and his wife (poison). The old lady
doesn't know anything about the third grave, but someone has
stuck a stake in the sand with an inscription penned in red: "2
Müllers." One of the single graves belongs to the woman who
jumped out the window when the Ivans were after her. It has a
kind of crooked cross fashioned out of two pieces from a door
panel—shiny white paint—and fastened together with wire. My
throat tenses up. Why does the sight of a cross affect us the way it
does, even if we can no longer call ourselves Christians? Memories of early childhood resurface: I see and hear Fräulein Dreyer,
tears in her eyes, describing our savior's Passion in infinite detail to
us seven-year-olds. For those of us in the West who were raised in
the Christian tradition, every cross has a God appended to it, even
if it's nothing but two splintered bits of door panel and a piece of
wire.

Everywhere there's filth and horse droppings and children
playing—if that's what it can be called. They loiter about, stare at
us, whisper to one another. The only loud voices you hear belong
to Russians. We see one coming our way, with some curtains
draped over his arm. He calls out to us, some obscenity. Now you
only see them occasionally or else in troops marching off. Their
songs strike our ears as raw, defiant.

I gave the baker seventy pfennig for the two loaves. A strange
feeling, as if I were handing him something completely worthless.
I just can't believe that our German money still has any value.
Erna the salesgirl was collecting all the ration books for the households still in the building, drawing up a list of names and the number of people in each apartment. Evidently new ration cards are

in the offing. She came by wearing a flowery summer dress, all done up—a rare sight. For the past two weeks none of the women dared go outside unless they were dressed like lowlifes. I'm in the mood for some new clothes myself. It's hard to grasp the fact there aren't any Russians knocking at our door, no one stretching out on our chairs and sofas. When I gave the room a thorough cleaning, I found a small Soviet star made of red glass and a condom in paper wrapping. I have no idea who might have left that. I didn't know they even knew there were such things. In any case, where German women were concerned they didn't feel it was worth the trouble.

They took away the gramophone, along with the record featuring an old ad jingle (". . . For the lady, for the child, everyone can find his style"). But they did leave a total of forty-three classical records, from Bach to Pfitzner, including half of *Lohengrin*. And the cover that Anatol had broken, which we gratefully toss into the stove.

It's already evening. I'm sitting on the window seat, writing. Outside it's summer, the maple is dark green, the street has been swept clean and is empty. I'm making use of the last bit of daylight, since we have to save on candles. No one's going to bring us any new ones.

So now it's over—no more liquor, sugar, butter, meat. If only we could get to our potatoes! But as of yet no one dares dismantle the basement barricade. We're not sure they won't be coming back or sending new troops in. The widow preaches one sermon after the other, although not about the lilies in the field, which would be the only apt example for us. She's spinning more gloom and doom, sees us all starving to death. When I ask for a second helping of pea soup she exchanges glances with Herr Pauli.

Antiaircraft fire is rattling my writing. People say they're practicing for a victory parade; the Americans are supposed to be

there as well. It's entirely possible. Let them get on with their celebrations; they don't concern us. We've surrendered. Nevertheless,
I do feel a new desire for life.

Moving along—now I'm writing at night, by candlelight, with
a compress on my forehead. Around eight o'clock someone
pounded on our front door, crying, "Fire! Fire!" We ran outside,
where everything was lit up and glaring bright. Flames were
shooting out of the ruined basement two houses down the street,
licking at the firewall of the neighboring house, which was still intact. Acrid smoke came streaming out of a hole in the ruins and
creeping up the street. The block was swarming with shadows,
civilians. Shouts and cries.

What to do? There's no water. The superheated air was blast-
ing out of the basement like a searing wind, exactly as during the
nighttime air raids, which is why no one got very excited.
"Smother it," people said. "Let's cover it with rubble." In no time
we'd formed two chains. People passed chunks of stone from hand
to hand, and the last person tossed them into the flames. Someone
called out to hurry, it was already nine, and all civilians had to be
off the streets by ten.

A few figures rolled a barrel of liquid over from somewhere; we
used buckets to scoop out the smelly stuff. In passing me a bucket,
one woman accidentally hit my temple with the metal rim. My
head spinning, I staggered over to a mound of stone on the grass
across from me, the circular patch with all the graves, and sat
down. A woman sat down next to me and told me in a monotone
that "the people under here" were an officer and his wife who
took cyanide. I knew that already, but I let her talk. "No coffin,
nothing," she said. "They were simply wrapped in blackout paper
tied up with string. They didn't even have sheets on their beds.
They'd just been relocated here when their own place was
bombed." But they must have had the poison ready.

I felt dizzy. I could literally feel the bruise swelling on my forehead. The fire was soon contained and smothered. I joined a group of people and at first couldn't understand why they were cursing the owner of the delicatessen in the ruined building. Then I learned the man had left some of his wine stores in the basement, which was partially intact. The Russians discovered the alcohol, or perhaps I should say they sniffed it out, and cleared off the shelves, candles in hand. By accident a spark must have landed in some of the straw used for wrapping the bottles, and that eventually led to the fire. According to one witness: "The boys were lying dead drunk in the gutter. With my own eyes I saw one of them who was still able to stand in his boots go down the row pulling watches off his comrades' arms." General laughter.

Now I'm lying in bed writing, cooling my bruise. For tomorrow we're planning a trip all the way across Berlin to the Schöneberg district.

Thursday, May 10, 1945

The morning went by with housework, breaking wood, fetching water. The widow soaked her feet in water with baking soda after trying out various hairstyles to find the one that shows as little gray as possible. Finally at 3:00 P.M. we were ready to set off on our first tour of the conquered city.

Poor words, you do not suffice.

We clambered past the cemetery in the Hasenheide park— long, uniform rows of graves in the yellow sand from the last big air raid in March. The summer sun was scorching. The park itself was desolate. Our own troops had felled all the trees to have a clear field for shooting. The ground was scored with trenches strewn with rags, bottles, cans, wires, ammunition. Two Russians were sitting beside a girl on a bench. It's rare to see one on his own; they probably feel safer in twos. We went on, through what were once heavily populated working-class streets. Now they seem so mute, the houses so locked up and shut off from the world you would think the ten thousand people who lived there had emigrated or were dead. No sound of man or beast, no car, radio, or tram. Nothing but an oppressive silence broken only by our footsteps. If there are people inside the buildings watching us, they are doing so in secret. We don't see any faces at the windows.

Onward to the edge of the Schöneberg district. We'll soon find out whether we can continue, whether any of the bridges leading west over the S-Bahn survived intact. Some of the buildings have red flags, the first we've seen. Actually they're more like flaglets, evidently cut from old Nazi flags—here and there you can still make out the line of a circle, where the white field containing the black swastika used to be. The little flags are neatly hemmed, undoubtedly by women's hands. How in our country could it be otherwise?

All along the way we see debris left by the troops: gutted cars, burned-out tanks, battered gun carriages. Occasional posters in Russian celebrating May Day, Stalin, the victory. Here, too, there are scarcely any people. Now and then some pitiful creature darts by—a man in shirt sleeves, a woman with disheveled hair. No one pays us much attention. A woman passes us, barefoot and bedraggled. She answers our question—"Yes, the bridge is still there"—and hurries away. Barefoot? In Berlin? I've never seen a woman in that condition before. The bridge is still blocked by a barricade of rubble; my heart is pounding as we slip through a gap.

Glaring sun. The bridge is deserted. We pause to look down at the railroad embankment, a jumble of tracks, straw-colored in the sunlight, pockmarked with craters a yard deep. Pieces of rail wrenched high above the ground, upholstery and scraps of fabric streaming out of bombed sleepers and dining cars. The heat is stifling. The smell of fire hangs over the tracks. All around is desolation, a wasteland, not a breath of life. This is the carcass of Berlin.

On into Schöneberg. Here and there we see people in the doorways—a woman, a girl, their blank eyes staring into space, their features vapid and bloated. I can tell by looking that the war has only recently ended here. They still haven't recovered from the shock; they're as numb as we were several days back.

We head down Potsdamer Strasse, past blackened offices, empty tenements, heaps of rubble.

A moving sight on one corner: two rickety old women standing in front of a pile of rubble so huge it towers above them. They scratch at the refuse with a coal shovel, load it onto a little cart. At that rate it will take them weeks to move the entire mountain. Their hands are knobby and gnarled; but perhaps they'll finish the job.

Kleist Park is a wasteland, with masses of rags, mattresses, and cushions torn from cars lying under the arcades, and piles of feces everywhere, swarming with flies. Right in the middle stands the half-finished high-rise bunker, like a hedgehog surrounded by iron spikes, that was intended to shelter us from bombs in the seventh year of the war. Two civilians are yanking away at a stack of beams, one of them sawing the timbers into more manageable pieces. Everything belongs to everyone. The saw cuts through the silence with its pitiful rasp. Reflexively, the widow and I drop our voices to a whisper. Our throats are parched—the dead city has taken our breath away. The air in the park is full of dust, all the trees are covered in white powder, riddled with bullet holes, badly wounded. A German shadow hurries past with a load of bedding. At the other end of the park we find a Russian grave surrounded by wire. Another set of gaudy red wooden steles and in the middle a flat granite slab bearing an inscription in lime paint: Here rest heroes who fell for the fatherland. The Russian word for hero is *geroi*. It sounds so Prussian.

Twenty minutes later we are in front of the house where the widow's friends live. "He was in the same brotherhood as my husband," she says of the man, a lecturer in classic philology. The building looks completely dead, the front door boarded up with lath. As we search for the back entrance we run into a woman who has lifted her skirt and is taking care of her needs in the corner of the courtyard, completely unembarrassed. I've never seen that in Berlin before either, not so publicly. Finally we find the entrance, climb the two flights of stairs, knock, and shout the widow's name as a password. Noises inside, steps and whispers, until they finally realize who it is. The door flies open, we embrace, I press my face against that of a stranger—after all, I've never seen these people before. First the wife, then her husband emerges, holding his hands out to us, asking us inside. The widow talks as if in a fever, her words a jumble, the other woman is talking as well and neither is listening. It takes a while before we're seated in the apartment's one inhabitable but very drafty room. We fish out the butter sandwiches we've brought along and offer them to the widow's friends. They're both amazed. They haven't seen any bread, and the Russians didn't leave any behind. In answer to the standard question "How often did they . . . ?" the lady of the house answers, with a broad East Prussian accent, "Me? Only once, the first day. After that we locked ourselves down in the basement. We had a wash-boiler full of water." The conquerors reached this neighborhood later and left earlier. Everything happened in a flash.

What are they living off? "We still have a sack of groats and a few potatoes. Oh, and our horse too!"

Horse? They laugh, and the woman explains with graphic gestures. While the German soldiers still controlled the street, someone came running into the basement with the good news that a horse had been killed, and in no time people were outside. The animal was still twitching and rolling its eyes as the first bread knives and pocket knives plunged into its body—all under fire, of course. Everyone sliced and dug at the first spot they found. When the philologist's wife reached over toward some shimmering layers of yellow fat, someone rapped a knife handle across her fingers and said, "You! Stick to your own place!" She managed to hack out a six-pound piece of meat. "We used what we had left to celebrate my birthday," she told us. "It tasted excellent. I pickled it in the last of my vinegar."

We wished her many happy returns. A bottle of Bordeaux appeared. We drank, raising our glasses to the wife. The widow talked about how she compares with a Ukrainian woman—we have lost all sense of moderation.

We said good-bye over and over. The philologist rummaged about the room, searching for something to give us in exchange for the bread but didn't find anything.

Then we moved on to the next district, the Bayerisches Viertel, to look in on my friend Gisela. The streets were blocked with row after row of German automobiles, practically every one of them gutted. One barber had reopened his shop; a piece of paper advertised that he cut men's hair and washed women's if they brought their own warm water. We actually saw a customer in the half dark, and a man jumping around with a pair of scissors. The first sign of life in the city carcass.

Up the stairs to Gisela's. I knocked and called out, shaking with excitement. Once again we pressed our cheeks together, though the most we ever used to do was give each other's hand a firm squeeze.

Gisela was not alone. She's taken in two young girls, students sent by an acquaintance, refugees from Breslau. They sat mutely in a nearly empty room that had no windowpanes but was nevertheless clean.

After the first eager exchanges a lull settled in the conversation. I could sense suffering in the air. Both young girls had black circles under their eyes. What they said sounded so hopeless, so bitter. At one point Gisela led me out to the balcony and whispered that both of them had been deflowered by the Russians; they'd had to withstand repeated rapes. Hertha, a blonde of twenty, has been having pains ever since and doesn't know what to do. She cries a great deal, according to Gisela. There's no word of her family; from Silesia they were scattered to the winds—who knows if they're still alive. She clings to Gisela hysterically. The other one, delicate Brigitte, is nineteen and defends herself psychologically with an angry cynicism. She's brimming with gall and hate: life is filthy and all men are swine. She wants to go away, far away, someplace where she won't see that uniform, the mere sight of which makes her heart lose a beat.

Gisela herself came through unscathed, using a trick I learned about too late, unfortunately. Before she became an editor, she had had ambitions to be an actress and had taken courses in which she learned a little about stage makeup. In the basement she painted a wonderful old-lady's mask on her face and tucked her hair under a kerchief. When the Russians came in and spotted the two young students with their flashlights, they pushed Gisela, charcoal wrinkles and all, back onto her bedding: "You, babushka, sleep." I couldn't help laughing, but I immediately had to rein in my merriment—the two girls looked too glum, too bitter.

These girls have been forever deprived of love's first fruits. Whoever begins with the last phase, and in such a wicked way, can no longer quiver with excitement at the very first touch. There's one boy I'm thinking of, Paul was his name. He was seventeen, just like me, when he pushed me into the shadows of an unfamiliar entranceway on Ulmenstrasse. We had been to a school concert—Schubert, I think—and were still warmed by the music, though we had no idea what to say about it. Both of us were inexperienced, teeth pressed against teeth, and I waited faithfully for the wonder you're supposed to feel when you kiss—until I realized that my hair had come undone. The barrette I used to keep it up was gone.

In a panic I shook out my dress and collar. Paul felt around in the dark on the pavement. I helped him, and our hands met and touched, but no longer with any warmth. We didn't find the barrette. I had probably lost it on the way. That was very annoying as my mother would notice right away, ask me what had happened, give me stern looks. And surely my face would betray what Paul and I had done in the entranceway. We parted in a hurry, suddenly at a loss, and never drew close to each other again. Even so, those shy minutes in the shadows have always kept their silver sheen.

We stayed at Gisela's an hour and spent a long time saying good-bye. These days it's so hard to separate from your friends; you never know whether and how you'll see one another again. So much can happen. Nonetheless I invited Gisela to visit us the next day. The widow had invited her friends as well. We want to see that they get a crust of bread.

Back home, the same desolate, long, dusty way. It turned out that the trip really was too much for the widow. Her feet were aching, and we had to make frequent stops to rest on the curb. I trudged along as if under a heavy load, the burdensome feeling that Berlin might never rise again, that we would remain rats in the rubble for the rest of our lives. For the first time I entertained the thought of leaving this city, of looking for bread and shelter elsewhere, someplace where there's air and open countryside.

In the park we rested on a bench. A young woman sitting next to us was taking a walk with two small boys. A Russian came by and waved his inevitable companion over, saying to him in Russian, "Come here, there are some children. They're the only ones you can talk to in this place." The mother glanced at us, anxious, and shrugged her shoulders. Sure enough, a conversation developed between the men and the two little boys, whom the soldiers took on their knees and bounced to a Russian knee-bouncing song.

Then one of the soldiers turned to me and said in the friendliest tone in the world, in Russian, "It's all the same who sleeps with you. A cock's a cock." (I'd learned that expression in all its country-boy crudeness from Anatol.) I had to strain to keep up my act of not understanding what he was saying—since that's what he was counting on. So I just smiled, which made the two men roar with laughter. As you please!

Home with tired feet. Herr Pauli had posted himself in an armchair next to the window and was keeping an eye out for us. He refused to believe that in three hours of trekking about we'd run into only a few wandering Russians. He had imagined the center of town would be abuzz with troops. After the fact we were surprised ourselves and wondered where all the victors might have gone. We gulped down the clean air of our corner, still shuddering at the thought of the dusty wasteland in Schöneberg.

I'm having a hard time falling asleep. Grim thoughts. A sad day.

Housework. We soaked our laundry, peeled the last potatoes from our kitchen stores. Fräulein Behn brought us our new ration cards, printed, in German and Russian, on newsprint. There's one type for adults and one for children under fourteen.

I have my card right here and am making a note of the daily ration: 200 grams of bread, 400 grams of potatoes, 10 grams of sugar, 10 grams of salt, 2 grams of ersatz coffee, 25 grams of meat. No fats. If they really give us all that it will be quite something. I'm amazed even this much order has been brought out of the chaos.

When I saw a line down in front of the greengrocer's I took my place and used our coupons to get some beets and dried potatoes. You hear the same talk in line as at the pump: everyone is now turning their backs on Adolf, no one was ever a supporter. Everyone was persecuted, and no one denounced anyone else.

What about me? Was I for . . . or against? What's clear is that I was there, that I breathed what was in the air, and it affected all of us, even if we didn't want it to. Paris proved that to me, or rather a young student I met in the Jardin du Luxembourg three years after Hitler came to power. We had taken shelter from a sudden shower under a tree. We spoke French and recognized right away that it was a foreign language for both of us. Then we had fun bantering back and forth and guessing where the other was from. My hair led him to place me as a Swede, while I pegged him as a Monegasque—I'd just learned what citizens of Monaco are called and found the name amusing.

The rain stopped as abruptly as it had begun. We started off, and I performed a little syncopation, so I would be walking in step with him. He stopped and proclaimed, *"Ah ha, une fille du Führer!"*—a daughter of Hitler, in other words, a German, unmasked the minute she tried to march in perfect step with her neighbor.

So much for fun and banter. For then the young man introduced himself not as a Monegasque but as a Dutchman and a Jew. And that was the end of our conversation. We went our separate ways at the next fork in the path. The experience left a bitter taste. I brooded over it for a long time.

I realized it had been ages since I heard about Herr and Frau Golz, my neighbors from my earlier building that burned down, who used to be faithful party followers. I went the few buildings' distance to find out. It took forever before their neighbors finally cracked open the door, keeping it on the chain, and told me that Herr and Frau Golz had snuck away unnoticed and how that was a good thing, since some Russians had been by looking for him. Evidently he'd been denounced.

Late in the afternoon someone knocked on our door, calling for me. I was amazed to see one of the figures, now practically forgotten, from our basement past: Siegismund, believer in victory, who'd heard from somewhere that I had connections to "higher Russians." He wanted to know if it was true that all former party members had to report voluntarily for labor or else risk being lined up against a wall and shot. There are so many rumors flying about, it's impossible to keep up with all of them. I told him that I didn't know anything and didn't think anything like that was planned, that he should wait and see. It was almost impossible to recognize the man. His pants were billowing loosely around his emaciated body, his whole person looked miserable and crumpled. The widow gave him a sermon about the dangers of fellow traveling, how he surely sees for himself what that can lead to. Siegismund—I still don't know his real name—swallowed it all meekly, then asked for a piece of bread. And he was given one, too, which caused a family row as soon as he left. Herr Pauli fumed and shouted that it was outrageous for the widow to give that man something—after all, he was responsible for the whole mess, and the worse off he was now, the better, they ought to lock him up and take away his ration cards. (Pauli himself was always against. He has a contrary character—dissenting, negating—a Mephistophelian "spirit that always denies." From what I've seen there's nothing on earth he's in complete and unreserved agreement with.) At any rate, no one wants to hear another word about Siegismund, and the man doesn't dare show himself in the house. Everyone would give him a tongue lashing; no one wants to have anything to do with him, especially not those in the same boat. He must find it all bleak as well as baffling. I also gave him a piece of my mind, which bothers me right now. Does that mean that I, too, am following the mob? "Hosanna! Crucify him!"—the eternal refrain.

Half an hour ago, in the evening twilight, sudden shots. Far off, a woman's scream. We didn't even look out the window. What for? But reminders like that aren't a bad thing—they keep us alert.

Saturday, May 12, 1945

This morning the entire community of tenants—as we are again officially called—gathered in the back garden, which I had at one point pictured as a cemetery. We were there to dig, all right, but only a pit for the building's garbage, which was towering over the bins. People were eager to work and had funny things to say. Everyone felt relieved, happy to be able to do something useful. It's so strange that no one has to go "to work" anymore, that we're all on a kind of leave, that the married couples are with each other from dawn to dusk.

After that I mopped the living room, scrubbed away all the Russian spittle and boot polish, and swept the last crumbs of horse manure off the floor. That left me good and hungry. We still have peas and flour. The widow has rendered what she could from the rancid leftovers of Herr Pauli's Volkssturm butter and uses it as fat.

The apartment was sparkling when our guests arrived from Schöneberg. They'd come together, even though Gisela had never met the widow's friends. All three were cleaned up and neatly dressed, their hair nicely done. They took the same route we did and saw the same thing—that is, hardly anyone except the occasional Russian, only silence and desolation. We showed them lavish hospitality: thin coffee and bread with a little fat for all of them!

I took Gisela into the living room for a chat. I wanted to know what she was thinking of doing. Her predictions were dire. She sees her world, the Western world, steeped in art and culture, as disappearing—and it's the only world she finds worthy. She feels she's too tired to start all over. She doesn't think that a discriminating individual will have any room to breathe, let alone do any kind of intellectual work. No, she's not thinking of taking Veronal or some other poison. She intends to stick it out, even if she has little courage and less joy. She spoke of trying to find "the divine" within her soul, of wanting to be reconciled with her innermost self, and of finding salvation there. She's undernourished, has dark shadows under her eyes, and will have to go on being hungry, along with the two girls she's taken in, whom I think she's feeding out of her own portion. Her small store of peas and beans and oats was stolen from her basement—by Germans, before the Russians invaded. *Homo homini lupus.* As she left I gave her two cigars that I quietly lifted from the major's box, which Herr Pauli has already half consumed. After all, I'm the one responsible for that gift, not Pauli; I deserve my share. Gisela can trade them for something to eat.

In the evening I went to get water. Our pump is a fine piece of work. The shaft is broken and the lever, which has come undone many times, has been lashed on cumbersomely with yards of wire and string. Three people have to hold the structure up while two pump. This collective effort is now taken for granted; no one says a thing. Afterward both my buckets are full of floating splinters and shavings from the pump. We have to strain the water. I'm once again amazed at the fact that "they" went to such effort to build barricades that proved useless but didn't give the slightest thought to ensuring we had a few decent water stations for the siege. After all, "they," too, put cities to siege, so they had to have known. Probably anyone in a position of power who'd talked about pump construction would have been dismissed as a defeatist and a scoundrel.

A quiet evening. For the first time in three weeks I opened a book—Joseph Conrad's *The Shadow Line.* But I had a hard time getting into it. I'm too full of my own images.

Sunday, May 13, 1945

A glorious summer day. Noises first thing in the morning—an optimistic clamor of beating rugs, scrubbing, hammering. Still, there's apprehension in the air, a looming fear that we'll have to hand our apartments over to the military. The rumor at the pump was that troops will be billeted on our block. Nothing in this country belongs to us anymore, nothing but the moment at hand. And all three of us chose to enjoy that by sitting down to a richly spread breakfast table, Herr Pauli still in his robe but already halfway healthy again.

Bells are ringing all over Berlin to celebrate the Allied triumph. Somewhere right now the famous parade is under way, a parade that doesn't concern us at all. They say that the Russians have a holiday, that the troops have been given vodka to celebrate the victory. The word at the pump is that women should do what they can not to leave home. We don't know whether to believe it or not. The widow shakes her head uneasily. Herr Pauli is again rubbing the small of his back, says he should lie down. I'll wait and see.

As it is, the subject of alcohol has been much on our minds. Herr Pauli heard about an order issued to retreating German soldiers to leave all liquor stores intact for the advancing enemy— experience shows that alcohol impairs the enemy's strength to fight and slows their advance. Now that's something only men could cook up for other men. If they just thought about it for two minutes they'd realize that liquor greatly intensifies the sexual urge. I'm convinced that if the Russians hadn't found so much alcohol all over, half as many rapes would have taken place. These men aren't natural Casanovas. They had to goad themselves on to such brazen acts, had to drown their inhibitions. And they knew it, too, or at least suspected as much, otherwise they wouldn't have been so desperate for alcohol. Next time there's a war fought in the presence of women and children (for whose protection men supposedly used to do their fighting out on the battlefield, away from home), every last drop of drink should be poured into the gutter, wine stores destroyed, beer cellars blown up. Or else let the defenders have their final spree, as far as I'm concerned. Just make sure there's no alcohol left as long as there are women within grabbing distance of the enemy.

Onward—it's now evening. The much-feared Sunday is over. Nothing happened: it was the most peaceful Sunday since September 3, 1939. I lay on the sofa; outside was full of sun and twittering birds. I nibbled on some cake the widow baked using a sinful amount of wood, and took an accounting of my life. Here's the balance.

On the one hand, things are looking pretty good for me. I'm healthy and refreshed. Nothing has harmed me physically. I feel extremely well armed for life, as if I had webbed feet for the mud, as if my fiber were especially supple and strong. I'm well equipped for the world, I'm not delicate—my grandmother used to haul manure. On the other hand, there are multiple minuses. I don't know what in the world I should do. No one really needs me; I'm simply floating around, waiting, with neither goal nor task in sight. I can't help thinking of a debate I once had with a very smart Swiss woman, in which I countered every scheme she put forward for improving the world by insisting that "the sum total of tears always stays the same"—i.e., that in every nation, no matter what flag or system of government, no matter which gods are worshiped or what the average income is, the sum total of tears, pain, and fear that every person must pay for his existence is a constant. And so the balance is maintained: well-fed nations wallow in neurosis and excesses, while people plagued with suffering, as we are now, may rely on numbness and apathy to help see them through—if not for that I'd be weeping morning, noon, and night. But I'm not crying and neither is anyone else, and the fact that we aren't is all part of a natural law. Of course if you believe that the earthly sum of tears is fixed and immutable, then you're not very well cut out to improve the world or to act on any kind of grand scale.

To summarize: I've been in twelve European countries; I've seen Moscow, Paris, and London, among other cities, and experienced Bolshevism, Parliamentarianism, and Fascism close up, as an ordinary person among ordinary people. Are there differences? Yes, substantial ones. But from what I can tell the distinctions are mostly ones of form and coloration, of the rules of play, not differences in the greater or lesser fortunes of common people, which Candide was so concerned about. And the individuals I encountered who were meek, subservient, and uninterested in any existence other than the one they were born to didn't seem any unhappier in Moscow than they did in Paris or Berlin—all of them lived by adjusting their souls to the prevailing conditions.

No, my current gauge is an utterly subjective one: personal taste. I simply wouldn't want to live in Moscow. What oppressed me most there was the relentless ideological schooling, the fact that people were not allowed to travel freely, and the absolute lack of any erotic aura. The way of life just wouldn't suit me. On the other hand, I'd be happy in Paris or London, although there I've always had the painfully clear feeling of not belonging, of being a foreigner, someone who is merely tolerated. It was my own choice to return to Germany, even though friends advised me to emigrate. And it was good I came home, because I could never have put down roots elsewhere. I feel that I belong to my people, that I want to share their fate, even now.

But how? When I was young the red flag seemed like such a bright beacon, but there's no way back to that now, not for me: the sum of tears is constant in Moscow, too. And I long ago lost my childhood piety, so that God and the Beyond have become mere symbols and abstractions. Should I believe in progress? Yes, to bigger and better bombs. The happiness of the greater number? Yes, for Petka and his ilk. An idyll in a quiet corner? Sure, for people who comb the fringes of their rugs. Possessions, contentment?

I have to keep from laughing, homeless urban nomad that I am. Love? Lies trampled on the ground. And were it ever to rise again, I would always be anxious, could never find true refuge, would never again dare hope for permanence.

Perhaps art, toiling away in the service of form? Yes, for those who have the calling, but I don't. I'm just an ordinary laborer, I have to be satisfied with that. All I can do is touch my small circle and be a good friend. What's left is just to wait for the end. Still, the dark and amazing adventure of life is beckoning. I'll stick around, out of curiosity and because I enjoy breathing and stretching my healthy limbs.

Monday, May 14, 1945

Last night the noise of motors tore me from my sleep. Hearing shouts and honking, I stumbled to the window and, lo and behold, there was a Russian truck full of flour. The baker already has coal, so now he'll be able to bake, to accommodate the ration cards and numbers. I heard him shout for joy and saw him hugging the Russian driver, who was also beaming. The Russians enjoy playing Santa Claus.

Then this morning at dawn I was wakened by the sound of chattering people queuing for bread. The line wound halfway around the block and it's still there now, in the afternoon. Many women have brought stools along. I can literally hear the hiss of gossip.

For the first time we have water from a proper hydrant, not far away at all. It's a mechanical wonder, an automatic pump with three spigots that deliver the water in a thick stream. Your bucket is filled in a flash. And you don't need to wait more than a few minutes. That really changes our day, making our lives easier.

On the way to the hydrant I passed a number of graves. Practically every front garden has these silent billets. Some are marked with German steel helmets, some with the gaudy red Russian stakes and white Soviet stars. They must have hauled along whole trainloads of these memorials.

Wooden plaques have been set up on the curbs, with inscriptions in German and Russian. One of them quotes Stalin to the effect that the Hitlers disappear but Germany remains. *Losungi*—that's the Russian word for such slogans, from the German *Losung*.

A bulletin has been posted next to the door of our building: "News for Germans." The last word sounds so strange in this context, almost like an insult. You can read the text of our unconditional surrender, signed by Keitel, Stumpff, Friedeburg, along with reports of arms being surrendered on all fronts. Göring has been captured. One woman claims she heard on a crystal set that he cried like a child at his arrest and had already been sentenced to death by Hitler. A colossus with feet of clay.

But there's another sheet posted up, which attracts far more attention and sparks more debate. Evidently the Russians are introducing new rationing regulations with larger allotments, but allocated according to group—heavy laborers, blue-collar workers, white-collar workers, children, and others. Bread, potatoes, concentrated foodstuffs, ersatz coffee, real coffee, sugar, salt, even fat. Not so bad, if it's true. In some cases the rations are more generous than we had lately under Adolf. This information is making a profound impact. I hear people say things like, "There's another example of how our propaganda made fools of us all."

It's true, too: the constant forecasts of death by starvation, of complete physical annihilation by the enemy, were so pervasive that we're stunned by every piece of bread, every indication that we will still be provided for. In that respect Goebbels did a great advance job for the conquerors: any crust of bread from their hands seems like a present to us.

This afternoon I stood in line for meat. There's nothing more instructive than spending an hour like that. I learned that trains are back up and running to Stettin, Küstrin, and Frankfurt an der Oder. On the other hand, our local public transportation is apparently still shut down.

One woman enjoyed telling the story of why the Russians chose to leave her building alone: on their first brief visit they found one family poisoned in their beds on the second floor and another, one floor up, all hanging from the transom of the kitchen window. The Russians took off, terrified, and never came back, and the residents decided to keep everything the way it was, as a kind of scarecrow, just in case . . . Anyway, I was able to get my meat without a hitch. All beef, no bones—that will help us out.

"Tenants' meeting in the basement, 4:30 P.M."—the word went from door to door: at last the basement barricade is being dismantled. A good thing, too: we'll be able to get to the rest of the widow's potatoes. We formed a chain along the hallway. A small candle stuck onto a chair gave a faint glow as bricks, boards, chairs, and mattress parts passed from one hand to the next.

The basement was topsy-turvy, a complete mess. The smell of excrement. Each person packed up his things. Unclaimed goods were supposed to be placed in the lightwell. (Despite this, the widow let some silk underwear that didn't belong to her quietly vanish into her sack. Later she remembered the Ten Commandments and put the piece of clothing, which had an embroidered monogram indicating the rightful owner, back where it belonged, claiming she had taken it "by mistake.") But all notions of ownership have been completely demolished. Everyone steals from everyone else because everyone has been stolen from and because we can make use of anything. So the only unclaimed goods were ones not worth the taking: threadbare slips, hats, a single shoe. While the widow kept poking around bitterly for the pearl tie pin—she'd forgotten where she hid it—I lugged the potatoes upstairs and dumped them next to Herr Pauli's bed. The widow followed me up and immediately started in like Cassandra with warnings of how we'd starve to death as soon as we finished the last of them. Herr Pauli vigorously seconded everything she said. This makes me think that the household is beginning to view me as a burden, one more mouth to feed, that they're counting each morsel I consume and begrudging me every single potato. Meanwhile Pauli is still happy to dip into my major's sugar. Nevertheless I want to try to get back on my own feet, as far as food is concerned—only how?

I can't bring myself to be angry with the two of them. Not that I've had to, but it could well be that in their situation I wouldn't be too happy to share my food either. And there's no new major on the horizon.

Tuesday, May 15, 1945

The usual tedious housework. Two roofers are stomping around in the attic apartment, which I entered for the first time since the Russians invaded. They're getting paid in bread and cigarettes. I can tell that the Russians never made it up here because the floors are covered with a fine layer of plaster dust that shows every footprint, and it was untouched when I let in the roofers. Presumably

I could have held out up here, if I'd had enough water and food—
an undiscovered Sleeping Beauty. But I'm sure I would have gone
crazy, all alone like that.

Once again we all have to report to the Rathaus. Today was
the day for people with my last initial. The street was unusually
crowded at registration time. A man in the town hall lobby was
chiseling away the relief of Adolf. I watched the nose come splin-
tering off. What is stone, what are monuments? An iconoclastic
wave such as we have never seen is currently surging through Germany. A new twilight of the gods—is it remotely possible that the
big Nazis could ever rise again after this? As soon as I've freed my
mind a little I really have to turn my attention to Napoleon; after
all, he, too, was banished in his day, only to be brought back and
glorified once more.

We had to go up to the fourth floor and wait in line. The corridor was pitch dark, packed with women you could hear but not
see. A conversation in front of me had to do with planting asparagus, a task several women had been assigned to do. That wouldn't
be so bad. Judging from their speech the two women behind me
were well-bred ladies. One said: "You know, I was completely
numb. I'm very small there, my husband always took that into
consideration." Apparently she'd been raped repeatedly and at-
tempted to poison herself. Then I heard her say, "I didn't realize it
at the time, but I later learned that your stomach has to have
enough acid inside for the stuff to work. I couldn't keep it down."

"And now?" the other asked, quietly.

"Well—life goes on. The best part was over anyway. I'm just
glad my husband didn't have to live through this."

Again I have to reflect on the consequences of being alone in
the world, in the midst of fear and adversity. In some ways it's easier, not having to endure the torment of someone else's suffering.
What must a mother feel, seeing her girl so devastated? Probably

the same as any one who truly loves another but either cannot help them or doesn't dare to. The men who've been married for many years seem to hold up best. They don't look back. Sooner or later their wives will call them to account, though. But it must be bad for parents—I can understand why whole families would cling together in death.

The registration was over in a flash. We all had to say which languages we know. When I confessed to my bit of Russian, I was given a paper requiring me to report tomorrow morning to Russian headquarters as an interpreter.

I spent the evening preparing lists of words and realized how paltry my command of the language really is. After that I ended my day with a visit to the lady from Hamburg downstairs. Stinchen, the eighteen-year-old student, has finally come down from the crawl space. The scars from the flying rubble have healed. She played the part of the well-bred daughter from a good home perfectly, carrying a pot of real tea from the kitchen and listening politely to our conversation. Apparently our young girl who looks like a young man also managed to come through safely. I mentioned that I'd seen her in the stairwell last night. She was arguing with another girl, someone in a white sweater, tan and quite pretty but vulgar and unbridled in her swearing. Over tea I found out that it was a jealous spat: the tanned girl had taken up with a Russian officer—in time more or less voluntarily—drinking with him and accepting food. This evidently irked her young friend, who is an altruistic kind of lover, constantly giving the other girl presents and doing this and that for her over the past several years. We discussed all of this calmly and offhandedly over a proper tea. No judgment, no verdict. We no longer whisper. We don't hesitate to use certain words, to voice certain things, certain ideas. They come out of our mouths casually as if we were channeling them from Sirius.

I got up at 7:00 A.M. Moscow time. The streets were quiet, with an early-morning stillness. The shops were empty; the new cards have yet to be distributed. A girl in uniform was standing by the iron-bar gate outside the headquarters; she didn't want to let me in, but I showed her my paper and insisted.

At last I was sitting in the office of the commandant, the present lord and master of at least a hundred thousand souls. A small, slender man, very much spit and polish, pale blond, with a conspicuously quiet manner of speaking. Russian is his only language, but he has an interpreter at his side, a bespectacled woman in a checked dress—not a soldier. Fast as the wind she rattles away in German and Russian, translating between the commandant and a sharp-nosed woman, the owner of a café. The woman wants to reopen? Excellent, she should go ahead and do so. What does she need? Flour, sugar, fat, sausage. Hmm, hmm. What does she have? Ersatz coffee? Good, she should serve that along with a little music, if possible, perhaps set up a gramophone—the goal is for life to return to normal very soon. The commandant promises she should have power back tomorrow, along with her street. The interpreter summons a man from the next room, most likely an electrical engineer; he brings in some blueprints and shows the commandant how power is being restored in the district. I crane my neck to look, but our block isn't there.

More petitioners follow. A man in blue overalls asks if he can take home a horse that's lying lame and bleeding in the park, to nurse it back to health. Please, go ahead—as long as he knows something about horses. I'm secretly amazed that the horse hasn't been cut up into pot-sized pieces by now. Or have we seen the last of those days, when animals were slaughtered right where they fell? It's astonishing to see all these people suddenly so fixated on obtaining permits just so they can cover their backs for anything they want to do. "*Commandant*" is clearly the word of the day.

A factory owner comes in with two stenotypists to register his small business, a stovepipe plant, temporarily closed due to lack of material. "*Budet*," says the commandant—It will be—a magic Russian formula that the interpreter consolingly translates as "Don't worry, there'll be new material coming in soon." Well, *budet* is definitely one of the words I can manage, along with the second magic formula, *zavtra*—tomorrow.

Next come two men, apparently managers of a chocolate factory. They've brought along their own interpreter, someone at the same level as me; the man must have spent time in Russia as a soldier or working there. Chocolate is still a long way off, of course, but the men want to bring some rye flour from a warehouse outside town and use it to make noodles. Go ahead! The commandant promises them a truck for *zavtra*.

The atmosphere is very matter-of-fact—no stamps and very few papers. The commandant works with small scribbled notes. I'm all eyes and ears watching the authorities in action; it's fun and exciting to observe.

Finally it's my turn. I jump right in and brazenly confess the obvious, namely, that my Russian isn't up to the complex task of interpretation. In a friendly way he asks where I learned Russian, what I studied. Then he says he's sure that in the foreseeable future there'll be a need for people trained in drawing and photography, that I should wait. That's fine with me.

Meanwhile two Russians have come in, boots gleaming, their

freshly pressed uniforms richly decorated. Being washed and groomed is a mark of *kultura* for them, a sign of a higher level of humanity. I still remember all the posters I saw hanging in offices and streetcars throughout Moscow. "Wash your face and hands every day, and your hair at least once a month," with cute little illustrations of splashing and sputtering and rinsing in washbasins. A religion of cleanliness. Polished boots are part of the same *kultura*, so I'm not surprised by how eager the men are to shine them up whenever possible.

The two men whisper with the commandant. Finally he turns to me and asks whether I could accompany First Lieutenant So-and-so (Ch-ch-ch . . . this time the name was clearly stated but I immediately forgot it) as an interpreter while he makes his rounds—he's been assigned to inspect the banks in the district. That's fine with me as well. I'm happy to do anything that isn't fetching water or scavenging for wood.

So I traipse through the Berlin streets alongside the swarthy, good-looking officer. He talks to me slowly, careful to pronounce every word, distinctly, the way you do with foreigners who barely speak your language, and explains that we first have to call on the district mayor, a German, to request a list of the various banks' branch offices.

Burgomistr is the Russian word for mayor, from the German *Bürgermeister*. Crowds of people are milling about the Rathaus and running up and down the dim corridors. Men dash from room to room, doors bang open and shut. Somewhere a typewriter is rattling away. Identical handwritten notices have been posted on the few pillars that have a little light: a family is searching for a woman who lost her mind on April 27 and ran away. "The person in question is forty-three years of age, has teeth in poor condition, hair dyed black, and wearing slippers."

In the mayor's office a swarm of men is buzzing around the

desk, talking and gesturing intently as an interpreter keeps chattering. Within minutes the first lieutenant is handed a list of the banks. A girl types out the addresses. The window seat is adorned with a bouquet of lilacs.

We set off. The lieutenant is reserved and very polite. He asks if he's going too quickly, if I know much about banking, if it really isn't a burden to accompany him.

At the Dresdner Bank we find things in good order: clean desks, with pencils placed at right angles. The ledger books are open, all the safes intact. The entrance to this bank is inside a larger entranceway; it was probably overlooked.

Things are different at the Commerzbank—a real pigsty, filthy, forlorn and empty. The vaults have all been broken into, as well as the deposit boxes, and cases have been slit open and trampled. There's human excrement everywhere; the place stinks. We flee.

The Deutsche Bank looks halfway decent. Two men are busying themselves sweeping the floor. The safes have been cleaned out, but very neatly, obviously opened using the keys from the bank. One of the men tells me how "they" had gotten hold of the director's home address and raced off with a truck to get him. When they arrived they found him dead, along with his wife and daughter—poisoned. Without wasting time they drove straight to the deputy director and demanded that he unlock the vaults. This bank has even opened for business. A sign states that the teller will receive deposits from 1:00 to 3:00 P.M. I'd like to see who's interested in making a deposit right now. The old-fashioned stocking or mattress method strikes me as decidedly more secure.

I can't quite figure out why the Russians burrowed their way into the banks like that, with such determination. Surely their orders did not include this sort of brutal safecracking—that's clear from the bank where the boxes were so ruthlessly smashed open and from the overwhelming fecal stench left by the robbers. It's possible the looters had been taught that banks in this country are the bulwarks of the evil capitalists, so that by plundering them they were performing a kind of expropriation of the expropriators, a deed worthy of praise and celebration. But it doesn't add up. This looks more like sheer unbridled looting, each man for himself, boldly snatching whatever he can. I'd like to ask the first lieutenant about it but don't dare.

A big cleaning operation is under way in the Städische Sparkasse. Two elderly women are scrubbing the floor. There are no vaults here. As far as we can see, the tills are completely empty. The lieutenant promises to send a guard tomorrow. But what is there to guard?

We spend a good while searching in vain for the Kredit- und Bodenbank. At last we find it in a back courtyard, safe and sound, peacefully slumbering away like Sleeping Beauty behind a folding security grate. I ask around in the building and eventually am able to give the first lieutenant the bank manager's address. No Russian ever even laid eyes on this bank. The glass sign out by the street that used to announce its presence is now nothing more than a few splinters dangling from a couple of screws.

There's one more branch of the Deutsche Bank, at the edge of our district. We make our way there. The sun is burning. I drag myself along, tired, weak, and weary. The first lieutenant kindly slows down to accommodate me. He asks some personal questions, about my education, what languages I know. And suddenly he says in French, very quietly and without looking at me: "*Dites-moi, est-ce qu'on vous a fait du mal?*"

I'm taken aback, stammer in reply, "*Mais non, pas du tout.*" Then I correct myself. "*Oui, monsieur, enfin, vous comprenez.*"

All at once there's a different atmosphere between us. How is it that he speaks French so well? I know without his telling me: he is a *byvshy*—someone from the "has been" class, the former ruling class in old Russia. He proceeds to tell me his background: he's from Moscow, his father was a doctor, his grandfather a well-known surgeon and university professor. His father studied abroad, in Paris, Berlin. They were well off, with a French nanny. The first lieutenant, who was born in 1907, was still able to imbibe something of the "has been" way of life.

After our first exchange in French, we grow quiet again. The man is clearly uncomfortable, unsure. All of a sudden he blurts out, staring ahead of him, "*Oui, je comprends. Mais je vous prie, Mademoiselle, n'y pensez plus. Il faut oublier. Tout.*" He looks for the right words, speaks earnestly and forcefully. I answer, "*C'est la guerre. N'en parlons plus.*" And we don't speak any more about it.

Silently we step into the bank lobby, which is wide open, utterly destroyed and looted. We trip over drawers and index files, wade through floods of papers, carefully stepping around the piles of excrement. Flies, flies, flies everywhere. I've never seen such massive swarms of flies in Berlin. Or heard them. I had no idea they could make so much noise.

We climb down an iron ladder into the vault, which is crowded with mattresses and strewn with the ever-present bottles, flannel boot liners, trunks and briefcases slit open. A thick stench over everything, dead silence. We crawl back up into the light. The first lieutenant takes notes.

Outside the sun is scorching. The first lieutenant wants to rest, have a glass of water. We amble a little down the street—the deserted, bleak, silent street that we have all to ourselves. We sit down on a garden wall beneath some lilacs. "*Ah, c'est bien,*" he says, but he prefers speaking Russian with me. Although he has a perfect French accent, it's clear he lacks practice, so that his French is quickly exhausted after the first questions and phrases. He finds my Russian quite valiant but smiles at my accent, which he finds— "*Excusez, s'il vous plaît*"—Jewish. That's understandable: after all, the Russian Jews speak Yiddish, which is a dialect of German, as their mother tongue.

I look at the lieutenant's brownish face and wonder if he isn't Jewish. Should I ask? Right away I dismiss the idea as tactless. Afterward I started thinking: with all the invectives and accusations the Russians heaped on me, they never once brought up the persecution of Jews. I also remember how concerned the man from the Caucasus was to let me know he wasn't a Jew—it was the first thing he said to me. In the questionnaire we all had to fill out in Russia when I was there, the word *Jew* was in the same ethnic column as *Tatar* or *Kalmuck* or *Armenian*. I also remember a female clerk there who made a great fuss about not being listed as a Jew, insisting that her mother was Russian. Still, in the offices where foreigners have to report, you find very many Jewish citizens with typically German-sounding surnames, names that have a certain flowery ring—Goldstein, Perlmann, Rosenzweig. Generally proficient in languages, most of these officials are devoted to the Soviet dogma—no Jehovah, no Sabbath, no Ark of the Covenant.

We sit in the shade. Behind us is yet another red column, another silent lodger, a Sergeant Markov. The door to the basement apartment opens a tiny crack, an ancient woman peers out, and I ask her for a glass of water for the Russian. Amicably she hands over a glass; it's cool, fogged up with condensation. The first lieutenant stands up and bows in thanks.

I can't help thinking of the major and his model etiquette. Always these extremes. Either it's "Woman, here!" and feces on the floor, or all gentleness and bowing. In any case, the lieutenant couldn't be more polite, couldn't treat me more like a lady—which I evidently really am in his eyes. In general I have the feeling that as long as we German women are somewhat clean and well-mannered and possessed of some schooling the Russians consider us very respectable creatures, representatives of a higher *kultura*. Even the lumberjack Petka must have felt something like that. Perhaps it's a matter of context, too, surrounded as we are by the remnant of well-polished furniture, the pianos and paintings and carpets—all the bourgeois trappings they find so splendid. I remember Anatol expressing his amazement at how well off the German farmers he met in the villages were as the front moved west. "They all had drawers full of things!" Yes, all the many things, that's new to them. Where they come from, people don't have as much; everything can be packed into a single room. Instead of an armoire many families just have a few hooks on the wall. And if they do acquire things, they manage to break them very quickly. Russians take no delight in all the mending and tinkering typical of German housewives. I saw with my own eyes how the wife of a Russian engineer swept the floor, then whisked the dirt right under the cupboard, where there was undoubtedly more than enough already. And hanging behind the door to their sitting room was a towel where all three children blew their noses—the smallest one at the bottom, the older ones higher up. Just like back in some poor rural village.

We spend a while sitting on the little wall, talking and resting. Soon the first lieutenant wants to know where I live and how I'm getting along. He'd like to get to know me better but right away wants to dispel any wrong ideas. "*Pas ça, vous comprenez?*" he says, and looks at me with foggy eyes. Oh yes, I understand.

We arrange to meet that evening. He'll call up to me from the street. I'm to be watching out for him at the arranged time. His name is Nikolai. His mother calls him Kolya. I don't ask about his wife. I'm sure he has a wife and children, but what does that concern me? In parting he says, "*Au revoir.*"

I go home and report the latest news to the widow. She's delighted. "You better keep him. Finally an educated man from a good home, someone you can talk to." (Pauli and the widow also know some French.) In her mind she's already seeing the provisions rolling in; she's convinced that Nikolai has access to food and that he'll do something for me—and by extension for all three of us. I'm not so sure. On the one hand, there's no denying that he's likable. Of all the Russian conquerors I've seen so far he's the most westernized. On the other hand, I don't have any desire to get involved with a new man. I'm still ecstatic at being able to sleep by myself between clean sheets. Besides, I want to finally move out of the second floor and away from the widow, above all away from Herr Pauli, who begrudges me every single potato. I'd like to resettle in the attic apartment, clean it up, make it livable. Why should I sleep with someone to procure food for that lazy Pauli? (Sleeping for food is another new concept, with its own vocabulary, its own specialized jargon, just like "my major's sugar," "rape shoes," "plunder wine," and "coal-filching.")

Moving on, late at night. Toward eight o'clock I was waiting by the window, as arranged, but there was no Nikolai. Herr Pauli made fun of me, saying my conquest was so unfaithful. The widow, still hopeful, kept her eye on the clock. Then, as it was getting dark, a call came from outside: "*C'est moi!*" I opened the door—now all worked up—and led Nikolai upstairs to our apartment. But he'd just come to say he couldn't stay longer than a quarter of an hour. He greeted the widow and Herr Pauli ceremoniously in French and left right away with his "*Au revoir.*" In the hallway he said, in Russian, as he shook my hand, "Until Sunday at eight." And then, again in French, "*Vous permettez?*" Since when are we in a position to permit or not permit? Maybe there really is a new wind blowing our way. Incidentally, Nikolai doesn't think there will be inflation or a new currency—I asked him this morning. He thinks the money we've been using will stay in circulation for the time being but that the banking industry will be overhauled and drastically simplified. "Probably socialized, right?" I asked. "No," he said, "not that. These are completely different conditions." And he changed the subject.

Thursday, May 17, 1945

Up early to get water at the new hydrant. There's a newspaper hanging in a shop window, the *Tägliche Rundschau*, printed by the Red Army for "the population of Berlin." We're no longer a people, only a population, present and accounted for but representative of nothing. This same linguistic differentiation—*Bevölkerung* as opposed to *Volk*—occurs in other languages, too, as in the French *peuple* and *population*. Reading about the victory celebrations in Moscow, Belgrade, Warsaw leaves a bitter taste. They say Count Schwerin-Krosigk has addressed the German people, called on them to face facts. Of course, we women have been doing that for a long time. But who knows what will happen once the generals and gauleiters and holders of the Knight's Cross start doing the same? I'd be curious to know just how high the suicide rate in Germany is at the moment.

Herr Pauli is sounding an optimistic note of late, talks about a rapid economic upswing, about Germany's being brought into world commerce, about true democracy and a spa cure in Bad Oeynhausen he'd like to treat himself to very soon. When, repeating what I'd gleaned from Nikolai, I poured a little water in his wine, and he turned genuinely irate, forbidding me to speak of things I know nothing about. I sensed that his anger went beyond this silly incident, that he's simply fed up with me. He used to have the widow all to himself, taking care of him day and night. I'm just a nuisance.

After dinner—pea soup, and I ate to stock up—Pauli calmed down and peace was restored. The widow even insisted I take a second helping. I can sense my star is on the rise again, thanks to Nikolai. Should that bother me? Should I hold my apartment mates to some specific moral standard? I won't. *Homo homini lupus.* It's true everywhere and always, these days even among blood relatives. At most I can imagine a mother going hungry to keep her children fed—but that's probably because mothers feel their children as their own flesh and blood. On the other hand, look how many mothers have been sentenced in recent years for selling their children's milk coupons or bartering them for cigarettes. Hunger brings out the wolf in us. I'm waiting for the first moment in my life when I tear a piece of bread out of the hands of someone weaker. There are times, though, when I think such a moment could never come: I can picture myself getting weaker and weaker, shrinking away, no longer having the strength to rob anyone. Strange thoughts to have on a full stomach and with a new Russian provider waiting in the wings.

The news in the stairwell is that they've ferreted a former Nazi party boss in our building, a *Reichsamtsleiter* or something like that—I don't know the Nazi rankings very well. I saw the man in the basement quite often, and I remember the blond woman who had been reassigned and whom no one really knew always holding hands with the man identified as her lodger, whom nobody knew either—two turtledoves, the cock being the boss in question. He didn't look like anything special, sitting around in his shabby clothes, and the few times he spoke he sounded stupid. That's what you call a good disguise.

I'd just like to know how word got out. It wasn't his mistress who denounced him: according to the bookselling wife she's howling pathetically in her fourth-floor apartment, where she managed to come through untouched except for two Ivans the first night. She doesn't dare go out anymore; she's afraid they'll take her away as well. They came for him in a military vehicle.

We have mixed feelings talking about this. A bit of schadenfreude cannot be denied. The Nazis were too pompous and subjected the Volk to too many harassments, especially in the last few years, so it's right that they should atone for the general defeat. Still, I wouldn't want to be the one to turn in those former martinets. Maybe it would be different if they'd actually beaten me or killed someone close to me. But what's playing out now is not so much grand revenge as petty malice, for the most part: that man looked down on me, his wife snapped her "Heil Hitler" at my wife, besides he earned more, smoked thicker cigars, so I'll bring him down a peg, shut him up along with his old woman . . .

Incidentally, I learned in the stairwell that next Sunday is Pentecost.

Friday, May 18, 1945

Up early to get water and look for wood. Slowly but surely I'm developing a real eye for firewood; I hardly miss a piece. I keep finding new places that haven't been combed over—in basements, ruins, abandoned barracks. Around noon Fräulein Behn brought us our new ration cards. For the time being the widow, Pauli, and I are in the fifth and lowest category—"others." Here are the allotments listed on my card: 300 grams of bread, 400 grams of potatoes, 20 grams of meat, 7 grams of fat, 30 grams of food items (semolina, barley, rolled oats, etc.), and 15 grams of sugar. On top of that there's a monthly allotment of 100 grams of ersatz coffee, 400 grams of salt, 20 grams of real tea, and 25 grams of coffee beans. By comparison, heavy laborers in group I, which also includes "well-known artists," technicians, factory managers, pastors, school principals, epidemiologists, and epidemiological nurses, receive 600 grams of bread daily, 100 grams of meat, 30 grams of fat, and 60 grams of food items, with a monthly ration of 100 grams of coffee beans. In the middle are group II (blue-collar workers) and group III (white-collar workers), with 500 and 400 grams of bread per day, respectively. Only potatoes are distributed with democratic equality to all stomachs. Second-string intelligentsia are supposed to be in group II. Maybe I can sneak in there.

You can sense that all this has had a calming effect. Everyone is sitting and studying their ration cards. We're being governed again; those in power are providing for us. I'm amazed we're supposed to get as much as we are, but I doubt it will be possible to distribute the rations punctually according to schedule. The widow is happy about the real coffee beans and promises to drink to Stalin's health with the first cup.

This afternoon I took a walk to the Rathaus, together with the woman from Hamburg and her daughter, Stinchen, on whose account she had asked me to accompany them. It seems that Stinchen was a leader of some kind in the League of German Girls and is afraid of possible reprisals, which I'm supposed to ward off by speaking Russian. The widow joined us as well.

On the way we saw many people back on the street, hustling and bustling about—even a lot of men, though women are clearly in the majority. I even spotted one woman wearing a hat, the first I've seen in a long time.

Some guards had been posted outside a few of the banks I inspected with the first lieutenant. Generally this meant two Russians with raised weapons. Definitely not the best way to attract customers.

Once again the Rathaus was like a beehive. We stood in the pitch-dark corridor and waited, surrounded by talk, the subject: pregnancy.

Yes, that's one topic of interest to every one of us they managed to get their hands on.

"They say every second woman is pregnant," claims one voice.

To which another voice, a shrill one, replies, "Even if that's true—surely you could go to anyone and have it taken care of."

"I heard that Stalin decreed that any woman with a Russian child gets counted as group number I," says a third voice.

General laughter. "Does that mean that for group number I you would . . . ?"

"Absolutely not—I'd sooner do something to myself." The widow poked me in the dark, trying to catch sight of my face. I didn't want her to see me. I don't want to think about that. This time next week I'll know better.

"Have you been to the hospital?" The question went down the line.

"No, what for?"

"Haven't you heard? They've set up an examination station for women who were raped. Everybody has to go. On account of venereal diseases."

Another poke. I don't know yet. I feel clean. I want to wait and see.

Everything went smoothly with Stinchen, of course: nobody asked about her glorious past. That's another joke, the idea of punishing minors for participating in things with the complete approval of their parents, teachers, and leaders. If our forebears once burned children as witches, and I've read that they did, it was at least because they thought the children had been possessed by grown-up devils who were inhabiting them, using them as a mouthpiece. It's hard to divine at what age our Western notion of responsibility for one's actions begins to apply.

A woman from the building next door walked back home with us. She told us about a lady in a neighboring apartment who had drunk and slept with the same Russian several times. Her husband, a clerk who'd been discharged from the Wehrmacht because of a heart condition, shot her from behind while she was at the kitchen stove, then took his pistol and shot himself in the mouth, leaving behind their only child, a girl of seven. "I've been keeping her at my son's place for all this time," the woman explained. "I'd like to keep her for good. And I'm sure my husband will approve when he comes back. He always wanted a girl as well as a boy." The neighbors wrapped the parents in woolen blankets and quickly buried them in the courtyard, along with the pistol. "Good thing there were no Russians in the building," says the woman. No doubt there would have been a to-do over the banned weapon.

We stood a while in front of the graves on the grassy knoll. The woman from Hamburg maintains that everything was bound to turn out this way—but if Hitler had been finished off on July 20, 1944, he would have kept some of his aura. Many people would have gone on believing in the dead man. Is he really dead now? Has he fled by plane? Escaped in a U-boat? There are all sorts of rumors, but no one is paying them much attention.

The woman with eczema came over in the evening, bearing sad news. She'd walked all the way to Lützowplatz to look up her boss, a lawyer for whom she had spent years taking down court statements. Because he was married to a Jewish woman and refused to divorce her, he'd had to endure a great deal, especially in recent years, when he could hardly find a crust of bread. For months the couple had been looking forward to the liberation of Berlin, spending entire nights huddled by the radio, listening to the foreign broadcasts. Then when the first Russians broke into the basement and went after the women, there was a scuffle. Shots were fired. One bullet ricocheted off the wall and hit the man in the hip. His wife threw herself at the Russians, begging them to help, in German. Whereupon they took her into the hallway, three men on top of her, as she kept howling and screaming, "But I'm Jewish, I'm Jewish." In the meantime her husband bled to death. They buried him in the front garden. His wife has fled, no one knows where. Writing this sends shivers down my spine. No one could invent a story like this: it's life at its most cruel—mad blind circumstance. The woman with eczema was crying, her tears catching on her crusted skin. She said, "If only it were over, this poor bit of life."

Saturday, May 19, 1945

We exist without newspapers and with no sense of time, following the sun like plants. After fetching water and wood I went shopping. The first things I got using the new ration cards were groats, pork, and sugar. The groats are full of husks, the sugar is lumpy, since it got wet, and the meat is stiff with salt. But it's food nevertheless, and we're happy with it. "I'm curious whether your Nikolai's going to show up tomorrow," the widow said as I was putting the bags and packages on the table.

In the afternoon we celebrated with a great housecleaning, set in motion when the widow cried out, "Look at that!" And lo and behold: water was dripping out of the faucet, genuine, thick drops of water trickling out of pipes that had been dry for such a long time. We opened the valves all the way and a strong stream came shooting out, first brown, but soon bright and clear. No more water shortages! An end to the ceaseless fetching! At least for us on the second floor—we found out later that those living higher than the third floor aren't so blessed. But even they can now get their water down in our own courtyard or else from those below them. I should note, however, that our vaunted community, the communal sense forged by national identity and living in the same building and sharing an air-raid shelter, is gradually eroding. In fine urban fashion everyone is locking themselves within their four walls and carefully choosing the people they mix with.

Our cleaning performance was first-rate—we turned our apartment inside out. I kept looking at the water, couldn't get enough of it, kept fiddling with the faucet. So what if it ran dry toward evening? We'd already filled the tub to the rim.

It's a strange feeling now, to have these technological wonders, these achievements of the modern age, reinstated one by one. I'm already looking forward to the day we get electricity back.

In the meantime, while we were hard at it, the blonde who'd been relocated here and whose high-ranking Nazi lover was taken away two days ago came by for a visit and subjected me to a tabloid tale of love and fidelity: "He told me our love was like nothing he'd ever experienced. He said it must be the greatest love ever." Maybe that really is how the greatest love ever talks. But to me it sounded atrocious, as if her lines had been lifted from a cheap movie or romance. She sat lamenting while I scrubbed the floor: "Where could he possibly be? What could they do to him?" I don't know. Anyway, she didn't dwell very long on that and soon turned the subject around to herself: "You think they'll come for me as well? Maybe I should get out of here? But where should I go?"

"Nonsense! They haven't posted any announcements saying party members have to report." Then I asked, "Do you know who squealed on him?"

She shrugged. "I assume it was his wife. She was evacuated to Schwiebus with their children but she's bound to have come back to Berlin, to the house they have in Tretow. So she probably heard from the neighbors that he'd often been out there with me, to pick things up."

"Did you know his wife?"

"A little bit. I used to be his secretary."

A typical example of what Berliners jokingly call a "refugee camp," a sheltering bed for husbands who'd been ordered to evacuate their women and children—and were all too happy to comply. Of course, plenty of stories are also being told about the husband-less evacuees, the "Mu-Ki's"—for *Mutter-und-Kind-Verschickten*, mothers and children sent away—about lovers climbing through windows and a lot of racy goings-on. You can't just transplant the average human with impunity, given all his moral weaknesses. The familiar worlds of kith and kin, of neighborhood, of polished furniture and hours chock full of activity serve as a strong moral corset. It seems perfectly plausible to me that the enraged wife turned her husband in, maybe because she assumed his emergency-shelter companion would be punished as well.

"Ach, he was so delightful," she assured me, when I finally managed to steer her to the door. And she wiped away a tear.

(July 1945, scribbled in the margin: She was the first woman in the house to have an American: a cook, big belly, fat neck, the man keeps lugging packages up to her.)

A glorious day. From very early on our street echoed with the footsteps of countless people marching off to visit friends and relatives in other parts of the city. We lingered over breakfast until eleven in the morning—cake and a mix of real and ersatz coffee. The widow regaled us with all sorts of family anecdotes—her strong suit. Her clan is truly and bewilderingly droll: her father-in-law was married three times, with long periods of bachelordom in between; he outlived two of his wives. So there are children and grandchildren running around from all the marriages, aunts younger than their nieces, uncles sitting in the same schoolroom as their nephews. On top of that, the widow confesses, the last wife, who outlived him, married again, and her second husband is Jewish. To be sure, this Jewish stepfather-in-law died long before the Third Reich, but there he was, a blot on the family record. Today, however, the widow goes out of her way to mention him, to the point of boasting about him.

After our midday meal I went up to the attic apartment, rummaged through the mountains of plaster and debris, carried buckets of trash downstairs, mopped the floors. I planted some chervil and borage in the rotting balcony boxes, that is to say I made some shallow grooves and sprinkled in the brown grains and tiny black seeds that are supposed to become my kitchen garden. I have no idea what these herbs look like except for the pictures on the front of the packages that the woman from Hamburg gave me, from some of her leftovers. Then I lay in the sun on the floor

of the terrace. A full hour of deep contentment—followed by un-
ease and restlessness. I feel something nagging at me, boring into
me. I can't go on living like a plant; I need to move, I have to act,
start doing something. I feel as though I've been dealt a good hand
of cards but don't know whether I'll be able to play them. And
who am I playing with? The worst thing of all at the moment is
our being so cut off.

I went back down to the widow's and found her absolutely ju-
bilant. Suddenly and completely by accident she turned up her
late husband's pearl tie pin—the one she'd stashed away and
couldn't find—in the toe of a much-darned sock. "How could I
forget something like that?" she wondered.

Pentecost Sunday passed peacefully. From 8:00 P.M. on I
waited for Nikolai the first lieutenant, who'd asked me on
Wednesday if he could drop by today. He didn't show up, nor is it
likely he ever will. Herr Pauli couldn't resist the occasion to make
a snide remark.

Monday, May 21, 1945

This Pentecost Monday didn't feel much like a holiday at all.
Hardly anyone is still employed. Berlin is on an extended vacation. While out for wood I stumbled on a notice calling on "cul-
tural workers"—artists, journalists, people in publishing—to
report to the town hall today at eleven. We are to bring records of
previous employment as well as samples of our work.

Off I go. The line on the third floor is unmistakable. Full-
fledged artists in their stubbornly unconventional clothes, theater

girls next to elderly female painters lugging paintings smelling of oil. Here a mannish woman, there a womanly young man with long lashes, probably dancers. I stand in the middle listening to the talk on either side about famous So-and-so, who was supposedly hanged. A woman's voice breaks in shrilly: "That's not right at all! Haven't you heard? It's just come out that he was half Jewish." That might be true, too. Everywhere you look, "non-Aryans" who'd been hidden deep in the family tree are being spruced up and put on display.

Registration was just a matter of form. An older woman with Jewish features took down our personal data in a thick notebook, giving each of us a certificate of registration, and that was that. Will anything come of this, some tip concerning work, some kind of assistance? Probably not.

For our main meal the widow opened one of the jars of chicken she put up in 1942 and has anxiously guarded ever since. Chicken it was, but chicken with a taste of mothballs. For years the jar has been sitting in the basement between mothballed rugs; by now it was completely permeated with the smell of naphthalene. That gave us a laugh. Even the gluttonous Herr Pauli abstained. The widow managed to get down a few bites and left the rest to me. I came up with a method of holding my nose and swallowing. But for hours afterward I was burping mothballs.

Around 3:30 P.M. I set off for Charlottenburg, to visit Ilse R., who worked as a fashion photographer and as an editor for a women's magazine until she married an engineer, a specialist in armaments and consequently someone they couldn't snatch and send off to the front.

After a protracted exchange of good-byes with the widow I started out. Long streets, desolate and dead. Inside the tunnel, where there used to be lamps both day and night, it was pitch-dark and smelled of excrement. My heart was pounding as I scurried through.

On toward Schöneberg. In a quarter of an hour I met only two people, both women, one barefoot, with varicose veins as thick as ropes. Everything looked so contorted and ghostly, possibly due to the sunglasses I'd put on because of the dust. A Russian woman in uniform with curly black hair was dancing on a wooden platform at the crossing, waving little red and yellow flags whenever a Russian car passed and giving a jolly, friendly greeting to the people inside. Her full breasts were dancing with her. A number of Germans carrying water buckets shyly squeezed their way past.

No end to the empty streets. Then, all of a sudden, a crowd of some twenty or thirty people streaming out of a cinema, where, according to the hand-painted signs, a Russian film called *Chapaev* was showing. I heard one man's voice, half in a whisper, pronounce the film "Absolute rubbish!" The walls are covered with colorful posters, scribbled and scrawled by hand, advertising variety shows in various pubs. The artistes are the first on the scene.

Bicycles were very literally clattering up and down the boulevard—on bare rims since there aren't any tires. This is a new and effective way to avoid Russian "confiscation." Incidentally, a number of Germans have recently been "finding" bicycles of their own, since the Russians abandon the ones they're riding at the first flat tire, then look for new and better models.

Onward, through green residential streets. All was silent, frozen, paralyzed. The entire district seems to have been scared into hiding. Now and then a young thing came mincing by, all gussied up. The widow heard at the baker's that people are even dancing again here and there.

My throat was dry with nervous excitement when I turned

onto my friend's street. When you haven't seen each other for two months—and what months!—you have no way of knowing whether the buildings are still standing or whether the people inside are still alive.

The building was there, safe and sound but locked shut, no signs of life. I wandered around for nearly fifteen minutes, shouting and whistling, until at last I managed to slip inside with one of the tenants. The familiar name was still on the apartment door upstairs. I knocked and shouted and called my name. I heard a shout of joy, and soon I was again embracing a woman with whom I had previously shaken hands at most. Her husband called out, "Imagine! She comes waltzing in here as if it were nothing at all!"

Ilse and I hastily exchange the first sentences: "How many times were you raped, Ilse?" "Four, and you?" "No idea, I had to work my way up the ranks from supply train to major."

We sit together in the kitchen, eating jam sandwiches and drinking real tea they fished out for the occasion, and exchange reports. Yes, we've all been through a lot. Ilse got it once in the basement, the other times on the second floor, in an empty apartment where they pushed her inside, using their rifle butts on her back. One of them wanted to keep his rifle with him when he lay down with her. That scared her, so she gestured to him to put his gun aside—which he did.

While Ilse and I discussed the subject, her husband stepped out to visit their neighbor, as he put it, to get the latest news for me off a crystal set. As he left, Ilse grimaced. "Yes, well, he can't really bear to hear about that." Her husband is tormenting himself with reproach for staying in the basement and not doing a thing while the Ivans took their pleasure with his wife. During the first rape, down in the basement, he was even within hearing range. It must have been a strange feeling for him.

We took advantage of Herr R.'s absence for a little female gossip. Ilse is a worldly, discriminating woman, very stylish. She's traveled all over the globe. So what's her opinion of the Russian cavaliers?

"Pathetic," she said, wrinkling her nose. "No imagination whatsoever. Simple-minded and vulgar, every last one, from everything I've heard around the building. But perhaps you had better experiences with your officers."

"No, not in that regard."

"Maybe they have the latest in socialist planned economies, but when it comes to matters erotic they're still with Adam and Eve. I told my husband that, too, to cheer him up." Then she says, with a wink, "with food so scarce a poor husband doesn't count for much. Mine is already getting a complex: he thinks that the Red Army with all its ladykillers really has a chance with us women." We laughed and agreed that as normal suitors, under normal conditions, ninety-nine out of a hundred of our worthy enemies wouldn't have the slightest chance with us. At most the hundredth might be worth a try.

We gossiped that way for a while, taking our mocking revenge on everyone who had humiliated us.

The engineer really did bring some news back from the neighbor's: evidently Berlin is to become an international city, for all the victors, and Leipzig will become the capital of the Russian areas. He also heard that Himmler has been caught. Still no confirmed news of Adolf. While Ilse seems very relaxed and manages to sneer at the recent state of affairs with ladylike superiority, her husband is dazed and distraught. His career has come to an end. They're clearing out what's left of his armaments factory. The Russians are hauling off the German machines. On my way over I saw several cargo trucks with huge wooden housings on top. Now I know what's inside. Herr R. is afraid of a social demotion, that he'll have to start over as a laborer. He craves contact and news, worries about surviving, is frantically looking for some job where he can earn his bread again, he's applied at the hospital for something in central heating. He's still stunned by the defeat. Once again it's clear that we women are dealing with this better; we're not as dizzy from the fall. Ilse and her husband are both learning Russian. Although reluctantly, he's contemplating a move to Russia, since "they'll be shipping all the means of production out of here." He doesn't believe that we Germans will be permitted to produce much worth mentioning in the foreseeable future; he also heard from the crystal-set neighbor that the whole country is to be converted into one great potato field. We'll see.

Repeated good-byes. After all, you never know when and whether you'll see each other again. On my way back I dropped in on the widow's shotgun-wed niece, the young mother-to-be who's living with her friend Frieda. She was lying on her back looking very sweet, glowing from within. But her body was far too thin for her vaulted belly, which was literally jutting out. You can almost see the baby draining all the juices and all the strength from the mother's body. Naturally no news of the father. He seems entirely forgotten amid the daily needs of finding food and fuel. Since there's only one electric cooker in the apartment, which is useless at the moment, the girls have built a kind of brick oven on the balcony and feed it with laboriously gathered fir branches. It takes forever for them to cook their bit of gruel. Moreover, Frieda has to constantly tend the fire, fanning it and adding wood. The place smelled of resin, like at Christmas.

Then the long march back home. A poster in German and Russian proclaims the imminent opening of a "free market." By whom? For whom? A "wall paper"—a newsheet posted on a wall—announces the new heads of the city—all unknown dignitaries, presumably repatriated Germans from Moscow. Colorful troops of Italians came stepping my way singing, loaded down with trunks and bundles, evidently for the journey home. More bicyclists rattled past on bare rims. Schöneberg was more forlorn, and the ghost tunnel by the S-Bahn was black and deserted. I was glad when it was behind me, when I saw the buildings on our block. I returned home as if from a big trip and divvied up my news.

Tired feet, humid day. Now the evening brings rest and rain.

Tuesday, May 22, 1945

By six in the morning the widow was already up and moving about the apartment. She'd received a note from the building chairman the previous evening. ("Building chairman" is another new invention. In our building the role is being played by the husband of the woman from Hamburg.) The note, which was on a mimeographed scrap of paper, instructed the widow to report at the town hall at 8:00 A.M. for work, nothing more. "It would be nice if it turned out to be cutting asparagus," she mused, making our mouths water at the prospect of a tasty dinner.

So today I played housewife and cooked some pea-flour soup for Herr Pauli and myself. At around 2:00 P.M. we heard loud shouting from down on the street outside our house—a kind of official town crier, exactly like a thousand years ago. He'd planted himself under the maple tree and was rattling off information from a piece of paper: all men and women between fifteen and fifty-five years of age capable of work and currently unemployed should report to the Rathaus at once for labor duty.

That set off a great debate in the stairwell: to go or not to go? The bookselling wife cast her vote for; she was afraid that otherwise they'd come and take us by force. I joined her, and together we set off. I asked her if she knew what was going on with their bookstore. "It burned down at the end of April," she answered tersely. Nevertheless she is pretty optimistic about the future and told me about a huge crate of books in the basement that she managed to keep safe throughout the Third Reich—mostly "forbidden" literature, that is, works that were banned in our country after 1933. At first this meant texts by Jews and emigrants, later by opponents of the war. "People have a craving for these things right now," she claims. "We're going to wall off a corner of the store and start a lending library—with a stiff deposit on the books, of course, or else they'll be gone in no time." I told her I'd be the first to sign up; I have a lot of catching up to do.

The steps outside the Rathaus were filled with women pushing and shoving one another—the men were few and far between. With a great deal of shouting and gesticulating, a youth took down our names. The patch of street in front looked like an extremely busy construction site. The trench in the middle of the boulevard, which was carved out for mysterious military purposes by a handful of Germans and several Russian girls in quilted jackets—forced labor—is now being filled in again, this time solely by Germans. This has a certain logic for me. Women are pushing carts loaded with sand, brick rubble, and fire-blackened debris up to the edge and tipping the contents into the trench. Bucket brigades have been lined up on all the side streets, and bucket after bucket is being passed up to the carts. I'm supposed to join in tomorrow morning at eight. I have nothing against that.

I looked for the widow among the women working but didn't

see her. At one point a car with a loudspeaker pulled up blaring the latest news in Russian-accented German. Nothing I hadn't heard before.

That evening we had bread with canned meat. The widow still hadn't come back—it was nine before we saw her red hat down on the street. She was absolutely beat, drained, done in. A few short, unintelligible angry sounds were all we got out of her—she refused to tell us what had happened. Finally, after an endless amount of time washing up, she managed to utter a few sentences, from which it was clear that there had been no asparagus. A Russian truck had transported the women to a machine works, where the widow and some two hundred others spent the whole day packing parts in crates, then unpacking them, repacking them, and wrapping them up—all under the eyes of stern Russian overseers. The widow had been jostled and shoved constantly; all they'd given her to eat was a crust of dry bread for lunch.

"And they call that organization!" She waxed indignant. "What a muddle, what a mess!"

Then she told us some more: "We pointed out to them right away that the iron parts were too heavy and would break the bottoms of the crates. And they just yelled at us to shut up and *'Rabota, rabota!'*—Work, work! So when the first crate broke into pieces as soon as it was lifted they really laid into us, and of course it was all our fault!" Shaking her head, she added: "It's a puzzle to me how these people managed to win the war. Any German schoolchild has more sense than they do." And she went on listing other examples of poor planning and stubborn insistence on the part of the Russians, to the point where she couldn't calm down. She'd had to come home on foot—which took a whole hour and a half—since they hadn't provided a truck to transport the women back after work. As a result she has

a blister on her toe; she yammers about that and about our fate
and the German defeat. Nothing can console her, not even the
hammer, the pliers, the dust rag, or the tin cup she smuggled out
of the factory under her dress.

Wednesday, May 23, 1945

Fitted out with bucket and dustpan, I marched off to the Rathaus
in the gray morning rain. Before I got there it was coming down
in sheets; I could feel my knit dress soaking up the water.

The rain kept coming—now a light drizzle, now a substantial
downpour. Nonetheless we kept on scooping and shoveling, filling
bucket after bucket with dirt so there wouldn't be a break in the
chain of hands. There were about a hundred women of all types.
Some proved sluggish and lazy and didn't move a muscle unless one
of our two German overseers was looking. (It's always the men who
get to do the supervising.) Others went at it like avid housewives,
with dogged determination. "Well, the work does have to get done,"
said one woman with great conviction. Once a cart was loaded four
of us shoved it up to the trench. I learned how to operate a swivel
plate. We worked until the heavy rain forced us to take a break.

We stood under a balcony, huddled close like animals, our wet
clothes sticking to our bodies. The women shuddered and shiv-
ered. We took advantage of the opportunity to eat our wet bread
as it was, with nothing on it. One woman muttered in a thick
Berlin accent, "Never ate the likes of this under Adolf."

She was challenged on all sides: "It's thanks to your Adolf
we're eating this."

Embarrassed, the woman said, "That's not how I meant it."

We stood like that for over an hour, in the pelting rain. When it began to taper off, our supervisor—a man with a Czech-sounding name and a Viennese accent—sent us back to the carts. We called these carts "lorries"—which sounded like a girl's name, and christened one "Laughing Laurie" and the other "Weeping Laurie." But someone scratched out "Weeping" and wrote "Smirking" instead.

Around three o'clock our Viennese overseer finally checked our names off his list and let us go home. On the way back I was swinging my bucket gaily, in the spirit of "what doesn't kill me makes me stronger."

At home I found the widow all keyed up. She confessed that for the past few days she'd been feeling "this itching and burning," so she'd consulted the encyclopedia under "syphilis" and "gonorrhea." As a pharmacist's wife she'd learned a great deal about human ailments, but this was one particular area where she lacked the necessary experience. "I have these little bumps," she declared, very sure of herself. According to the encyclopedia little bumps like that are symptomatic of early syphilis, breaking out three to four weeks after infection. The widow calculates that it was exactly four weeks ago that her stairwell rapist, that little, beardless boy, had his way with her.

"What? Vanya? That child?" I can't believe it. "You mean you think that he—?"

"Why not. Exactly, a stupid little boy like that. Besides, I'm not sure if that really was Vanya. How could I know? And then that Pole!"

The widow starts sobbing miserably. What am I supposed to do? There's no point in my taking a look, since I don't know a thing about it. And she fiercely dismisses my suggestion that she ask Herr Pauli. So all that's left is to wait till tomorrow and get to the hospital as early as possible, to the special clinic that's been set up for women who've been raped. Then I remember how my ears started to ache back in school when we were studying the human ear, with the help of oversized anatomical models. It's likely that the widow's symptoms flared up when she read the description in the encyclopedia. We'll just have to wait until tomorrow. I may have to go and get examined myself soon. I'm one day late.

Thursday, May 24, 1945

The alarm jangled—time to get up for shoveling. Today I dressed in my blue training pants and tied on a kitchen apron. Once again the sky was overcast. It was drizzling when we arrived. We shoveled diligently. This time there were even two men shoveling alongside us, at least when the supervisor was watching—otherwise they didn't do a thing. All of a sudden around ten o'clock we heard some shouting, and a Russian voice: "Woman, come! Woman, come!" A command that's been all too popular. In a flash all the women disappeared, hiding behind doors, crawling under carts and piles of rubble, squatting to make themselves as small as possible. But after a moment most of them, including me, reemerged. "Surely they're not going to—? At least not here, in the middle of the street. Besides, there's only one of them."

And he now went into action. A lieutenant, evidently equipped with orders, rounded up the remaining women and herded us together. We trudged along behind him, in front of him, while he raced around us like a sheepdog, brandishing his rifle. We cut across the garden plots and finally wound up in front of a machine tool factory.

The large halls lay empty, the hundreds of workbenches deserted. A German shout of "Heave-ho!" came echoing off the walls—a team of German men under Russian command were using cranes to hoist a disassembled forging press onto some train cars. The parts were bigger than they were. Everywhere you looked you saw men unscrewing things, turning switches off, oiling machines, hauling parts away. The siding outside the factory was lined up with one freight car after the other, several already piled high with machine parts.

What were we women supposed to do here? We loitered about, not knowing where to go. We realized right away we couldn't leave, since all the gates were guarded by soldiers.

Finally we were ordered to the assembly hall, where we were told to collect all the brass and other "bright metal" we could find and haul it, in crates, to the freight cars.

Together with another woman, who stubbornly refused to respond to my attempts to strike up a conversation, I dragged out a box and went around picking up shiny bits of metal—copper thread, brass ingots—just like a magpie. I rummaged through the workers' lockers, finding pipes, crumpled handkerchiefs, neatly folded sandwich paper—all as if they'd just finished yesterday. Then we tossed our magpie booty onto the floor of a train car, where two women were clambering about sorting the metal like proper housewives, nicely according to size.

At noon we were ordered into a different hall, a kind of storage shed, with high shelves holding metal bars of every type, threading and bolts and nuts as big as a fist. We spent an eternity passing them all from hand to hand. The woman at the end of the line stacked everything in crates, as ordered.

I thought about what the widow had experienced yesterday and waited with some suspense for the bottoms to break when the crates were moved. But it never came to that. As soon as they started to lift the first crate, it was clear that it was too heavy. Not even our slave driver, a squinty-eyed NCO with a chest like a cupboard, could make it budge. There were no wheelbarrows or anything of that nature. The man muttered a few crude curses and ordered everything taken out of the crates and passed hand to hand all the way to the freight cars. In that way a minimal amount of work was accomplished with a maximum of effort.

New labor details showed up, mostly young women but with quite a few older ones as well. Word went round that we were to be fed. And indeed after 3:00 P.M. they ordered us into the factory canteen, where we found some steaming thick bread soup. But there was a shortage of tin plates and spoons, so that each woman had to wait for the woman next to her to finish. Hardly any of the women ran up to use the faucet; most just gave their spoons a quick swipe on their skirts or aprons and then took the plate from the person before them.

Back to work! *Rabota!* There was a considerable draft in the shed. This time we spent hours passing zinc fittings down the line. Finally, it most have been around eight, our squinty-eyed task master showed up and shouted, "Woman—go home!" and started shooing us out with his arms, as if we were a flock of chickens. A happy cry of relief. Then we went to the canteen, where we were given another 100 grams of bread. After that a cask was rolled in, with a thick white liquid streaming out of it—some kind of syrup. We stood in line. "Tastes great," the first women to try it reassured us. I didn't know how to handle it until one woman gave me a piece of bilious green paper she'd found in the shed that I could fold and use as a container. The green comes off, the woman said, but claimed that it wasn't poisonous.

I showed up at the widow's around ten and proudly displayed my booty. I scraped the gluey liquid off the green paper and the widow merely shook her head. I took a spoon and licked it and wound up with a mouth full of paper. No matter—it tasted sweet. Only after a while did I remember about the encyclopedia and the widow's "little bumps."

"Oh, it's nothing," she said, in answer to my question. "The doctor told me I'm all right."

I drilled her a bit more, wanting to know what it was like at the clinic.

"There were two other women there apart from me," the widow reported. "The doctor was a cheery sort. He fiddled around a bit and then said, 'Green light, track's all clear!'" She shook herself. "Nope, I'm through with that." Incidentally, an official expression has been invented to describe the whole business of raping: "forced intercourse." Maybe they ought to include that phrase next time they print up the soldiers' phrase book.

Friday, May 25, 1945

Up again early and off to work in the clear morning. Women marching in from all directions. Today most brought their own dishes; I, too, had a soldier's mess kit dangling from my belt. We lined up as ordered, first in rows of three, then four—after which they spent an interminable time counting, sorting, and registering us. Our supervisor was the same Viennese man who had been in charge at the carts; they say he's a musician. It took him nearly an hour to list all of us. Some women were new recruits. "Well, we have to work one way or the other," I heard one of them say. "At least here we'll get something to eat."

Sure enough, we started off with some thick barley soup. Then we crossed over the railroad embankment to the work halls, where we saw German prisoners slaving away—old men in shabby clothes, probably Volkssturm. They groaned as they lifted heavy gear wheel flanges onto the train cars. They milled about alongside us, eyeing us intently. I didn't catch on, but some others did and slipped them bits of bread on the sly. That's not allowed, but the Russian guard looked steadfastly the other way. The men were unshaven and emaciated, with the gaping eyes of wretched dogs. They didn't look like Germans at all to me. They resembled the Russian POWs we used to see while the fighting was still on, the ones forced to clear rubble from the ruins. This, too, is a logical reversal.

Back in the hall our first task was to haul unwieldy iron bars, in groups of two or three; after that we passed rods and pieces of plate metal down the chain out to the freight car. A Russian came in, looked us over, waved two women aside and then a third. The third was me. We trotted after him. Where to? One of us speculated: "Maybe to peel potatoes?" They'd already taken a dozen women to do exactly that out by the railroad embankment, where the Russian trailers with fancy curtains are located.

No, he was taking us someplace else, over to a dilapidated shack and down a dreary corridor where the fecal stench grew more and more unbearable. One woman decided to take off; she simply bolted back, cutting across the landing. After that the Russian made the two of us who were left march in front of him. He led us into a room with a stone floor. We saw a wash boiler, tubs, washboards, buckets. He pointed at the equipment and made a gesture of washing laundry.

That was fine with us, but not there in that hovel. The other woman, a pert little person with lively eyes, helped me drag the largest washtub outside the shed, onto a kind of porch. We felt safer there, and it didn't stink so much. The Russian didn't object. He brought us two pieces of hard soap and a number of previously white overalls, shirts, and handkerchiefs, and signaled to us to wash them. Although his tone was curt, he wasn't unfriendly, and he didn't grope us in any way, not even with his eyes.

My fellow washerwoman revealed that she was from Danzig and exchanged a few snippets of Polish with the Russian. So much the better! That way I don't have to talk, I can keep my Russian hidden. I don't want to speak with them as a washerwoman.

Other soldiers kept coming over in groups, lounging around the washtubs and gossiping about us. Two of them debated how old we might be. After much back and forth they decided I was twenty-four. Not bad!

The hours crawled by. We soaped and rubbed and fetched warm water from the company kettle, cold water from the hydrant on the street. I rubbed my fingers raw on all the filthy clothing. The towels were rigid with grease. They were all monogrammed hand towels from German families—war booty. I scrubbed away with a hairbrush—quite a struggle. Meanwhile the Russians refused to leave us in peace, pinching us where they could. I batted them away like a horse switching at flies, and sprayed them with water from my hairbrush, but didn't say a word. Now and then our boss came over and chased off the Romeos. Then he brought us some underwear—fastened with laces instead of buttons.

The whole time the woman from Danzig was telling me in a monotone how several Ivans went at her mother, who already has grandchildren. Using her Danzig Polish, she had asked if the men weren't ashamed to rape such an old woman.

To which they gave the classic answer, in German: "You old, means you healthy."

I was on the verge of keeling over right at the washtub when our boss showed up and announced it was time for lunch. He brought each of us a mess tin full of rich, fatty soup with meat, cucumbers, and bay leaves, and a tin plate of pea porridge well laced with bacon. It seems he is a cook, and a good one at that. The food tasted fabulous. I could feel my strength reviving.

We went on washing for an eternity. Two o'clock, three, four, five, six. We washed without a break, under constant supervision. We soaped the clothes and wrung them out and fetched water. Our feet ached; our knuckles were close to bleeding. The Russians watching us enjoyed the spectacle; they rubbed their hands in gleeful revenge, thinking they'd really gotten to us with the washing. "Ha ha ha, now you have to wash for us, serves you right!" The woman from Danzig merely grinned. I played deaf and dumb, smiled all around, and washed and washed. The men were amazed. I heard one say to another, "They work well. Always cheerfully, too."

We dragged out the work on the last hand towels until it was six, then cleaned the washtubs and wandered over to the canteen, where everyone was given a dollop of mush. After that all the women started to head home, us included, but when we reached the gate the guards chased us back, crying, *"Rabota!"* The women started screaming and pushed their way to the gate, ready to mutiny. But the eight-hour day doesn't apply to the vanquished. A soldier pushed at us, brandishing his rifle and calling out threateningly, "Woman! *Rabota!*" That's one Russian word everyone's learned by now.

Everyone had to return to the hall and load more iron parts. Silent and worn out, we passed one another the rods and plates. Handling cold iron when your hands have been washing all day hurts something fierce.

Finally, toward eight, our overseer called out that the train car was full. That was an understatement: it literally groaned when the locomotive hauled it away. Perhaps the floor will give way before the train reaches Moscow. One old worker, who'd been sitting on top of the car, jumped off as it was moving. He claimed they should have let him stay right where he was, so he could go with the rest of the transport; after all, "what's left for us here?" And he pointed at the hall, deserted and stripped bare. "Where are our husbands going to work now?" the women asked.

An hour later I was home, dead tired this time, with hands so stiff I don't feel much like writing. At the same time I'm still a little intoxicated by the rich meal and the size of the portions. Tomorrow we go on washing: our boss already informed us that there's more laundry waiting.

Saturday, May 26, 1945

Once again the cattle count at the factory yard took forever, though our Viennese should have mastered it by now. And once again the day started off with some hot barley soup; the women were pleased to see whole pieces of meat. And I'm happy not to have a Herr Pauli keeping track of every bite I put in my mouth.

In vain I looked around for my co-washer, but the small, pert woman from Danzig didn't show up. So I persuaded two other women—one very young, the other around forty, both friendly looking—to join me at the washtubs. The uniforms were waiting, having already been put to soak. They were full of grease stains, since this is a motorized unit.

The day passed just like yesterday. The new washerwomen were nice and hardworking. Once again the Russians crowded around us. We fended them off with our elbows and silly laughter. One slit-eyed individual was determined to provoke us. He took a few tunics already hanging on the line to dry and tossed them back in the tub, pointing out several stains that were still visible. Of course the stains were still there. The pitiful bit of soap we had wasn't enough, and all our brushing couldn't make up for that. Other men were friendlier, placing pieces of bread next to their tunics.

Toward noon our boss rigged up a kind of dining room in front of the building, consisting of a crate and two overturned drawers. He asked us to sit down and served us a large pot of the rich stew—always with the same friendly but deadpan expression. We sat in the sun and took our time eating, enjoying the meal greatly. Both my fellow washers gave evasive answers to my usual question about how often it had happened to them. The older of the two, a spirited woman with bad teeth but humor very much intact, said that it was all the same to her—as long as her husband didn't find out about it when he came back from the western front. Apart from that, she subscribes to the saying "Better a Russki on top than a Yank overhead." She's in a position to know, too; her building was hit head on and she and the other residents who had retreated to the basement were buried in rubble. Several people were wounded and one was killed. It took two hours for help to arrive and dig them out. She became very agitated when she started speaking about the person killed, an old woman. "She was sitting by the wall, right in front of a mirror." The builders had hung the mirror low because the basement was originally intended as a shelter for the children from the kindergarten housed in the ramshackle building next door. When children were evacuated from Berlin, the kindergarten was closed and the basement was freed up for the people in the building. "The mirror exploded into a thousand pieces, which flew right into the old woman's back and neck and head. And in the dark and with all the to-do no one noticed she was quietly bleeding to death." Still outraged, the woman waved her soup spoon in the air. "Fancy that, a mirror."

An amazing death, no doubt about it. Presumably the children for whom the basement shelter was designed were supposed to comb their little locks in front of the mirrors each morning after the nightly air raid—a luxury clearly installed back when the raids first started, when the shelters still offered a measure of comfort as well as confidence.

We scrubbed the afternoon away, rubbing tunics, trousers, and caps with our wrinkled, swollen hands. Around seven we were able to sneak out onto the street through a side gate. A wonderful feeling of freedom—a combination of finally getting off work and playing hooky.

At home the widow, Herr Pauli, and I drank what was left of the Burgundy I'd stolen from the police barracks. Tomorrow is Sunday, but not for me. The Viennese gave a little speech today, the gist of which was that if we didn't show up for work tomorrow they would come to our apartments and take us to the factory by force.

Sunday, May 27, 1945

A long, bleak, and weary day, the longest Sunday of my life. We worked without stopping in the factory yard from eight in the morning until eight in the evening under the glaring sun. No laundry today. Our Russians have the day off. We stood in a chain across the yard, passing zinc ingots and sharp jagged bits from hand to hand, while the sun beat down on us without mercy. Our chain, which spanned about a hundred yards, was stretched thin, so that you always had to carry the heavy metal two or three steps to hand it off to the next woman. My head was soon aching from the sun. On top of that my back hurt and my hands were still raw from all the washing.

At first there was just stupid gossiping and bickering on all sides, until finally a kind of singing started up, more like a droning, the same verse over and over: "Shine on, dear sun, we don't give a whit, the mayor is sitting and taking a sh——ine on dear sun." And on and on. That's how the women vented their anger over their stolen Sunday.

Every now and then a tall, bony woman would reach into some cranny of her undergarments, fish out a wristwatch wrapped in a handkerchief, and announce the time. The hours crept by, interrupted only by a hasty serving of gruel.

Back into the shadeless blaze. Zinc, more zinc, and no end in sight. By around four o'clock we had filled the first freight car until it was gleaming silver. Then with a "heave-ho" we shoved the car a way up the track and rolled the next one into place, a French boxcar from Bordeaux with the SNCF lettering I knew so well. It gave off a horrible stench—the men had used it as a latrine. The women laughed. One of them called out, "Looks like the shit's being freighted to Moscow as well."

Onward, no end of zinc. Finally even our two overseers grew bored. We know them pretty well by now. We call one "Teddy" and the other "Squint." Today they weren't as strict as usual; twice they even shouted the lovely word "Break." Squint went so far as to risk a dance with one of our girls while the rest of us clapped time. Both soldiers suddenly disappeared around five, but just because they were off duty didn't mean we were, unfortunately. All at once the whole place was unnaturally quiet—no shouts driving us on, no chatter, no moaning, nothing at all. Only the grating of our feet and the occasional weak cry of "Watch out" when one of the women dozed off. And of course someone was always asking what time it was.

Word came from the basement—where the women were also on their feet all day—that the masses of zinc ingots still stored there were inexhaustible. Around seven we heard a rumor that we were done for the day, but that proved false. Zinc, zinc, and more zinc . . . Finally, at eight, a Russian showed up and waved us over to the canteen. We gulped down the rich soup and trudged home. I was keeling over; my hands were dark gray. When I washed up, the water was full of thick gray flakes. I lay down for a bit and let the widow pamper me with tea and cake.

The electricity is back on as of yesterday. The time of candles is over; now people can ring instead of knocking—the quiet has come to an end. The Berlin station is broadcasting on the radio, generally news reports and disclosures that reek of blood, corpses, and atrocities. They say that millions of people—mostly Jews— were cremated in huge camps in the East and that their ashes were used for fertilizer. On top of that everything was supposedly carefully recorded in thick ledgers—a scrupulous accounting of death. We really are an orderly nation. Late in the evening they played Beethoven, and that brought tears. I turned it off. Who can bear that at this moment?

Back in the laundry. Today our Ivans were in particularly high spirits. They pinched and pawed us and repeated their standard offer in German: "Bacon and eggs, sleep at your home," and then, just to make sure we understood, they rested their heads on their arms like Raphaelesque angels.

Bacon and eggs—we could certainly use that. But delicious as the prospect was, there were no takers as far as I could see. And rape seems pretty much out of the question here in the wide-open factory yard, in broad daylight, with so many people milling about. People are busy everywhere you look, there's no quiet corner to be had. That's why the boys add the bit about where they'll sleep— what they want are willing, bacon-craving girls who'll take them home. I'm sure there are plenty that fit that description here in the factory, but they're also afraid, and fear is an effective damper.

Once again we washed tunics, shirts, and handkerchiefs, one of which turned out to be a little rectangular bedside table cover, hemmed in red and embroidered with the cross-stitched words "Sleep Well." For the first time in my life I was washing handker- chiefs sneezed in by strangers. Was I nauseated by the enemy snot? Yes, even more than by the underwear—I had to struggle not to gag.

Evidently my fellow launderers didn't have the same reaction—they went on washing with great vigor. By now I've come to know both of them fairly well. Little nineteen-year-old Gerti—gentle, reflective—half whispered a confession involving all kinds of amorous mishaps. One boyfriend left her; another fell in the war. . . . I steered the conversation to the end of April. Finally, her eyelids lowered, she described how three Russians had hauled her out of the basement into a stranger's apartment on the first floor, threw her on a sofa, and had their way with her—first one after the other, then in no particular order. Afterward, the three of them turned into jokesters. They rummaged through the kitchen, but all they found was some marmalade and ersatz coffee—in other words, the typical pantry fare at that time. Laughing, they spooned the jam onto Gerti's hair, and once her head was covered they sprinkled it generously with ersatz coffee.

I stared at her as she told the story, quietly and ashamed, speaking to her washboard. I tried to picture the horrible scene. No one could ever invent such a thing.

Our taskmasters spurred us on all day with cries of *"Davai, pustai, rabota, skoreye!"* Move, get on with it, work, faster! All of a sudden they're in a tremendous hurry. Maybe they're planning to leave soon.

One problem for us washerwomen is how to use the toilet. The place is so awful you can barely set foot inside. We tried cleaning it out with our laundry water the first day, but the pipes are clogged. Moreover there are always Russians lurking around. So now two of us stand watch at either end of the corridor while the third uses the toilet. We always take along our soap and brushes, since otherwise they disappear.

At noon we spent an hour lingering at our upturned-drawer dining table, enjoyed the sun, ate rich soup, and took a nap. Then we went back to washing, and washed and washed. We were soaked with sweat by seven, when we headed home, once again sneaking out the side entrance.

A bath at home, a nice dress, a quiet evening did some good. I have to think about things. Our spiritual need is great. We're waiting for some heartfelt word, something that would touch us, some declaration that would bring us back into the stream of life. Our hearts have run dry, they're hungry for what the Catholic Church calls "manna for the soul." I think I'd like to find a church next Sunday, if I get the day off and if they're having services. I'd like to see whether churchgoers are finding manna like that. Those of us who don't belong to any church have to suffer alone in the darkness. The future weighs on us like lead. All I can do is brace myself for what's to come, and try to keep my inner flame alive. But why? What for? What task awaits me? I feel so hopelessly alone.

Tuesday, May 29, 1945

Another wash day, long and hot. This time it was positively raining trousers and tunics. One tunic disappeared off the line, apparently a particularly fine item that belonged to an officer. The idea that one of us might have filched the thing didn't occur to anyone, not even the man who was robbed. The men let out the inevitable hue and cry, but it was clear they accepted the theft as a natural occurrence. Thieving has deep roots among these people. Back when I was traveling in Russia I was robbed of nearly everything that could be stolen, especially during the first part of my stay: my purse, briefcase, coat, gloves, alarm clock, even the stockings I'd hung in the bathroom to dry. One time I was in an office with three people who worked there. I bent down for a moment to open a drawer and look for a photo, and when I turned back again I saw that someone had taken my pair of scissors. It had to have been one of the three of them, all friendly, well-mannered clerks. I didn't dare say anything; I simply poked around the desk some more, my face blushing instead of the thief's, while they calmly went about their business. To this day I don't know which one it could have been. I only know that ordinary Russians couldn't find scissors like that in the stores. No doubt about it, poverty breeds theft; it's catching on here as well. But the Russians have their own style, a kind of innocent approach, as if stealing were something completely acceptable. That's just the way it is, what can you do about it?

The men paid court to us all day long with their rote proposition: "Bacon and eggs, sleep at your home." One of them kept following me around. He showed me a German 20-mark bill on the sly and laid another one on top, as a promise, if I'd step in the shed with him, real quick, and . . . He'd already made the same offer to little Gerti.

Today we had a Russian woman washing alongside us, the wife or girlfriend of a captain, a busty blonde. She was washing some men's shirts made of rayon, humming a German hit she'd probably picked up from a record. Gerti and our fellow launderer—both with perfect pitch—sang along. The Russian woman smiled at us. The atmosphere was friendly.

It's sunny and breezy outside, nice weather for drying. Most of the Russians were dozing in the yard. For a while no one came to pinch or pester us. We just went on washing. Somehow our talk shifted to poetry. It turns out that Gerti knows half of her school reader by heart. I joined in, and for a while you could hear poems by Mörike, Eichendorff, Lenau, and Goethe—all declaimed over the washtubs. Eyes down, Gerti recited: "Just wait, for soon / you, too, will rest." Then she sighed and said, "If only that were true." Our fellow washer shook her head. She's more than twice little Gerti's age, but dying is the last thing on her mind. Her constant refrain: "Everything passes, time goes by."

Around eight, tired and worn out, I arrived home. Except it turned out it wasn't home anymore. Our accidental family has fallen apart. In view of the dwindling supply of potatoes in the basket, Herr Pauli finally blew up at the widow—it was a long time coming—and demanded she stop sharing their room and board with me. My stock has gone down since Nikolai vanished into thin air and there's no other prospect in sight, no viable candidate for "sleeping up" some food. The widow met me in the hallway, hemming and hawing, to deliver the bad news. On the one hand, she likes me. The bad times have brought us together. On the other hand, she's known Herr Pauli longer than she's known me, feels bound to him, and is also counting on him to provide some sort of guarantee for the future. She doesn't want to antagonize him.

I said, "Thank God I know where I stand. I haven't exactly been savoring the meals here for some time. To tell the truth I was glad to be eating with the Russians this past week."

Of course, I have no idea what I'm supposed to live off next week, once the work for the Russians is finished and I'll be sitting alone upstairs in the attic apartment, forced to rely on the little bit we've been allotted but have yet to receive. I packed my belongings—a few spoons and a handful of old clothes—and trundled upstairs, though as I'm writing this I'm back in the widow's apartment, where I'm spending the last night. It's an orphan's lot to wander, I suppose. The most bitter thing in the life of a single woman is that every time she enters some kind of family life, after a while she ends up causing trouble: she's one too many, someone doesn't like her because someone else does, and in the end they kick her out to preserve the precious peace.

And still this page is smudged with a tear.

Our last wash day. Starting tomorrow we're free, all of us. The Russians were tying up their bundles, the air was full of imminent departure. Inside the shed they'd lit a fire under the wash boiler because some officer wanted to take a bath. The others scrubbed themselves in the open, using bowls they set on chairs and rubbing their broad chests with wet hand towels.

Today I made a conquest: using gestures and broken German, our amorous young pursuers led me to understand that "that one" was in love with me and was willing to do anything I wished, if I would . . . "That one" turned out to be a tall, broad soldier with a peasant's face and innocent blue eyes; his temples were already gray. When I glanced his way he coyly looked away, then moved a few tiny steps closer, took the heavy bucket of water from me, and carried it over to the tub. An entirely new model! What a brilliant idea—to think it never occurred to any of the others. I was even more surprised when he spoke to me in perfect, Russian-free German: "We're leaving tomorrow, someplace far away from here." Moreover he pronounces his *h* like *h* and not *kh*—he says "here" and not "khere." I figured out right away that he was an ethnic German from the Volga basin, one of the Volga-Germans. Yes, he said, he was from the Volga region and German was his slightly rusty mother tongue. He followed me around the whole day, with friendly, fatherly eyes. He wasn't the pinching type, more on the shy side, a farmer. But he had this fawning, doglike look in his eyes that he used to express any number of things. As long as he was near me the men by the washtubs refrained from pinching and jostling.

Once again the three of us worked like slaves. Little Gerti was in fine spirits, warbling away. She's happy because as of today she's sure there won't be any little Russian, from back then on the sofa—which makes me think about the fact that I'm a week late now. Even so I'm not worried; I still believe in my inner No.

But happy Gerti had bad cramps. We tried to help her a bit, washing some of her things. The day was gray and humid; the hours passed very slowly. Toward evening the Russians trickled in to pick up their clothes, which had dried in the meantime. One of them took out a dainty lady's handkerchief with a crocheted hem, held it to his heart, rolled his eyes romantically, and spoke a single word, "Landsberg"—the name of a place. Looks to me like another Romeo. Perhaps Petka, too, will one day press his lumberjack paws to his heart, roll his eyes, and murmur my name—unless, of course, he's still cursing me with every chop of the ax.

In all the chaos of departure the cook didn't serve us from his own stores today; we had to report to the canteen and slurp down the barley soup. There the word was going round that we'd never see the eight marks per day we'd been promised, that the Russians were taking all the money with them. Then there was a second, even wilder rumor on top of that: supposedly the radio had warned of a Mongolian horde about to pour into Berlin, men so fierce even Stalin was unable to keep them in check and had been forced to grant them three days of freedom to plunder and rape and had advised all women to hide in their homes. Utter nonsense, of course. But the women believed it and kept jabbering and moaning, all riled up, until our interpreter intervened. A battle-ax of a woman who addresses everyone with the familiar form and sings the same tune as our overseers even though she was sent here to do forced work just like the rest of us. She wangled her position thanks to her scanty bits of Russian (she's from Polish Upper Silesia). Well, I passed her level of ability long ago, but I'm very glad I didn't let them know it. I would have hated having to translate all the orders and shouts of our taskmasters. The whole group is afraid of the woman. She has pointy canine teeth and a piercing, malicious gaze—exactly how I imagine a female guard in a concentration camp.

In the evening they announced in the canteen that we were being dismissed. They also told us we could pick up our pay next week in room number such-and-such in the Rathaus. Maybe it will be there, maybe it won't. I shook hands with little Gerti and the other woman—gingerly, since the three of us are very sore—and wished them all the best. Gerti wants to go back to Silesia, where her parents live. Or lived. No one knows anything for sure.

Thursday, May 31, 1945

Today I began my solitary, hungry existence in the attic apartment. It must have been some instinct that made me eat the way I did at the widow's, with no holding back. After all I knew it couldn't last. That's why I stuffed myself with as much food as I could. No one can take that away from me now. But the shift from the good life to nearly nothing is all the harder. I have no supplies laid up, and as of yet they've hardly doled out a thing. That leaves bread, which we do receive promptly—in my case 300 grams, i.e., six rolls of gray rye bread—and which I easily eat up just for breakfast. As it happens, today there weren't any rolls, so I had to take a kilogram loaf. I made a cross over it the way my mother's very devout mother used to do. May I never lack for bread up here. I notched the crust to mark off three daily portions. There's no fat of any kind to spread. The widow gave me some dried potatoes and the remaining pea flour, but those won't last more than two midday meals. For supper there's really nothing except for nettles. It makes you so listless. As I write this I feel as if my head were a balloon that might fly away any minute. I get dizzy if I bend over; the change is too drastic. Nevertheless I'm glad I had those few fat weeks. They've left me some strength. Presumably food will be doled out sooner or later. I can't count on a Russian provider—that's all over.

I spent the whole day slaving away in the attic, a day of complete silence and solitude, the first in a long time. At one point I noticed that the real tenant's radio had disappeared. There were handprints on the whitewash where the radio should have been. Proper fingerprints, too—good specimens for a Sherlock Holmes. I deduced that the roofers were expanding their own inventory, taking one piece here, one piece there. Well, I intend to give them a piece of my mind. I can get their address from the housekeeper of the landlord, who took off toward the west. She's running things on his behalf, already collecting rent for June. The May rent was canceled: in the official records for 1945, that month won't count.

Friday, June 1, 1945

The chervil in my balcony flower boxes is sprouting in curly shoots; the borage has little round leaves. The bit of green brightens my morning. For breakfast I had three pieces of bread, spread with a paste I made from dry yeast and water. Pretty short rations.

Despite that I set off on a long trek, this time to Steglitz, to visit a young secretary from my old firm.

Berlin is cleaning up. Children are looking scrubbed again. Everywhere you see caravans of families with handcarts—refugees from outside the city heading home. Here and there notices are pasted on the walls and lampposts calling on the Silesians and East Prussians to join the group transports for the trip back east. They say it's more difficult to travel west, since the Elbe is still impassable. That's where the Russkis met up with the Yanks: according to the radio they're still celebrating and fraternizing.

On my way to Steglitz I passed long chains of women, all dressed in blue and gray, stretched out across the mountains of rubble. Buckets were going from hand to hand. A regression to the time of the pyramids, except we're hauling material away instead of constructing something.

The building was still standing but looked blown out and bare. The walls inside the apartment were full of cracks, and you could still see signs of fire. The wallpaper was in tatters, but in her little room Hilde had flowers in all her vases. She seemed strangely quiet, so I babbled away, trying to think of something to amuse her, just to make her laugh. Finally she started talking on her own, and I fell into an embarrassed silence.

She was wearing a dark blue dress because she doesn't have a black one. On April 26 she lost her only brother—seventeen years old. While she and her mother stayed behind in the basement, he went up to see what was going on, and a piece of shrapnel tore through his temple. His body was looted—by Germans. Then his undressed corpse was carried into a nearby cinema. Hilde searched all over but it took her two days before she finally found him. She and her mother put him in a cart and wheeled him off to the Volkspark, where they used a spade to scratch out a shallow grave. They buried him in his rain jacket.

He's still there: Hilde's mother had just left to take some lilacs to the grave site.

Both mother and daughter managed to escape the Russians. They were protected by the four flights of stairs and by the fact that the fourth-floor landing is damaged, so that it seemed as though no one was living on the higher floors. Hilde reported that a twelve-year-old girl in the basement who was tall for her age got dragged off in all the commotion and "used up" by the Russians along with some other women. Luckily there was a doctor on hand who was able to help her afterward. One Russian who came roaring through accidentally left a woman in the building a dirty handkerchief with all kinds of jewelry knotted up inside, a treasure that spawned fabulous rumors about its value.

Hilde related all this without emotion. Her face has changed; she looks as if she's been singed. She has been marked for life.

I took a detour on my way back to see my friend Gisela. She's still putting up the two forsaken ex-students from Breslau. All three of them were pretty grimy—they'd had to pass rubble down a chain for several hours that morning. Blond Hertha was lying on the sofa, her face flushed and hot—the lady doctor next door diagnosed an inflammation of the ovaries. On top of that she's most likely pregnant. She throws up the little bit of dry bread she gets for breakfast. The Mongol who forced her open had her four times in a row.

For their midday meal the three women served a thin flour soup. I had to eat as well, so as not to offend them, and I was very hungry. Gisela snipped in a few nettles. They're growing wild in the flower boxes on her balcony.

Then it was back home and up the stairs to my attic. A snapshot from along the way: a black coffin, smelling strongly of tar, tied to a cart with string, pushed by a man and a woman, with a child perched on top. Another snapshot: a municipal garbage wagon with six coffins on top, one of them serving as the drivers' bench. The men were eating their breakfast as they drove, passing a bottle of beer and taking turns drinking.

Saturday, June 2, 1945

I called on one of the roofers and when he opened the door I came right out and told him that I'd come for the radio that had disappeared from my apartment. At first the good man acted as if he had no idea what I was talking about: he didn't know anything about any radio, I must be mistaken.

Then I played a dirty trick. I showed him my old paper from the town hall, assigning me as an interpreter to the local commandant, and told him that I could get a Russian to conduct a house search anytime I wanted. At that the man immediately recovered his memory: oh, right, it was possible that his colleague, who happened to live in the same building, might have taken the radio, which had been sitting unattended, back home for safekeeping. The roofer asked me to wait, then he climbed up a flight of stairs and came back three minutes later with the radio—still packed in paper and tied with string. I see they took the packing paper from the apartment as well.

Authority as a means of applying pressure. And here I was, using a little piece of paper to pretend I had authority. The trick produced prompt results, too. I'm convinced that otherwise I would have never gotten the radio back. Still, it left me feeling slimy. However, it appears that most of life's mechanisms rely on similar tricks—marriages, companies, nation-states, armies.

Around noon I went out onto the balcony to sun myself. From there I could see straight into the window across the way, where a woman was working at her sewing machine stitching red and white stripes. Then she started cutting circles out of a white sheet and trimming them into stars. Stars and stripes. It's supposed to be an American flag. Earlier the woman with eczema asked me on the stairwell how many stars the American flag ought to have. I didn't know for sure whether it was forty-eight or forty-nine, so I told her to look it up in the widow's encyclopedia. It's a difficult flag for our German seamstresses to sew, because of the colors and particularly because of the design. Compared to that the Russian flag is a cinch; all you need is to take an old swastika flag—available in every unbombed household—remove the black-and-white swastika pattern, and sew a yellow hammer, sickle, and star onto the red background. I've seen some touchingly crooked hammers and twisted sickles. The *tricouleur* works best (the French are victors as well). Just stitch together three vertical strips of blue, white, and red, and you're done. For red most of the seamstresses use ticking or scraps from Nazi flags. White's easy enough to find, too—an old sheet does the trick. Here again the problem is the blue. I've seen people cutting up tablecloths and children's clothes for that. The widow sacrificed an old yellow blouse for a hammer, sickle, and star. Her encyclopedia also came in handy for the Union Jack. The only problem is that ours doesn't wave very well; it sticks out from the flagpole like a board, thanks to several yards of flat braid sewn behind the blue background—made from an apron—in order to keep all the crosses and stripes in place.

This could only happen in our country. An order came—I have no idea from where—to hang out the flags of the four victorious powers. And lo and behold, your average German housewife manages to conjure flags out of next to nothing. If I were one of the victors looking for a souvenir, I'd go around after all the celebrations were over and pick up some of these amazing rags—all so different in color, fabric, and form. All throughout the afternoon, these bits of cloth kept popping out of the buildings on our street, like pennants stuck on a dollhouse, touchingly crooked and faded.

Around 5:00 P.M. Ilse R. stopped in unexpectedly—the woman I visited in Charlottenburg almost two weeks ago. She walked here the long way, in high heels, too, since that's all she has, elegant lady that she once was. She came with a plan. Her husband knows a Hungarian who somehow wound up in Germany shortly before the war broke out. She says that this Hungarian has a wad of U.S. dollars that he wants to use as start-up money. He thinks a press would be the most lucrative venture—he's published newspapers, magazines, and books. According to him, all the old publishing houses are dead because they made deals with the Nazis. So the field is wide open to the first person who comes along with a clean slate and some paper. They'd like me to go in on it since I have publishing experience and know how to do layout. But I don't know the Hungarian, I've never even heard of him, and it all sounds to me like so much hot air. Then again I might be wrong. Anyway, I said I'd go along. As soon as the company is set up I'd get an employment card and along with that a group II card and 500 grams of bread per day instead of 300. It staggers the mind!

The widow came by while Ilse was visiting. The three of us chatted away like a ladies' tea club. All that was missing was coffee and cake; I had nothing to offer. Still, all three of us were pretty merry, outdoing one another with our rapish wit.

Then I spent a quiet evening, brightened by the radio I recovered from the roofers. But I turned it off right away. After jazz, more disclosures, some Heinrich Heine and sweeping statements about humanity, they started broadcasting tributes to the Red Army, a little too saccharine for my taste. Better nothing at all or else a straightforward "Let's just declare the matter closed and start a new chapter."

Sunday, June 3, 1945

A peaceful morning, hot sun, the pitiful little homemade flags dotting the street with color. I puttered around the room and cooked my barley soup on the electric hot plate, which kept going out. Two more soups and that's the end of the barley. There's no fat left, and they have yet to distribute any. But in the shop they said that Russian sunflower oil is on its way. I saw before me the golden sunflower fields of the Ukraine. That would be nice.

After I ate I made my second trek to Charlottenburg, cutting across the hazy, desolate city. My legs moved of their own accord. I'm like an automatic walking machine.

I met the Hungarian at Ilse's apartment; he really is very keen to start something. A swarthy type with a rectangular forehead. He was wearing a freshly pressed shirt and looked so well fed that I had no doubt about his dollars. In rather broken German he presented his plan, which consists of first setting up a daily paper. He even has a name picked out, *Die neue Tat*—the *New Deed*, because right now everything has to be new. We talked about the content of the paper, what line it should take. A graphic artist was there as well; he's already sketched out the masthead, very bold.

In addition to that the Hungarian would like to start up a number of magazines, one for women, one for older youth, to help with democratic reeducation (a phrase he picked up from the radio). When I asked how far he'd come in his dealings with the Russians, he answered that there was still time for that, the first order of business was to buy up all the paper left in Berlin to nip any competition in the bud.

It's clear he thinks of himself as a future Ullstein and Hearst all wrapped up in one. He sees skyscrapers where we see rubble, and dreams of a giant consortium. A pocketful of U.S. dollars is a powerful inspiration.

Despite my doubts and reservations I immediately sat down with the artist and made up a front page. The Hungarian wants a large format and lots of photos. As far as the actual printing is concerned, we all defer to Ilse's engineer husband. He knows of a print shop that's still half buried in loose rubble from a fire. He thinks the presses could be excavated, easily repaired, and put back into use. I suggested that they probably can't be retrieved until after the Russian troops have left. But Herr R. smiled and said that machines like those are too old-fashioned for the victors, who have their own specialists and are interested only in the newest and best.

The trip home went fine. My legs are just a little sore from walking so fast. But I feel cheery and even sense there's a chance this just might work.

Now it's up to me. Tomorrow we're supposed to begin planning for the magazines. For the moment our office is the engineer's apartment. I'm supposed to have my midday meal there as well. Ilse managed to smuggle in a sack of peas. Good thing, too.

To round off the evening I concocted a small dessert. I took a teaspoon of what sugar was left in the bag and sprinkled it into a little glass. Now I'm dipping my index finger into the glass, slowly and deliberately, so that my fingertip picks up a few grains at a time. I look forward to every lick, enjoying each sweet morsel more than I ever did a whole box of prewar chocolates.

Up early and off to Charlottenburg, very humid outside. Our magazines are already beginning to take shape. I gathered what I could find in the way of texts by banned authors—either from Herr R. or others in the building: Maxim Gorky, Jack London, Jules Romains, Thomas Wolfe, as well as older writers like Maupassant, Dickens, Tolstoy. The only question is how to acquire the rights for works not in the public domain, since none of the old publishing houses are still in existence. But our Hungarian isn't concerned with minor details like that. He's all for printing. "If someone shows up demanding money, then we'll just pay," he says, and pats his pocket. He's gotten hold of a bicycle and has generously put it at the disposal of the "publishing house," which for the time being exists in name only.

We really did have pea soup for our main meal of the day, although unfortunately it didn't turn out right. Ilse said she boiled the peas but they refused to soften, so she put the whole mess through the mill. The result was rough as sand, but we managed to swallow it down. She'd cooked it with a bit of bacon; they gave the rind to me since I have so far to walk. I should check my weight—I have the feeling I'm rapidly wasting away. My skirts are getting baggy.

I marched home around six. The streets were filled with small, tired caravans of people. Where were they coming from? Where were they going? I don't know. Most were headed east. All the vehicles looked the same: pitiful handcarts piled high with sacks, crates, and trunks. Often I saw a woman or an older child in front, harnessed to a rope, pulling the cart forward, with the smaller children or a grandpa pushing from behind. There were people perched on top, too, usually very little children or elderly relatives. The old people look terrible amid all the junk, the men as well as the women—pale, dilapidated, apathetic. Half-dead sacks of bones. They say that among nomadic peoples like the Lapps or Indians old people used to hang themselves on a tree when they were no longer of any use or crawl off to die in the snow. Our western Christian civilization insists on dragging them along for as long as they can breathe. Many will have to be buried in shallow graves along the roadside.

"Honor your elders"—yes, but there's no time or place for that on a cart full of refugees. I've been thinking about how our society treats the elderly, about the worth and dignity of people who have lived long lives. Once they were the ones in possession, the masters of property. But among the possessionless masses—which at the moment include nearly everyone—old age counts for nothing. It's something to be pitied, not venerated. But precisely this threatening situation seems to spur old people to action, seems to spark their urge to live. The deserter in our building told the widow that he had to keep every bit of food locked away from his elderly mother-in-law because she steals whatever she can get her hands on and devours it in secret. Without a second's hesitation she would eat up all his rations as well as his wife's. If they say anything to her she starts moaning that they want her to starve to death, that they're trying to kill her to inherit her apartment. And in this way dignified matrons are turning into animals, greedily clawing at what's left of their lives.

I slept poorly because of a toothache. Despite that I got up early and set out for Charlottenburg. Today the flags are out again everywhere. The Allies are said to have flown in by the thousands, English, Americans, French. And all these comical, motley flags waving them welcome—products of German women and a week-end's hard work. Meanwhile the Russian trucks never stop rolling, carrying our machines away.

I trudge along, as always the automatic walking machine. I'm putting in about twelve miles a day, with the barest nourishment. The work itself is fun. The Hungarian is always cooking up something new. He heard somewhere that for now the only available paper will go for schoolbooks. So he adds schoolbooks to the publishing program. He's guessing there'll be a great demand for contemporary German primers and Russian grammars; my assignment is to rack my brains about that. Today Ilse actually treated us all to a cup of real coffee. At six I headed home, on paper-thin soles. Along the way I met the first German public service vehicle to resume operation, a bus that runs every half hour. But it's hopelessly packed; there's no way to get on. I also saw some German policemen, newly commissioned. They seemed oddly undersized, determined not to stick out.

By the time I got home my feet were aching and I was dripping with sweat. The widow met me on the stairs with some surprising news: Nikolai had been there and had asked after me! Nikolai? It took me a moment to remember. Oh yes, Nikolai from the distant

past, Nikolai the first lieutenant and bank inspector, Nikolai who
wanted to come but never came. "He said he'd check in again at
eight," the widow said. "He'll go straight up to the attic and ring
for you. Are you glad?"

"*Je ne sais pas,*" I answered, remembering Nikolai's French. I really didn't know whether to be glad or not. After Nikolai twice dissolved into thin air, the idea that he'd actually show up seemed
highly implausible. What's more, that was a bygone era, and I
didn't want to be reminded of it. And I was so tired.

I had barely managed to take a quick wash and lie down for an
hour, as I always do after the forced march from Charlottenburg,
when the doorbell rang. And there, indeed, was Nikolai. We exchanged a few phrases in French in the dim hallway. When I invited him in and he saw me in the light, he was visibly startled.
"Just look at you. What's the matter?" He said I was all skin and
bones. How, he wanted to know, could that have happened in such
a short time? What can I say? All the work and the endless marching around and that degree of hunger and just a little dry bread
are a formula to make anyone waste away. What's odd is that I
hadn't realized that I'd changed that much myself. You can't check
your weight anywhere, and I never give the mirror more than a
fleeting glance. But have I changed so much for the worse?

We sat facing each other at the smoking table. I was so tired I
couldn't suppress my yawning, couldn't find the words in my
head, so drowsy I had no idea what Nikolai was talking about.
Now and then I pulled myself together, ordered myself to be nice
to him. For his part he was friendly but distant. Evidently he had
counted on a different reception, or else he simply no longer felt
any attraction for the pale ghost I have become. Finally I understood that, once again, Nikolai had only come to say good-bye.
He's already stationed outside Berlin and came in on duty for just
this one day, for the last time, as he put it. So there's no need to put

on a friendly show for him; I don't have to pretend I'm interested. By the same token I kept feeling a quiet regret that things turned out as they did. Nikolai has a good face. In parting, in the hallway, he pressed something into my hand, with a whisper: "*En camarades, n'est-ce pas?*" It was money, over 200 marks. And he hadn't gotten anything from me apart from a few half-yawned words. I'd happily use this money to buy something to eat, if only some supper for tonight. But in times like these everyone clings to what they have. The black market is dying.

Wednesday, June 6, 1945

Once again it's evening, and the walking machine has come back home. The rain is streaming down outside, and inside—oh, joy!—the water is streaming from the faucet in my apartment. I fill the tub and shower myself with water. No more lugging those heavy buckets up the stairs.

Another day hard at work. I went with the Hungarian to look into renting office space. Our first stop was the Rathaus, where he obtained some official papers, stamps, and signatures that are meant to authorize his plans and attest to his clean record. There were a number of amazing characters there, types you haven't seen for years, people who've been staying out of sight and are now crawling out of the woodwork everywhere you look. I saw young male dancers, a Jewish woman who'd gone underground and was talking about her nose operation, an older man with a bright red "Assyrian" beard who was a painter of "degenerate" art.

After a cup of real coffee Ilse and her husband had a heated discussion about whether he should accept a job in Moscow. They're offering him a high-level position, good pay. But Ilse is dead set against it, if for no other reason than that he would have to make the move by himself at first. He doesn't want to go either. He'd prefer to keep breathing western air, our publishing plans have helped him take heart, and he's hoping to get back in the usual boys' game of money and power and big cars.

Today the Allies are conducting negotiations. The radio is spitting speeches, brimming with the tributes our ex-enemies are paying one another. All I know is that we Germans are finished. We're nothing but a colony, subject to their whims. I can't change any of that; I just have to swallow it. All I want to do is steer my little ship through the shoals as best I can. That means hard work and short rations, but the old sun is still in the sky. And maybe my heart will speak to me once more. One thing's for sure: my life has certainly been full—all too full.

Thursday, June 7, 1945

Today the walking machine had the day off. I got up early to stand in line at the greengrocer's for some pickled pumpkin. Unfortunately the stuff proved too briny for me to get down. Luckily I got two bunches of dried vegetables—known as "shredded wire"—and a bag of dried potatoes. On top of that I picked a purseful of nettles in the gardens outside the ruined buildings, elegantly plucking them using the fishnet gloves I saved from my air-raid gear. I devoured them greedily, even drinking the greenish stock I'd boiled them in, and felt properly refreshed.

After that I calculated that my period was over two weeks late, so I strode seven buildings down to where a woman doctor had hung out her shingle, though I'd never seen her before and didn't even know if she had started practicing again. Once inside I met a blond woman, not much older than me, who received me in a wind-battered room. She'd replaced the windowpanes with old X-rays of unidentified chests. She refused to engage in small talk and got right down to business. "No," she said after examining me, "I don't see anything. Everything's all right."

"But I'm so late. I've never had that before."

"Do you have any idea how many women are experiencing the same thing? Including me. We're not getting enough to eat, so the body saves energy by not menstruating. You better see that you get a little meat on your bones. Then your cycle will get back to normal."

She asked for ten marks, and I handed them to her. But I felt bad—after all, what could she do with that? After we were through I risked asking whether there were indeed lots of women who'd been raped by the Russians and were now pregnant coming and asking her for help.

"It's better not to speak of such things," she said curtly, showing me out.

A quiet evening all to myself. Gusts of wind are sweeping through the empty window frames, swirling dust into the room. Where can I possibly go if the real tenant shows up one day? What's certain is that, if I hadn't been here, the apartment would long since have been cleared out by the roofers and other fellow citizens. When it comes to heating, other people's furniture burns better than your own.

The walking machine is back at it. An amazing event today: a section of the S-Bahn has resumed operations on a trial basis. I saw the red-and-yellow cars up on the track, climbed the stairs, paid two old groschen for a ticket, and got on board. The passengers were sitting on the benches with an air of ceremony—two of them immediately moved closer together so I could squeeze in. Then we went hurtling through the sunny wasteland of the city, while all the endless, tedious minutes I had spent marching flew by the window. I was sorry I had to get out as soon as I did. The ride was so nice, a real gift.

I put in a lot of work. Ilse and I sketched out the first number of our planned women's magazine. We still haven't decided on a name for it, so we put our heads together on that. Each periodical definitely has to contain the word *new*.

The day was strangely dreamlike; people and things appeared as if behind a veil. I walked back home on sore feet, listless from hunger. All we had to eat at Ilse's was more pea soup—two ladlefuls apiece, since we're trying to make the supplies last. It seemed to me that every person I passed had hollow, hungry eyes. Tomorrow I'm planning to go pick some more nettles. I kept my eyes peeled for every spot of green along the way.

Everywhere you turn you can sense the fear. People are worried about their bread, their work, their pay, about the coming day. Bitter, bitter defeat.

A day off for me. We agreed that for as long as I don't have anything to eat I'd make the twelve-mile trek only every other day.

In the store where I'm registered they gave me groats and sugar in exchange for coupons—enough for two or three meals. Then with my elegantly begloved hands I picked an entire mountain of nettle shoots, orache, and dandelions.

In the afternoon I went to the hairdresser's for the first time in ages and asked for a shampoo and set. They washed about a pound of dirt out of my hair. The hairdresser had popped up from somewhere to take over the shop of a colleague who was pressed into the Volkssturm at the last minute and is missing in action. Supposedly the man's family was evacuated to Thuringia. The place had been pretty well ransacked, but one mirror is still intact and one dryer is still halfway serviceable, if rather dented. The man's speech was very prewar: "Yes, ma'am. Why of course, ma'am. I'd be happy to, ma'am." I find all overly solicitous and polite phrases somewhat alien now. "Yes, ma'am" is for internal use only, a currency of no value except among ourselves. To the rest of the world we're nothing but rubble women and trash.

They've announced on the radio that the Russians are going to set up their military administration in Berlin after all, so that Russia will now stretch all the way to Bavaria, Hanover, and Holstein; the English are supposed to get the Rhine and the Ruhr, and Bavaria goes to the Americans. It's a topsy-turvy world with our country all sliced up. We've had peace for a month now.

A reflective morning, with music and sunshine, which I spent reading Rilke, Goethe, Hauptmann. The fact that they were also German is some consolation, that they were our kind, too.

At 1:30 P.M. I set off on a humid march through a Berlin that's still silent and empty. In Charlottenburg we sat down again and planned. A new man has joined our group, a professional printer. He thinks obtaining paper shouldn't be our first order of business, since anyone who has paper is going to hold on to it and even hide it for fear of confiscation. And if even someone were willing to part with some, we have no way to pick it up and no place to store it until we can start printing. At the moment our entire automotive fleet consists of two bicycles—and that's more than most firms. The printer thinks our primary task should be to acquire a license from the authorities—for an official allocation of printing paper. The engineer has already made the rounds of every conceivable German or Russian office and collected a lot of empty promises—he gave a rather depressing account. Only the Hungarian is bursting with optimism. He's a sly dog, no doubt about it. I happened to mention a crate of framed photos that was still in the basement of my former firm, portraits of men who'd received the Knight's Cross that were intended to be handed out as prizes at some ceremony. His eyes grew bright and he immediately asked, "Pictures? With glass?"

"Yes, all framed with glass."

"We'll go and get the glass," he decreed. He's found some potential office space, but like most spaces in Berlin it has no windowpanes. As far as I'm concerned he can go ahead and break in. I'll gladly act as a lookout. But my guess is that the crate has long since gone.

On my way home I dropped in on Gisela. Hertha was lying sick on the sofa again, but this time her face was no longer a glowing red—it was snow white. She'd had a miscarriage, Gisela told me. I didn't ask any questions, just gave each of the girls one of the chocolates the Hungarian had given me on my way out "as a thank you for the good tip about the glass." Filled mocha beans, very tasty. It was nice to see the girls' tense, bitter faces relax when they tasted the sweet filling.

I told Gisela about our publishing plans, thinking that she could join us as soon as one of them becomes concrete. Gisela was skeptical. She can't imagine that we'll be able to print the kind of thing we want to, not here in Germany right now. She thinks that they won't allow anything that doesn't follow the Moscow line, which isn't her own. She's too embarrassed to mention the word *God* in front of me, but that was the gist of what she was saying. I'm convinced that she prays and that this gives her strength. She doesn't have any more to eat than I do. She has deep circles under her eyes, but hers are lit up, whereas mine are simply bright. We can't help each other now. But the simple fact that I'm surrounded by other hungry people keeps me going.

Another day to myself. I went to the police to try to get some kind of official permission to use the abandoned garden in back of the burned-down house where Professor K., once a close colleague of mine, used to live. I showed them a letter the old man had mailed from the Brandenburg Mark, where he had found a refuge asking me to look after his garden. I was sent from pillar to post. Nobody claimed to have the authority. Dingy cubbies with cardboard in the windows, musty smells, low-level bickering. Nothing has changed.

On the way home I picked my quota of nettles. I was very low on energy; my diet has no fat. There's always this wavy mist in front of my eyes, and I feel a floating sensation, as if I were getting lighter and lighter. Even writing this down takes effort, but at least it's some consolation in my loneliness, a kind of conversation, a chance to pour my heart out. The widow told me she's still having wild dreams of Russians. I haven't had anything like that, probably because I've spewed everything onto paper.

My potato supply looks pretty grim. The rations they've given us have to last through the end of July. We were forced to take them now, and anybody can smell the reason why: the tubers, which had just been dug out of the pit, are fermenting, so that half the potatoes are already a stinking mash. I can hardly stand the smell in the kitchen, but I'm afraid they'll spoil even more quickly if I keep them on the balcony. What are we supposed to live off come July? What's more, I'm worried about the gas stove. When there's enough pressure in the gas line to use it, the pipes start banging like gunshots. And the electric cooker, patched up as it is, doesn't want to run anymore.

I have to guard the bread against myself. I'm already 100 grams into my next day's ration—I can't let that become a habit.

Tuesday, June 12, 1945

The automatic walking machine was back in Charlottenburg. No more joyrides on the S-Bahn. Something went wrong after the first few runs and the streetcars are once again out of commission. We worked hard; now our designs and proposals must be submitted to all the various offices.

On the way I had a new experience. Bodies were being exhumed from a grassy lawn, to be reinterred in a cemetery. One corpse was already lying on top of the debris—a long bundle wrapped in sailcloth and caked in loam. The man who was doing the digging, an older civilian, was wiping the sweat off with his shirtsleeves and fanning himself with his cap. It was the first time I had ever smelled a human corpse. The descriptions I've read always use the phrase "sweetish odor," but that's far too vague, completely inadequate. The fumes are not so much an odor as something firmer, something thicker, a soupy vapor that collects in front of your face and nostrils, too moldy and thick to breathe. It beats you back as if with fists.

At the moment, the whole city of Berlin is reeking. Typhus is going around, and hardly anyone has escaped dysentery—Herr Pauli was hard hit. I also heard that they came for the lady with eczema; apparently she's been quarantined in a typhus barracks. There are fields of garbage all over, swarming with flies. Flies upon flies, blue-black and fat. Must be the life for them! Each bit of feces is covered with a humming, swarming mass of black.

The widow heard a rumor that's going around Berlin: "They're making us starve as punishment because a few men from Operation Werewolf recently shot at some Russians." I don't believe it. You hardly see any Russians at all in our district, so the werewolves wouldn't have anyone to prey on. I have no idea where all the Ivans have disappeared to. The widow claims that one of the two drink-and-be-merry sisters who moved to our building—Anya with the cute little son—is still receiving Russian callers with packages. I'm not so sure that's a good thing: I can picture her lying across her sofa, her white throat slit.

(Scribbled in the margin at the end of June: Not Anya and not the throat, but a certain Inge, two buildings down, was found this morning with her skull bashed in, after a night of boozing with four unknown men, still at large. She was beaten with a beer bottle—empty, of course. Probably it wasn't malice or even a lust for murder. More likely it just happened that way, perhaps after an argument over whose turn it was. Or maybe Inge laughed at her visitors. Russians are dangerous when drunk; they see red, fly into a rage against anyone and everyone when provoked.)

Wednesday, June 13, 1945

A day to myself. The widow and I went out to look for nettles and orache and roamed through the professor's ruined garden, now run wild. Even if I did receive permission to tend the garden, I would be too late. Strangers have broken off whole branches of the cherry tree, picking the cherries just barely turned gold. Nothing will ripen here; hungry people will harvest everything before its time.

Cold, storms, and rain. The streetcar drove down our street again for the first time. I jumped on right away, just for the ride, but once on board I realized it would be a good time to go to the Rathaus and ask whether we really could expect pay for our week's labor for the Russians. It turned out my name was indeed on the list, along with all the others, with every workday neatly recorded. They'd even entered the amounts to be withheld for tax. I am to be paid 56 marks—though not until there's money in the coffers again. The clerk asked me to check back next week. At any rate, they're keeping the books and adding amounts and collecting the money, so I'm bound to get something.

While I waited in the rain for the streetcar to take me back, I spoke with two refugees, a married couple. They'd been traveling for eighteen days from Czech territory and had bad things to report. The man told how the Czech at the border was stripping Germans of their shirts and hitting them with dog whips. "We can't complain," his wife said wearily. "We brought it on ourselves." Apparently all the roads from the east are swarming with refugees.

On the way home I saw people coming out of a cinema. I immediately got off and went into the half-empty auditorium for the next showing. A Russian film entitled *At Six P.M. after the War*. A strange feeling, after all the pulp novels I've been living, to sit in the audience again and watch a film.

There were soldiers in the audience, alongside several dozen Germans, mostly children. Hardly any women, though—they're still reluctant to venture into dark places with all the uniforms. But none of the men paid any attention to us civilians; they were all watching the screen and laughing diligently. I devoured the film,

which was full of salt-of-the-earth characters: sturdy women,
healthy men. It was a talking movie, in Russian—I understood
quite a bit, since it takes place among simple people. The film had
a happy end—victory fireworks over the turrets of Moscow,
though it was apparently filmed in 1944. Our leaders never risked
anything like that, for all their promises of future triumphs.

Once again I feel oppressed by our German disaster. I came
out of the cinema deeply saddened but help myself by summon-
ing things that dull my emotions. Like that bit of Shakespeare I
jotted in my notebook back then in Paris when I discovered Spen-
gler and felt so dejected by his *Decline of the West:* "A tale told by an
idiot, full of sound and fury, signifying nothing." Losing two world
wars hits damned deep.

Thursday, June 14, 1945

And once again the walking machine was back in Charlottenburg. If only our firm were already in operation and I had my
group II ration card, with 500 grams of bread per day, so that I
could save a little of it for the evening. As it is I sacrifice all six of
the rye rolls I get every morning for breakfast. That is to say, I
pack two with me and eat them at the two breaks I allow myself;
otherwise I'd give out. Despite my "frying" them in ersatz coffee,
the rancid-tasting potatoes are difficult to get down. I should pick
them over again; the little pile is melting away at an alarming rate.

Dozens of telephones were lining the hallway outside the engineer's apartment. They're being collected from everywhere,

supposedly for the Russians. Berlin without phones! Looks like we'll go back to being cavemen.

The evening brought a nice surprise: I finally procured my ration of fat for the past twenty days at the corner store—20 times 7 equals 140 grams of sunflower oil. Reverently I carried home the little bottle I'd been toting around all week in vain. Now my apartment smells like a Moscow *stolovaya*, one of those cafeterias for ordinary people.

Friday, June 15, 1945

I went down very early to get my six rolls. They're dark and wet—we never had anything like them before. I no longer dare buy a whole loaf, because I'd eat up the next day's portion.

Today we broke into my old employer's basement. The Hungarian, the engineer, and I slipped in through the back, through the laundry room. We had managed to prize open the crate, which was standing untouched in the shed, when the wife of the company's representative appeared on the basement stairs. They're still living in the building. I mumbled something about having left some files and papers lying around. The men hid behind the crate. Then we broke off the frames, tore out the pictures—photographs signed by young men decorated with the Knight's Cross—and stacked the glass panes; we had brought some packing paper and string with us. After that we were able to make our getaway through the back entrance. I don't really care if they notice the loss; after all, I lost my camera and all my equipment, which I had left at work at my boss's request, when the place was destroyed by a bomb. What are a few panes of glass compared with that? We absconded with our loot as fast as we could, each of us lugging a heavy stack of glass to my place, where the men had parked our two valuable company bicycles. I was given four panes' commission; I could have glazed one whole window in my attic apartment—if I'd had any putty.

In the evening I read some of the rather random selection of books belonging to the apartment's rightful tenant. I found a copy of Tolstoy's *Polikushka* and read that for the umpteenth time. Then I plowed through a collection of plays by Aeschylus and came across *The Persians*, which, with its lamentations of the vanquished, seems on the surface well suited to our defeat. But in reality it's not. Our German calamity has a bitter taste—of repulsion, sickness, insanity, unlike anything in history. The radio just broadcast another concentration camp report. The most horrific thing is the order and the thrift: millions of human beings as fertilizer, mattress stuffing, soft soap, felt mats—Aeschylus never saw anything like that.

Saturday, June 16,
to Friday, June 22, 1945

I haven't been writing. And I won't be, either—that time is now over. It was around 5:00 P.M. on Saturday when the doorbell rang. "The widow," I thought to myself. But it was Gerd, in civilian dress, suntanned, his hair lighter than ever. For a long time neither of us said a thing; we just stared at each other in the dim hallway like two ghosts.

"Where have you come from? Have you been discharged?"

"No, I just snuck off. But now would you let me in?" He was dragging a sled behind him, mounted on small wheels and loaded with a trunk and a sack.

I was feverish with joy. No, Gerd wasn't coming from the western front. His antiaircraft unit had been shipped out to the east at the last minute. After an enemy shell hit their position three of them went off and parked themselves in an abandoned villa, where they found suits, shoes, a bale of tobacco, and sufficient food. The situation got dicey, though, when the local authorities, a mixture of Russians and Poles, started going through the houses. The three joined a group of Berlin evacuees and marched home with them. Gerd knew my current address from the red-bordered field post he received about my apartment being hit. Of course, he fully expected to find my new lodgings destroyed as well and me who knows where. He's amazed I'm here and in one piece. When I told him about my starvation rations he shook his head and claimed that from here on out he'd take care of getting what was needed. He had some potatoes in his sack, in perfect condition, and a piece of bacon. I started cooking it immediately and invited the widow to join us. She knows Gerd from my stories, greeted him with an effusive hug, even though she'd never seen him before, and in her torrent of words was soon showing him her thumb-and-finger trick: "Ukrainian woman—like this. You—like this."

I could see that Gerd was taken aback. With every sentence he grew colder, pretended to be tired. We tiptoed around each other and were sparing with any words of affection. It's bad that Gerd doesn't have anything to smoke. He had expected a flourishing black market, like Berlin of old.

After the unaccustomed rich food I felt flushed and high-spirited. But in the night I found myself cold as ice in Gerd's arms and was glad when he left off. For him I've been spoiled once and for all.

Disrupted days, restless nights. All sorts of people who were on the march with Gerd came by, and that led to constant friction. He wanted the guests to be fed. I wanted to save as much bacon and potatoes as I could for the two of us. If I sat there and didn't speak, he yelled at me. If I was in a good mood and told stories about our experiences over the past few weeks, then he really got angry. Gerd: "You've all turned into a bunch of shameless bitches, every one of you in the building. Don't you realize?" He grimaced in disgust. "It's horrible being around you. You've lost all sense of measure."

What was I supposed to say to that? I crawled off in a corner to sulk. I couldn't cry, it all seemed so senseless to me, so stupid.

Do you remember, Gerd? It was a Tuesday toward the end of August 1939, around ten in the morning. You called me at work and asked me to take the rest of the day off to go on an outing with you. I was puzzled and asked why, what for. You mumbled something about having to leave and again insisted, "Come, please come."

So we went out to the Mark and roamed through the piney woods in the middle of a working day. It was hot. One could smell the resin. We wandered around a lake in the woods and came across whole clouds of butterflies. You identified them by name: common blues, brimstones, coppers, peacocks, swallowtails, and a whole gamut of others. One huge butterfly was sunning itself in the middle of the path, quivering slightly with outspread wings. You called it a mourning cloak—velvet brown with yellow and blue seams. And a little later, when we were resting on a tree trunk and you were playing with my fingers, so quietly, I asked you: "Do you have a draft notice in your pocket?" You said, "Not in my pocket." But you had received it that morning, and we sensed it meant war. We spent the night in a remote forest inn. Three days later you were gone and the war was here. We have both survived. But is that a good thing for us?

I gave Gerd my diaries. (There are three notebooks full.) He sat down with them for a while and then returned them to me, saying he couldn't find his way through my scribbling and the notes stuck inside with all the shorthand and abbreviations.

"For example, what's that supposed to mean?" he asked, pointing to "Schdg."

I had to laugh: "*Schändung,*" of course—rape. He looked at me as if I were out of my mind but said nothing more.

Yesterday he left again. He decided to go with one of his antiaircraft buddies, to visit that man's parents in Pomerania. He said he'll bring back some food. I don't know if he's coming back at all. It's bad, but I feel relieved. I couldn't bear his constant craving for alcohol and tobacco.

What else? Our publishing plans are stalled. We're waiting for an official reply. The Hungarian is showing the first signs of growing tired; lately he's been talking about a political cabaret that absolutely ought to be started up right now. Nonetheless we continue working diligently on our program and do what we can to combat our general sense of paralysis. I'm convinced that other little groups of people are starting to move here and there, but in this city of islands we know nothing about each other.

Politically things are slowly beginning to happen. The émigrés who came back from Moscow are making themselves felt; they have all the key positions. You can't tell much from the newspapers, assuming you can even find one. I usually read the *Rundschau* on the board next to the cinema, where it's pinned up with thumbtacks for the general public. Our local district administration has a curious program—apparently they're trying to distance themselves from the Soviet economic system, they call themselves democratic, and are endeavoring to get all "antifascists" to come together.

For a week now it's been rumored that the southern parts of Berlin will be occupied by the Americans and the western parts by the English. The widow, duly illuminated by Herr Pauli, thinks that an economic upswing is near at hand. I don't know; I'm afraid it won't matter which of the Allies will be in charge, now that the victors have embraced so warmly at the Elbe. We'll wait and see. I'm not so easily shaken anymore.

Sometimes I wonder why I'm not suffering more because of the rift with Gerd, who used to mean everything to me. Maybe hunger always dulls emotions. I have so much to do. I have to find a flint lighter for the stove: the matches are all gone. I have to mop up the rain puddles in the apartment; the roof is leaking again; they merely patched it up with a few old boards. I have to run around and look for some greens along the street curbs and stand in line for groats. I don't have time for feeding my soul.

Yesterday I experienced something comic: a cart stopped outside our house, with an old horse in front, nothing but skin and bones. Four-year-old Lutz Lehmann came walking up holding his mother's hand, stopped beside the cart, and asked, in a dreamy voice, "*Mutti*, can we eat the horse?"

God knows what we'll all end up eating. I think I'm far from any life-threatening extreme, but I don't really know how far. I only know that I want to survive—against all sense and reason, just like an animal.

Does Gerd still think of me?

Maybe we'll find our way back to each other yet.